# MURDER CITY

The Untold Story of Canada's Serial Killer Capital, 1959-1984

Michael Arntfield, PhD

Research Assistant: Lee Mellor
Original Artwork: Nikolina M. Wallis
Cover Images: Courtesy of Western University Archives

Suite 300 - 990 Fort St
Victoria, BC, Canada, V8V 3K2
www.friesenpress.com

Copyright © 2015 by Michael Arntfield
First Edition — 2015

All rights reserved.

No part of this publication may be reproduced in any form, or by any means, electronic or mechanical, including photocopying, recording, or any information browsing, storage, or retrieval system, without permission in writing from the publisher.

ISBN
978-1-4602-6181-1 (Hardcover)
978-1-4602-6182-8 (Paperback)
978-1-4602-6183-5 (eBook)

1. True Crime, Murder, Serial Killers

Distributed to the trade by The Ingram Book Company

# TABLE OF CONTENTS

**Acknowledgements** ................................................... ix
**Prologue**
*Kingdom Hall* ............................................................... 1

**Chapter 1**
*Canadian Horror Story* .................................................. 9
    A City in the Forest .................................................. 11
    The Basement Book of the Dead .............................. 14
    Portrait of a Serial Killer ........................................... 18
    Psychotic vs. Psychopathic Killers ............................. 19
    Organized vs. Disorganized Killers ........................... 20
    Process-Focused vs.
    Act-Focused Killers .................................................. 22
    MO vs. Signature ...................................................... 23
    Preparatory Paraphilia vs. Attack Paraphilia ............ 24
    Rapist Typologies ..................................................... 29

**Chapter 2**
*The Truscott Hangover: 1959-62* ................................. 35
    Stranger Danger ....................................................... 37
    Innocence Lost ......................................................... 41
    "A Miscarriage of Justice" ......................................... 43
    A Wolf in Ass's Clothing ........................................... 45
    The Big Chill ............................................................ 50

**Chapter 3**
*Flashpoint: 1963-67* .................................................... **57**
    14 King .................................................................59
    Victims: Margaret Sheeler, Age 20 & Unborn Child ............60
    Shadow Play ..........................................................63
    Victim: Victoria Mayo, Age 32 ...............................64
    While the City Sleeps ............................................66
    Victim: Georgia Jackson, Age 20 ...........................72
    Boxtown ................................................................75
    Codebreaker .........................................................78
    Victim: Glenda Tedball, Age 16 .............................81
    Combing the Jane Does .......................................82
    Tip of the Iceberg .................................................84

**Chapter 4**
*The Tissue Slayings: 1968* ........................................... **87**
    Dead of Winter .....................................................89
    Victim: Jacqueline Dunleavy, Age 16 .....................90
    "Perverts Destroy" ................................................94
    Jalopy ....................................................................99
    Victim: Frankie Jensen, Age 9 .............................104
    Victim: Scott Leishman, Age 16 ..........................110
    Water's Edge .......................................................112
    The Neighbour ...................................................117
    Victim: Helga Beer, Age 31 .................................123
    Quarantine ..........................................................125
    Victim: Lynda White, Age 19 ..............................128

**Chapter 5**
*Critical Mass: 1969* ................................................... **133**
    March of Time ....................................................135
    Victim: Jane Wooley, Age 62 ...............................136
    Victim: Patricia Bovin, Age 22 .............................138
    Victim: Robert (Bruce) Stapylton, Age 11 ...........142
    The Lords of Hellmuth .......................................146
    Victim: Jackie English, Age 15 ............................150

"Buried With Me" ............................................................. 160
The Telephone Man ........................................................ 162
Hinterland ....................................................................... 169

**Chapter 6**
*Lost and Found: 1970-75* ............................................... **175**
The Porn Man ................................................................. 177
Victim: Soroya O'Connell, Age 15 ................................... 185
Victim: Edith Authier, Age 57 .......................................... 188
Victim: Belva Russell, Age 57 .......................................... 190
Intentional Walk .............................................................. 191
The Sectionman .............................................................. 194
Victim: Priscilla Merle, Age 21 ........................................ 200
The Taxi Driver ............................................................... 202
Hillcrest .......................................................................... 206
Victim: Mary Hicks, Age 21 ............................................. 209
The Gore ......................................................................... 210
Victim: Judith Barksey, Age 19 ........................................ 212
Victim: Eleanor Hartwick, Age 27 ................................... 214
Victim: Suzanne Miller, Age 26 ....................................... 215
Victim: Irene Gibbons, Age 66 ......................................... 216
Victim: Louise Jenner, Age 19 ......................................... 219
Hunter's Moon ................................................................ 220

**Chapter 7**
*The Slasher and the Strangler: 1976-79* ......................... **223**
Moving the Needle .......................................................... 225
Victim: Susan Scholes, Age 15 ......................................... 227
Victim: Luella George, Age 23 ......................................... 229
Victim: Donna Veldboom, Age 22 ................................... 230
The Ridge ........................................................................ 233
Victim: Irene MacDonald, Age 31 ................................... 234
Corpus Delicti ................................................................. 235
Three Decades On ........................................................... 236

**Chapter 8**
*Ebb Tide: The 1980s* ................................................................... **239**
    A New Era ................................................................. 241
    Victim: Donna Jean Awcock, Age 17 ......................... 244
    Hot Potato ................................................................. 250
    "Who Killed Me?" ..................................................... 253
    Ties That Bind .......................................................... 255

**Chapter 9**
*Aftershocks* ................................................................................ **263**
    Typecast .................................................................... 265
    Reindeer Games ........................................................ 266
    London Calling ......................................................... 267
    Project Angel ............................................................ 270
    Unlocking the Past .................................................... 275
    A Better Mousetrap .................................................. 285

**Conclusion**
*London Reign* ............................................................................ **291**
    Crimes of Opportunity ............................................. 293
    Blacktop .................................................................... 293
    Generica ................................................................... 296
    Sister Cities & Serial Murder .................................... 299

**Postface**
*The Last Detective* ..................................................................... **303**
    Notes ......................................................................... 307
    Conclusion ................................................................ 316

**Selected Bibliography** ........................................................... **317**
**Index** ....................................................................................... **325**

*For the victims and their families,
and for the Dennis Alsops
—Senior and Junior—
who together carried the fire for over fifty years.*

# ACKNOWLEDGEMENTS

It's difficult to know where to start in terms of acknowledging all of the people who provided inspiration, support, and source material for this personally transformative book—my personal *Caine Mutiny*. In writing this book I have been inspired by the remarkable bravery and resilience of many. Ironically, and for very different reasons, I have also been motivated by the indifference and incompetence of an unduly influential but woefully ineffectual handful of pretenders.

During the course of my research, which broadly transcends my own investigative police work, academic teaching, scholarly and forensic research pursuits, and media productions, I have either directly or indirectly met some truly remarkable people. The academic, scholarly, and scientific collaborators, supporters, and intellectual contributors are the most obvious. The soon-to-be Dr. Lee Mellor—friend, colleague, and stalwart research assistant—is first up in this category, followed in short order by Dr. Eric Hickey—a true luminary and the original "public" criminologist—whose wisdom and insight are truly unrivalled on a global scale. Moving on, Dr. D.J. Williams at Idaho State University, Dr. Jonathon Vance, Dr. Tim Blackmore, Dr. Kim Luton, and Dr. Regna Darnell at Western University, together with Dr. Marcel Danesi at the University of Toronto, all played enormous roles in seeing the vision for this book through to completion. Detective Ken Maines of the American Investigative Society of Cold Cases—at once a sleuth and a forensic entrepreneur with a vision—as well as Dr. John Olsson of the British Institute for Forensic Linguistics and

Deneen Hernandez of the FBI's Forensic Cryptanalysis Unit also merit thanks, as do Dallas Drake of the Homicide Research Institute, Enzo Yaksic of the Multidisciplinary Collaborative on Sexual Crime and Violence, and Jeffrey Christian, an independent researcher and hired-gun armchair sleuth in the field of Canadian crime history, genealogy, and victimology. Other experts and trailblazers whose work is cited here—David Canter and D. Kim Rossmo—also deserve recognition for their calling as pioneers in helping to try to solve serial cases and unsolved crimes. Their research has played a significant role in advancing a number of the cases discussed in this book.

I also need to acknowledge the extraordinary support and commitment of countless police officers of varying rank, with whom I have worked and who have supported not only this book but also a wider vision regarding cold case closure in Canada. More specifically, from the London Police, I acknowledge Sergeant Dave Staines (ret.), Detective Constable Zaia Lazar (ret.), Sergeant Dave Gilmore, and from the OPP, Sergeant Barry Ruhl (ret.) Detective Constable John Veilleux, and Detective Shawn Mather. From the RCMP, I offer special thanks to Assistant Commissioner Cal Corley (ret.) and Staff Sergeant Gerard MacNeil (ret.), as well as Corporal Bob Basanti and Inspector Tino Liokossis, all of whom were early adopters and huge supporters of my teaching and research, first undertaken while still a cop myself. I'd also like to recognize and offer specific thanks to Detective Chris Neal and others with the Toronto Police Cold Case Unit for their tireless efforts and appreciation of my work. Beyond this list of names, there are another two-dozen officers between five police services I would like to thank and whose stories I'd also like to one day tell, as well as several Crown prosecutors who asked not to be mentioned by name for fear of predictable bureaucratic blowback. By extension, the crime reporters of the world, including Jane Sims at the *London Free Press*, who I credit with coining the term "the Truscott hangover" used in Chapter Two of this book, all deserve recognition for keeping public interest in these cases alive.

I also want to acknowledge and thank the extraordinary families who have met with me during my research and whose perseverance in the face of horrific tragedy, dashed hopes, questionable investigations, and sense of abandonment is the true inspiration for this book. The Jensen, White, English, Franklin, and Awcock families in particular are remarkable inspirations, and along with Dennis Alsop, are the real heroes of this dark age in London and Canadian history alike. I met a number of these very brave and tenacious people through Dennis Alsop's son—Dennis Jr.—who is fulfilling his father's tireless wish for closure and justice, and has done a great public service in the process. I also met some of them through the work done by the studios and networks affiliated with the production of the internationally syndicated mini-series *To Catch a Killer*. Further, Niki Wallis, who single-handedly captured the true essence and veritable innocence of those victims whose families, for the most part, I've met over recent years deserves tremendous gratitude for her vision, compassion, and acumen.

Lastly, the wonderful and dedicated students, faculty, and staff who volunteer their services, scholarship, and insights as part of my Cold Case Society at Western University deserve special thanks, especially my 2IC, Professor Neisha Cushing, my virtual assistant Brikena Qamili, and Barry Arnott with the Western University Archives Collection. Some of the students attached to the Society aspire to go on into policing, the practise of law, and victim services and counselling. Some simply have a passion for history and social justice. Others are logicians inevitably fascinated by the puzzles presented by cold cases and the challenge of building a better mousetrap—often at the expense of their own studies or personal lives. Regardless of what drives them, they are truly an inspiration and demonstrate how future generations of knowledge users will help shape the discourse of criminal investigation and improved professionalization of policing in Canada.

Lastly, with respect to Dennis Alsop Sr., my sentiments are perhaps best summarized with the words of epic crime novelist James Ellroy. In eulogizing Jack Webb (*Dragnet*'s iconic Joe Friday) in the revised 2005 edition of the Los Angeles crime anthology *The Badge*, he affectionately laments that "he kicked too soon…I never got a chance to thank him. I never got a chance to say, 'you got me hooked, I just followed your lead.'" While dying at age 92 is not really "too soon" in the grand scheme of things, the point is that I never had the chance to meet Dennis Alsop, something I regret. If I had, I would have told him that this is his book as much as mine, just as it is the book of any real cop who ever stuck with a case in spite of the odds and even after being told to drop it and move on. There's not too many of them left.

With thanks,

Michael Arntfield, PhD

# -PROLOGUE-
# KINGDOM HALL

"The angels will ferret him out."
– Jehovah's Witness Overseer Arthur Powley, 1966

Slouching back behind the wheel of a '57 Ford Meteor, he lay waiting. Closing time was 6:00 p.m., but nightfall was already half an hour past, the streets of a sleepy town devoid of witnesses—sitting eerily still at the edge of infamy.

The darkness and the cold was proof positive of a typical February night, but proof positive also of something else: his wait was over at last. There was no more putting it off. The mask of normalcy and conformity he had worn for so long would finally be removed to unveil the grotesque aberration that lay beneath. The conditions were too optimal not to act, to not follow his fiendish calling. Tonight would be the night he would surrender to the obsessions that for so long had consumed him—to the dark forces that had tormented him.

Three kids and a doting wife at home, including a newborn hurled headlong into an already screwed-up world—no matter. A dinner invitation offered and accepted he would have to miss and pretend forgetting if later asked—no matter. A moonlighting gig cleaning the local Bank of Montreal for which he would pull an uncharacteristic no show—no matter. Triple-booked solid on a Friday night, he had left himself plenty of options for juggling future alibis. But only arrested men need alibis, he thought, and only men who make mistakes get arrested—at least in the counties. For the most part, he was right.

From fifty paces out, as the clock struck 6:01 p.m., he watched through the frosted-over glass in the door as a sign on a string swung from "open" to "closed," the owner threw the switch, and darkness fell on the Aylmer Dairy Bar for the night. He had been to this same place many times before. It was an innocent and yesteryear "drug store" of the Norman Rockwell type—more milkshakes and fellowship than pharmaceuticals—that only seemed to exist in other peoples' idealistic memories, but which in this case, at least for a little while, was real.

He had been there under false pretences more than enough times to know the nighttime closing routine—to know *her* routine. She had been kind to him too. Extra scoops of ice cream each time he patronized the joint, whether on his lunch break, between odd jobs, on weekend dates with his wife, or after worship. It was all part of his cover—the believable but tenuous veneer of normalcy that bought him precious time between then and now. It was this same precious gift of time that allowed him to plan his attack, at last now just minutes away. With each visit to the dairy bar, their cross-counter chitchat inevitably turned time and again to the Jehovah's Witnesses, the local Kingdom Hall, and his recent, mysterious absences. She had tried to reignite his interest in worship, his faith in the Creator. She had implored him to attend the Hall more regularly, to reconnect with the group, to commit to the doctrines, and to read *The Watchtower*. He sat, listened, and feigned interest, but his mind wandered elsewhere, creeping farther with each visit toward a foreboding place.

All the while, for months on end he had sat in the same swivel stool and peered over the same coffee-stained linoleum counter, watching her work—watching her serve him. Each subtle movement, each passing glance and genuine smile only fuelled his increasingly cruel fantasies, endlessly intensifying his longing for this night of all nights. The antecedents of his obsession, the starting point for the terminus that was about to reveal itself, he could never fully recall. All he could remember is that he had been sowing the seeds of this very opportunity for longer than he ever thought possible. Here and now, at this place, at this time, and on this frigid and otherwise unremarkable night, his mission would finally come to fruition. If he pulled it off, it would not be the last—that much he knew for sure. This was the night his betrayal of her trust would be complete, as would his own conversion of another kind. It would be a metamorphosis into a twisted monster of such folkloric proportion that even his elders and the overseers at the Kingdom Hall would later struggle to find the appropriately hellish metaphors to describe him, and to describe what happened that night.

Through the clouded windshield of the Meteor, he saw two plumes of steam in the cold night air as the front door to the diner opened and then closed again, the owner and the girl talking—exchanging goodnights and see you tomorrows—before they abruptly split up. It was now a quarter past the hour. The owner, still wearing a counterman's visor, struggled to slip the key in the latch and spin the frozen tumbler to lock up for the night. At the same time, the girl tenuously gripped her blue peacoat and headed due south into a freezing headwind—directly into his path. The hunt was canned.

The monster rocked the key in the column until the engine turned over. The vents blasted hot air in his face; London AM radio crackled in at *mezzo forte* through the single speaker in the dash. With headlights silhouetting a petite, solitary figure shuffling down an ice rink walkway, the Meteor crept up John Street as he swung left and slowed into the oncoming lane. Whitewalls snagged the curb; he hand-cranked the driver's window as the girl—head down—meandered towards him. "Georgia?" he called out innocently, while fiddling with the radio volume as if both surprised and concerned. It was Act One of what would be, until that time, the performance of his life.

The girl looked up from beneath her propped-up coat collar as if startled, but then recognized the figure in the driver's seat as her eyes adjusted and he came into focus. Her concern soon morphed into confusion. In looking at him alone in the Meteor—no wife or kids on board, nothing but a glib smile—she must have thought that his being there was inherently strange. But then again, she knew he likely just finished putting in a full day at the Canadian National yard just one town over. After all, that same nomadic and unpredictable job was why he always seemed to be "in the neighbourhood" whenever she was working the closing shift alone at the dairy bar—which was pretty much always.

It was a seemingly random evening encounter, but there was actually nothing random about it. So the twisted game played on, and right on cue, he insisted that she get in and take a ride. While it was a comparatively short trek home to her parents' house, where she lived with her little brother and sister, it was also too cold to be out walking if there were alternatives, or so he reminded her. He was convincing to say the least. And then, of course, there was the recent string of murders just a few minutes down the highway in infamous London. Even in the proverbial Sleepy Hollow of Aylmer, everyone knew of the most recent London and area cases—all London women and little girls, all horrifically murdered in the last few years—all *unsolved*. With so many potential killers still on the loose, once daylight dies, as it does so early in February, there was no safe place to be walking alone, at least in theory. That much the girl remembered. The monster in the mask driving the Meteor reminded her of it once again—and again.

But socializing with men—married men at that—outside of the Kingdom Hall, let alone getting into a car with one of them alone, was forbidden in the girl's world. It was a world of innocence and kindness where, amidst the hippie rhetoric of the time, genuine niceties and traditional decorum still prevailed. What people might think of seeing her riding shotgun, unaccompanied in a fellow Witness's car, and the potential that she might indirectly offend someone immediately trumped any consideration for her own safety. On the other hand, she thought to herself, what was there to really be afraid of? After all, she had known his wife as a friend and fellow Witness since she was in the 7$^{th}$ grade. She had been to their wedding two years earlier, in April of '64, at the same Kingdom Hall where the girl was fast becoming a favourite of the overseers. After toggling her eyes back and forth between the darkened, ice-laden street and the warm and idling car, she stepped off the sidewalk and made her way towards the Meteor as a type of unlikely oasis. It was a decision that would help change the criminal complexion of one town forever, and would set into motion a series of events that would destroy countless lives and rewrite the Canadian history books all at once.

Seeing her moving towards the Meteor, he eagerly reached over to prop the passenger side open from the inside. The heavy door swung open against a freezing southern headwind and the girl grabbed it by the window on the rebound. She then gingerly sat down on the seat, and with a frozen and ominous "clunk" she unknowingly sealed herself inside a six-cylinder, two-door tomb. The door was barely sealed before the monster headed off north-bound at a spirited pace, assuring her that he would turn around and head back south to her house the first chance he got. But he didn't turn around. He headed for the county road 73 exit to the highway—the highway west, toward London.

Momentarily confused, the real situation soon dawned on the girl and a formless terror that she'd always known existed—since her childhood when she learned of the evil in the world from the overseers—was now finally coming into focus. That terror, at the age of twenty, was finally taking on a discernible form, and it was all around her. It would eventually consume her. As she began to fidget, coming to recognize her impending death sentence for the crime of being nothing more than a trusting small-town waitress, he wrapped his right arm around her, grabbed her shoulder, and pulled her across the front bench seat, tightly beside him, with a grip that told her everything about what was to come. With one hand on the wheel and the other keeping a crushing grip on her fragile body, he kept her plastered to his side as he floored the rusted wreck out of town. In the rear-view mirror, she watched as the only world she ever knew soon disappeared into a narrowing point amidst the black of night behind her. In that same mirror, she could also see the look of abject horror on her own face for the first time. The fact that she knew him, his wife, and everything about him was precisely what made this a one-way trip. There was no way he would ever let her speak a word of what was about to happen to anyone. He would make sure of it. From the moment she recognized and spoke to him on the street, for reasons beyond her control, she was already doomed. She now knew that for certain.

Struggling for her life, she began to scream and thrash wildly as she tried to inch her way towards the passenger door, the car veering shoulder to shoulder and fishtailing on the black ice as its rear bumper swayed side to side like the pendulum on a clock. Escape at any cost, even if it meant bailing from a speeding car onto a frozen county road, was the only option left. But he had other plans. Every contingency had been accounted for, including where he was going to dispose of her when he was done with her and where he would later deliberately lead the Witnesses and local cops to search for her in vain. In that final mile to the destination, the harder she pushed, and the louder she screamed, the angrier he became.

He had a vision for how the night was supposed to play out, but he also knew that reality seldom measured up to the fantasy. He was, after all, a realist as much as a monster—at least under pressure. An unconscious body was just as effective for what he had envisioned, so once they hit the highway, it was time to escalate to Plan B. Westbound in the shoulder lane, at just over the speed limit, he reached into the back seat, grabbed a leaded soda bottle, and brained the trusting virgin with it—not once, but twice. Through it all, the bottle remained intact, its reinforced glass base opening up the base of her skull beneath a quintessentially 60s up-do as blood started pooling out onto the vinyl backrest.

Ferrying a motionless and near lifeless body down the winter highway, with the girl slumped forward in the seat beside him, he then opted for Plan C and took a sudden detour to the adjoining countryside of Malahide Township, an area which would become a future favourite of his as he fantasized about the thrill of this first kill again and again. Pulling off onto an unploughed rural switchback, he killed the headlights and threw the Meteor into park. It was here where it would end. The girl, now semi-conscious and likely resigned to what was about to happen, looked him in the eye and spoke her final words before he set upon her. "My parents are waiting for me." It was at once a plea for mercy and a warning of the inevitable eventuality of his being caught. She was right on both accounts, but he didn't care. Not then. Not now.

An hour later, he was home again—back to wearing the mask of normalcy, with souvenirs of his horrific acts in hand, and trophies from the girl's body hidden at his secret lair elsewhere. It was, for the time being at least, back to pantomiming the family man—the man of newly restored faith, the rail worker, the night janitor, the handyman, the jack-of-all-trades and master of one: invisibility. His ability to hide in plain sight was, by then, his one and only transferable skill, and one that would continue to serve him well. It was a ruse that ended up working for the better part of six years, before being finally revealed for who he really was—*what* he still remains.

It was the winter of '66 and a storm was gathering. Thirty minutes down the road in London, it had already arrived. Before anyone could forecast it, the two fronts would collide. Then everything changed.

# -CHAPTER 1-
# CANADIAN HORROR STORY

"A city is more than a place in space, it is a drama in time."
-Sir Patrick Geddes, *Cities in Evolution*

# A CITY IN THE FOREST

For decades, the city of London, Ontario trumpeted itself as the "Forest City." It was one of those pseudonyms that seemed to have no known first instance, but which persisted for generations until it came to replace London's actual name in most public dialogues, like Chicago as the "Windy City" or Detroit as the "Motor City." From day one, the alias stuck, and it was quickly used to showcase the city's unique geography and ecology, to shrewdly brand London as a place surrounded by trees and nature. It was used to frame the city as a tranquil and peaceful setting respectful of its origins as a forested settlement—as Pleasantville writ large. Over the years, this same nickname was parlayed into an even shrewder marketing strategy to attract tourists, draw new residents, and spur economic development as the city sought to conjure an unrivalled blend of the urban and the bucolic. The motto was used to accentuate the city's abundance of parks, gardens, and what was for several generations an unprecedented number of hardwood trees. For a long time people believed the myth. Many still do. In reality, that forest for many years served as little more than camouflage—a veneer that hid what lay beyond. As the Brothers Grimm knew all too well, and aptly warned us about through their macabre fairy tales, forests—while outwardly picturesque and innocent places—harbour dark and foreboding characters. And even darker secrets.

This is a book about a city under siege. More than that, it's a snapshot of a specific time and place that many would like to forget and others never knew existed. It's a book that serves as an exposition on what should have been the best kept secret in Canada, but which is now almost without question the worst. What is detailed in the pages that lay ahead has never been told before. For the better part of a quarter century, an unassuming city that was considered to be the epitome of Mainstreet Canada managed to secure one of the most dubious distinctions of our era—being the serial killer capital of the nation and, more likely, beyond.

Admittedly, this is a provocative and controversial proclamation to make. Investigation was therefore first focused on an examination of resources that might *exclude* the city of London, Ontario as being the prime suspect, the recipient of this unwanted and unenviable mantle. I have therefore repetitively sought to uncover verifiable data that would refute what initial observations seemed to suggest, or at least to locate what we might call exculpatory evidence—facts that might allow me to alibi London and move on in my search. I could not.

In scrubbing countless databases and in consulting decades worth of data with respect to both solved and unsolved murders, as well as examining offence-specific details distilled from the array of sources cited throughout this book, I could find no competing case study over such a fixed interval of time. I have consulted with investigators and behavioural scientists with the FBI and its National Centre for the Analysis of Violent Crime, as well as from both law enforcement agencies and universities from Europe to Australia. I have engaged members and stakeholders with various research groups and think tanks, such as the Centre for Homicide Research, the Northeastern University Multidisciplinary Collaborative on Sexual Crime and Violence—arguably the most exclusive guild of criminology and serial offender subject matter experts in the world—as well as the American Investigative Society of Cold Cases. Translation: There are few if any true crime books anywhere that have been sourced and extensively peer reviewed to this degree. Conclusion: The London case study cited here remains unrivalled.

The reality is that, based on all of the available and verifiable data, it would seem that no other city or single location comes close—not by a long shot. After nearly three years' worth of collective research, London, Ontario—current population of roughly 470,000 residents in its *census metropolitan area* (CMA)—still holds the Canadian, North American, and seemingly global record for spawning, housing, or otherwise inviting in the greatest number of serial killers, as currently defined, over a prescribed period. It has hosted the greatest number of serial offenders either living or killing—or both—in one place and at one time relative to the total population.[1] On a per capita basis, during the historical period under scrutiny here, London had the greatest ratio of citizens to serial killers anywhere since firm statistics on violent crime have been credibly tabulated. Today, it remains a seemingly unbroken record—a seldom talked about chapter in the city's sordid past, and by extension, Canada's collective criminal heritage. This is now: London is a safe and prosperous, as well as a technologically and economically diverse city that boasts a violent crime rate well below the national average. But that was then—the will to forget or ignore won't change it.

There have been about sixty known serial killers in the history of Canadian crime. As is explained in this book, a total of at least six and as many as nine serial sexual murderers—ten to fifteen percent of the national total since Confederation—emerged from London's CMA over a comparatively compressed historical period. As a sedate city when this all began, one of just over 160,000 permanent residents, these figures are unrivalled even by cities as large as New York and Los Angeles, both of which have had up to four confirmed serial killers active at any given time. By way of comparison, if London had a population on par with these cities at that same point in history, one can extrapolate, on a per capita basis, the equivalent of eighty to one hundred killers walking the streets at any one time. Thirteen of the twenty-nine canonical victims slain during this period in London are accounted for by three previously identified killers—Russell Johnson, Gerald Thomas Archer, and Christian Magee. It provides no comfort to know that the sixteen other unsolved killings are then attributable to at least three other serial murderers, rather than sixteen individual murderers each killing one victim in discrete incidents. That said, neither prospect is any less horrific than the other. These figures, of course, also don't include the litany of other "routine" murders that occurred in London during this same period, most of which—by comparison at least—have since been solved.

It should however be noted that London, although the apparent national capital of serial homicide, has never been the Canadian "murder capital," a title frequently obsessed over by the press and the Canadian public at once. Over the last several decades, and since firm numbers have been tabulated by the Canadian Centre for Justice Statistics on homicide in Canada, the city of Winnipeg has consistently overshadowed all other cities as the murder capital of the nation. This refers to the greatest total number of murders per capita annually. Winnipeg has earned this classification a total of sixteen times, more than twice the total of Ottawa-Gatineau as the distant runner-up. Toronto, on the other hand, has never even charted, although watching or reading national news reports with a decidedly Toronto-centric crime narrative might suggest otherwise to the untrained eye.

There has always been a sort of oral history about London's place in the narrative of crime and sexual violence in Canada—about it, once upon a time, being an unlikely and unprecedented haven for serial killers. When I began my policing career in the late 1990s, this distinction was talked about by various people in legal and academic communities as though it were common knowledge—a widely known fact, albeit one not found in any book. Nearly twenty years later, that book has now been written, all of the supporting data compiled in a single volume of work, here for the first time. In comparing London, Ontario to other Canadian cities over this same period, the numbers quite simply speak for themselves. That said, this book is not about fixating on numbers but is instead about providing the necessary *context* for these numbers—an understanding of the fixations and paraphilias of serial killers and what either brought them to London or how the city turned them out. Above all, it is about victims, families, and loss—the human stories behind the statistics.

# THE BASEMENT BOOK OF THE DEAD

The realities of serial killers operating in London and area, and the details to follow about paraphilias and signatures of those killers, is no doubt disturbing, but in the context of today's advances, this same information is in most part available through various public databases, books, and scholarly journals for those motivated to find it. Sadly, such motivation has often not been bestowed upon those tasked—and trusted—with investigating the associated crimes.

Such realities were certainly *not* lost on one Dennis Alsop, a celebrated career case man with the Ontario Provincial Police (OPP), who retired a Detective Superintendent in 1979 and who later died in 2011, at the age of 92. Before he died, Dennis knew, much ahead of his time and without knowledge of future terminology and investigative advances, that the potential answers to the cases that had haunted him his whole life could not die with him. These were cases of the murdered London and area women, teens, and children whose deaths seem to have defied everything he thought possible about civilized society and police work at once. He consequently got his affairs in order and consolidated a lifetime's worth of data familiar to him and boxed it up—literally. He knew that whether it were the pages of a definitive case study or criminology textbook, or the pages of one of his own key reports that he wrote as the lone warrior against London's cabal of serial sex killers decades earlier, none of it was likely to be read by his erstwhile peers if he ever left it to the police. So, he didn't.

During his storied career, for nearly twenty of the twenty-five years covered in this book, he had single-handedly inherited most of the murders occurring in London and region. Other murders outside his jurisdiction were followed up by him off the books. He had started as a junior crime scene tech on the Lynne Harper murder in the summer of '59 and checked-out following the reign of the so-called "Bedroom Strangler" in 1979. He had investigated the murders of the London schoolboys, which started the nation's Block Parent program, and had managed, while sequestered in an office in Toronto, to assist the OPP investigators assigned to the "Mad Slasher" task force in the late 1970s by submitting his insights and hunches through the now extinct police teletype system. Dennis was the point man for what remains the most strange and unsettling era of crime in one city in Canadian history. The London region over the troubling quarter-century covered in this book was certainly a place where men of action were in short supply. During the city's darkest hour, however, it was Dennis—from Constable to Corporal to Detective Sergeant to Detective Inspector to Detective Chief Inspector and ultimately to Detective Superintendent—who today prevails as the unlikely, and really, the sole protagonist of this era. Fighting against unimaginable bureaucracy within his own organization and deadly denial within the same city and region he swore to protect, he went at it alone and would spend the rest of his career and even his life hunting the hunters. For a while, it seemed, the hunters even tried hunting him back, not to mention his own family. Yet he remained undaunted and immovable in an age of silent fear and in the face of looming danger. Today, his assemblage of accumulated writings, clippings, and photographs prevails as what is likely one of the most important private historical collections available with respect to crime in Canada, and serves as a decoder ring that unlocks a dark and forgotten past.

Although a veteran cop myself, I had admittedly never heard of Dennis Alsop prior to 2011. The OPP history books and museums are defined by savvy sloganeering and are full of dates and superfluous details about when new equipment was acquired or when new buildings were opened, but there are few (if any) stories about men like Dennis. When he retired, he went away quietly and did the friendly fade with the OPP, most or all of his hunches having been ignored and his pleas for assistance overlooked by his own organization. But old Dennis still had one final trick up his sleeve.

Secreted away in the basement of his London home during his final years, Dennis engineered the criminological equivalent of the Paris Opera Vault—arguably one of the most famous time capsules ever made. But while the Parisian version housed rare recordings to be opened up by future generations, Dennis Alsop's capsule housed rare and forgotten files containing the answers to murder mysteries and unspeakable crimes that had long since gone cold. As a veritable Pandora's Box, which, once opened, would pick the scabs off the city's bloody past, it contained a ledger of names that had long since become a listing of ghosts, and which he would soon take to his grave with him. London's book of the dead listed both the victims and their killers, whether known or suspected, many of whom found a way to escape justice and get away with it, some of whom were never so much as identified, and some of whom are still alive today—roaming free. It infuriated Dennis in life, but in death he would find some solace by finally passing on the torch.

A few months after his death, and while his house was being cleaned out of its final effects, this same box was found by Dennis Alsop's son—Dennis Jr.—just as his father had intended. The secret cache was not limited to diaries, logs, notes, reports, and interview transcripts. It also contained carbon and Photostat copies of original case files and crime scene photos, all believed to have been long since lost to history. The documents told a story never before known about what *really* happened in London. The story, told as a type of epistolary novel through clippings, memos, reports, and teletype transmissions started with the infamous murder of Lynne Harper in Clinton, an hour north of London and where Dennis's investigative career began. It seemed that, from there on, much of what happened in London appeared to be intertwined or connected. Dennis Jr., knowing the significance of what he had found, also knew that his father left the box to be found by him and him alone. He further knew that he had some tough decisions to make. In the end, he contacted me.

I would like to say that the rest was history, but it turned out to be only the beginning. Dennis Sr. had some remarkable insights and was able to connect the dots in ways that, I'm almost certain, baffled and intimidated his colleagues and handful of loyalists before he was shipped out of London towards the end of his career. I'm certain that Dennis himself was not sure how he knew it or how to make sense of it but he intuitively did nonetheless—decades ahead of the forensic advances of today. In the 1887 novel *A Study in Scarlet*, Sir Arthur Conan Doyle's first full book depicting the savant sleuth, Sherlock Holmes says: "It was easier to know it than to explain why I know it. If you were asked to prove that two and two made four, you might find some difficulty, and yet you are quite sure of the fact." Indeed, in my first look through that box of decades' old clues, on yellowed paper and in dusty hardcover diaries, it's clear that by the end of his career—and even more so at the twilight of his life—Dennis knew he was close to breaking the London and area cases that had rewritten the record books, but for which he had been sidelined for years by bureaucratic drones higher-up. He just didn't know how to explain it. Now, it's my turn.

Dennis knew that the box contained information that was not only unsettling but also damaging. It was, for all intents and purposes, a radioactive package that needed to be handled with care and could never fall into the wrong hands. By the time he died, he had resigned himself to the fact that those wrong hands might include the same types of police managers who had constrained him the first time around. He was once bitten twice shy, even from beyond the grave. He knew that, as the song by The Who cautions, the new boss really is the same as the old boss.

Today, those files from that box have travelled a circuitous and dramatic route back to the OPP. Time will tell what they will be able to make of them. In the meantime, the story of the Forest City, its people, and what happened there over an unprecedented quarter century, is told here for the first time, with overdue answers revealed, original theories introduced, and all of the old-time cop's hunches and obsessive gumshoeing overlaid onto the latest analytic and scientific methods in the study of crime and serial offending. The box and its book of the dead unites Dennis and me across time and space as two men mutually consumed with the search for the truth. I would be lying if I said that inheriting the box was not something of a cross to bear—one half curse, one half blessing. Knowledge is power, they say, but at the same time ignorance is also bliss. I guess you can't have it both ways.

MICHAEL ARNTFIELD

# PORTRAIT OF A SERIAL KILLER

Serial killers are a complex lot—one size does not fit all. They have been both lionized and demonized as uncanny other-worldly beings, in part because of their statistical rarity and the fact that their methods and motives remain mysterious to so many. A closer look confirms that most are as pathetic as they are horrific, and that it is in fact the unremarkable and pointless nature of their own lives that fuels their actions and their need to destroy the lives of others. Such destructive behaviours are, it seems, in the absence of proper investigations and a willingness by communities to recognize their existence in the first place, the one area of their lives where they can achieve some degree of "success." Extensive study and research on serial offenders by countless experts has subsequently determined categories and sub-categories of organization, methodology, mobility, and violent fantasy that prompt these behaviours. Further, since sexual assault plays a part in most, albeit not all, serial killings, there are also rapist typologies, which measure degrees of sexuality and rage. It is intended that what follows provide a basic definitional tutorial and lead to a better understanding of the chapters ahead, terms used, and above all, the phenomenon of serial killing in general. This examination of serial killers and their choice of victims, through the lens of modern criminological theory, criminal investigative analysis, and forensic victimology—all disciplines that have come of age since many of the unsolved cases cited here have gone cold—reveals specific and individuating behavioural discriminators that are much better understood today.

In brief, a serial killer—the definition having been revised in 2006—is someone who has murdered on two distinctive occasions and who generally displays certain sexual, ideological, compulsive, and even psychopathic characteristics that can be identified subsequent to that second killing. By contrast, a mass murderer can be generally defined as someone who has killed three or more people in a single incident, whether at a fixed location or as part of a mobile killing spree. The terms are, in fact, mutually exclusive.

What also separates serial killers from mass murderers is the frequent presence of psychopathic as well as paraphilic compulsions that precipitate offending. Paraphilia is the experience of intense and often dangerous sexual arousal in response to atypical objects, situations, or individuals, while the definition of psychopathy is more complicated, and is often used interchangeably—and erroneously—with psychosis. I will begin with a quick discussion of the latter.

## PSYCHOTIC VS. PSYCHOPATHIC KILLERS

In simplest terms, psychosis is a condition that can be either acute or chronic in nature, and which amounts to a disorder of the mind or some other cognitive abnormality that presents itself in an obvious—or clinical—fashion. This might include a diagnosed mental illness such as schizophrenia or bipolar disorder, and which might be associated with delusions, hallucinations, or states of altered reality that are substance or stress-induced, or just hereditary.

Psychopathy on the other hand is slightly more complicated. By definition, a clinical or criminal psychopath is an individual who scores 30 or higher on a standardized test known as the Psychopathy Checklist Revised (PCL-R), which was designed and later revised by Dr. Robert Hare, a Canadian experimental psychologist and pioneer in the field. The PCL-R, sometimes cited as the Hare Checklist in reference to its creator, measures four types of distinct behaviours known as facets, and which gauge dominant features ranging from impulse control problems and malignant narcissism to manipulative character traits and a general lack of empathy. Hare's work in this area builds on an earlier version developed in the 1950s known as the Cleckley Checklist, similarly named for its creator Hervey Cleckley, and whose research suggested that the psychopath could in part be summed up by what he called an "innate fearlessness." This might mean a fearlessness of taking risks, pushing the limits, hurting people, or getting caught—or all of the above.

Beyond the distinction between psychosis and psychopathy, it should be noted that a psychopath is also different from what is known as a sociopath, though the difference is more subtle. Prior to the 1980s, when Dr. Hare helped clean up the nomenclature, the terms psychopath and sociopath were routinely and wrongfully used as synonyms. Even today, the distinction is lost on many people who should know better, including those in law enforcement. There are countless studies and even full university courses on distinguishing the two, but for the purposes of this book the easiest way to differentiate a psychopath from a sociopath is to think of a sociopath as someone who often possesses psychopathic *traits* and who exhibits evidence of what's known as anti-social personality disorder, but who does not necessarily meet the threshold of clinical psychopathy. In other words, they might be malicious and even sexually or interpersonally treacherous, but they may not necessarily obtain a sufficiently high score on the PCL-R to merit classification as a psychopath. Phrased differently, one might say that a sociopath is a type of psychopath-lite; or, that while a sociopath has major behavioural problems, sexual perversions, and impulse control issues, they lack the psychopath's grandiosity or simply do not know any better. The psychopath, on the other hand, often knows better and simply does not care—they know and *like* what they are.

# ORGANIZED VS. DISORGANIZED KILLERS

The level of organization shown by a serial murderer, even a one-time killer, at a crime scene and the specific activities conducted with the victim either before or after death—or during the act of murder itself—make strong statements about the offender's motives, level of intelligence, and whether they may be either psychotic or psychopathic. With few exceptions, an *organized offender* is closely correlated with psychopathy, while a *disorganized offender* is associated with psychosis. Crime scene data and biographical details relating to offenders, collected over the last several decades in both North America and the United Kingdom, point to overwhelming commonalities among organized offenders and disorganized offenders to the extent that what a killer does *not* do can be as revealing as what he or she (generally *he*) *does* do in terms of specific crime scene behaviours. This includes whether he acts with planning, premeditation, and is in control of his actions, or whether he acts impulsively and opportunistically and worries about the consequences later—if at all. Organization levels can also reflect factors as simple as offender mobility, including access to a car, which in itself is a variable that can be used to narrow the field of suspects.

<u>Organized</u>
Medium to high intelligence
Socially and sexually capable
Employed with a stable work history
Controlled during the crime
Living with someone, likely an intimate partner

Highly mobile with regular access to a vehicle
Follows the police investigation in the media
Interest in police gadgets, weapons, and investigative techniques
Previous or ongoing interest in becoming a police officer
Uses alcohol prior to the crime and a habitual drinker
Premeditated crime stemming from specific fantasies
Victim is a random stranger or targeted stranger fitting a certain preference
Conversation/seduction with/of victim
Uses restraints and seeks dominance/compliance
Possible captivity of victim
Crime scene cleaned and/or weapon(s) removed
Victim's body transported/concealed
May participate in search for victim or aid in investigation
May move or change routine after the crime

<u>Disorganized</u>
Low to medium intelligence
Socially and sexually incapable
Unemployed and lack of a stable work history
Anxious or panicked during the crime
Lives alone or has no fixed address
Lives near the crime scene/attack location
Limited mobility, has no immediate access to a vehicle
Little interest in media attention or investigative status
Limited alcohol use
Crime is spontaneous and opportunistic
Victim is usually a random stranger, location not predetermined
Little to no conversation with the victim
Attack is sudden, explosive, and excessive
No use of restraints
Postmortem sexual acts or mutilations are common
Body left at scene in plain view, usually on back (supine)
Weapon left at scene, crime scene messy and obvious

Some serial offenders, such as "Night Stalker" Richard Ramirez—whose horrific home invasion, Satanic-themed murders terrorized Los Angeles in

1985—confirm that a comparatively rare breed of killer can toggle back and forth between both organized and disorganized traits. We now recognize this type of hybrid killer as belonging to a third "mixed" category of offender, and who exhibits one or both organized and disorganized behaviours based on immediate circumstances. These cases are rare, however, and do not reflect an attempt to use profiling countermeasures or toy with investigators as much they do the fact that some killers have a personal level of organization that is variable and reactive, often reflecting responses to the specific behaviour of their victim.

## PROCESS-FOCUSED VS. ACT-FOCUSED KILLERS

Whether organized, disorganized, or mixed in their behaviours, serial and sexual murderers can be further separated into one of two methodological categories that involve the commission of the crime itself, known as the offender "focus." In Canada, whether a killer is *process-focused* or *act-focused* is supposed to be determined through the completion of the Violent Crime Analysis System (ViCLAS) questionnaire, which is discussed again later, and which includes a series of 262 questions to be completed by investigators and then uploaded to a national database for comparison. While the RCMP, which administers the database in all provinces except Ontario and Quebec, claims that 3200 linkages among some 300,000 violent crimes have been made to date, the system and its skyrocketing licensing and maintenance costs have been met with great public and media criticism. This is in part because many of these purported linkages are thought by some to represent overstatements of the system's abilities. This issue will also be discussed later along with the U.S. equivalent, the Violent Criminal Apprehension Program (ViCAP), which predates the Canadian version.

Without compromising the required secrecy of the ViCLAS questionnaire, it could be said that a process-focused murderer, with rare exception, is one who fits one of the following subtypes: the hedonist-thrill killer, the hedonist-lust killer, and the power-control killer. The act-focused serial murderer is instead one of either a hedonist-comfort killer, a visionary killer, or a missionary killer.

As we move forward, consider that a process-focused killer is—as the term suggests—a murderer who is focused or fixated on the actual process of killing; he enjoys it and seeks to prolong the experience, extend the victim's terror or suffering, and the emotional and sexual satisfaction he obtains from it. Strongly affiliated with organized offenders and psychopaths, process-focused killers are typically sexual sadists whose fantasies are built around extreme violence and deep-seated paraphilias.

An act-focus killer, on the other hand, is a comparatively clinical and efficient killer who—with some rare but notable exceptions—dispatches his victims to fulfil some ulterior motive such as financial gain or as part of some grand (and usually delusional) vision. Another way to describe the difference between the two types is to say that victims of process-focused victims show evidence of *expressive* violence—acts that serve a symbolic or intrinsically gratifying purpose and that are carried out solely to express the killer's paraphilic fantasies, such as mutilation, amputation, torture, or posing. Victims of act-focused killers tend to instead show evidence of *instrumental* violence, or acts carried out solely to bring about death, and which offer no additional symbolism for the killer.

## MO VS. SIGNATURE

Assessing acts of expressive versus instrumental violence at crime scenes or during subsequent autopsies is also a key step in separating a killer's *modus operandi*, or method of operating (usually abbreviated as simply MO) from what's known as a criminal signature. Police have traditionally placed great emphasis on a killer's MO, and this over-reliance has been played out in countless crime films and television series where "matching" MOs seems to be enough to break a case. The reality is that MOs are highly unstable and can change as frequently as the killer's mood, level of sobriety, access to weapons, the behaviour of a victim, or even the weather. Edmund Kemper, the "Co-Ed Killer"—a wannabe cop who picked-up, murdered, and frequently decapitated hitchhiking college girls in northern California from 1964 to 1973, in addition to murdering his mother and both grandparents in separate incidents—got away with his crimes for so long in part because his MO varied so wildly. A process-focused killer at heart, Kemper preferred to strangle his victims if possible and prolong the rush of the kill. But if things didn't go as planned, when victims resisted and things quickly spiralled out of control, he would stab them as a matter of convenience, taking on a more act-focused MO. The police at the time fell into a trap of what we call "linkage blindness" by failing to connect victims bearing signs of different MOs, which had for years been how crimes were solved. A decade later, this same linkage blindness and a lack of standardized law enforcement training with respect to signature analysis was exploited by another serial killer targeting college girls named Ted Bundy. In roaming the United States from as early as 1961 to 1978, from the Pacific Northwest to the Florida Panhandle, Bundy changed weapons and body-disposal tactics to present the illusion of different killers employing different MOs in different jurisdictions. While Kemper's MO fluctuated as a matter of convenience and circumstance, and Bundy's variance was used for strategic purposes and to exploit police communication deficiencies, the bottom line is that MOs evolve, devolve, and sometimes change entirely. Signatures, on the other hand, are a different story entirely.

The MO describes all of the elements required to carry out the act of murder—the instrumental violence. Every killer, serial or otherwise, has an MO, as does nearly every habitual criminal from the most petty of shoplifters to the most brazen of armoured-car robbers. A signature, by comparison, is limited in most cases to sexually-motivated and process-focused killers, and is what the killer does to realize his fantasy and feel fulfilled and satiated until his next crime. Whether it involves the collecting of souvenirs (a victim's identification, jewellery, or clothing) or trophies (body parts, flesh, or hair), or involves elaborate posing or ritualistic activities, signatures are just that—unique and individuating characteristics that are difficult to fake, and which are the tell-tale indicators of a killer's mindset and the nature of their underlying paraphilias.

## PREPARATORY PARAPHILIA VS. ATTACK PARAPHILIA

Signatures are sometimes referred to as paraphilic footprints because, in their elaborate or grotesque design rests the unique impression left by a killer's life story. The first season of the critically acclaimed HBO series *True Detective* remains one of the only fictional crime narratives, in either film or television history, to credibly discuss the origins of paraphilias and how they escalate and become more elaborate with each new victim. From the Greek word *"para,"* meaning "beside" or "other," and *"philia,"* meaning "love," the term describes an attachment to or fixation on objects, images, people, or circumstances that is either forbidden by conventional society or prohibited by law—often both. Many paraphilias are harmless and strictly reflect sexual preferences and desired "types" while others are so bizarre and offensive that indulging them inevitably violates laws and social norms.

Most paraphilias are thought to develop in early childhood, usually as part of some emotionally or sexually traumatic experience. By the time a child—in most cases a male—reaches puberty, these paraphilias are hardwired into their personality and sexuality. Many of these paraphilias never escalate beyond the primary or preparatory stage, where an individual experiments with different scenarios or sexual partners and objects. A psychopath, however—especially one who also happens to be a paraphiliac and who consistently places their own sexual gratification, need for power, and selfish interests ahead of the feelings or safety of others—will often progress to experimenting with secondary paraphilias, often called attack paraphilias.

Attack paraphilias are indulgences in fantasy enactment that require violence against others, or non-consenting partners, in order to complete. The term is used interchangeably with criminal paraphilia in that these acts, by their very nature, violate one or more criminal statutes. The need to act on these impulses is often not a well thought-out decision. It is instead a compulsion that dates to an offender's formative years, when his personality and sexual self-image was first imprinted. Because attack paraphilias—acquired or developed when preparatory paraphilias become boring or outmoded—involve non-consenting partners, murder is often not surprisingly connected to the fantasy itself. As rightfully described in *True Detective*, these murders that are the result of attack paraphilias "don't just happen in a vacuum," and in looking at London during the period in question, we therefore have to ask what collective social forces were behind the recurring patterns seen in both preparatory and attack paraphilias at work in such a closed community.

*Preparatory paraphilias* routinely seen in London during the period in question and cited in this book include:

- Exhibitionism: Arousal or obsession channelled by exposing oneself or committing indecent acts in front of strangers and in public places. Correlated with scatologia and a known early indicator of numerous attack paraphilias, including both pedophilia and necrophilia.
- Mechanophilia: A sexual fixation on machines and repeating devices, usually nondescript and functional in their design. A known predictor of necrophilia and other necrophilic spectrum behaviours.
- Partialism: A sexual or fantasy-oriented obsession with single, usually atypical, body parts (eyes, ears, fingers, etc.). Correlated with necrophilia and a known predictor of necrosadism.
- Placophilia: A sexual fixation on tombstones, crypts, mausoleums, and memorials. Correlated with taphophilia and a known predictor of necrophilia.
- Scatologia: Also known as telephone scatologia, it describes arousal and empowerment obtained by anonymously making obscene or frightening phone calls—usually repeated—to unsuspecting victims. Correlated with exhibitionism, and a known predictor of numerous attack paraphilias.
- Scopophilia: Also known as voyeurism, it describes arousal and empowerment obtained by covertly watching or photographing persons engaged in sexual or other intimate behaviours. Common among Peeping Toms and a known predictor of a variety of attack paraphilias. A sub-category that involves watching persons engaged in non-sexual behaviours and conducting surveillance of their everyday activities is known as *crytoscopophilia*.
- Taphophilia: Sexual excitement from being in or near cemeteries, mortuaries, and funerals. Correlated with placophilia and a known predictor of necrophilia.
- Zoophilia: Sexual excitement or empowerment obtained through either visual or physical contact with animals, or by engaging in sexual acts with animals. Correlated with exhibitionism and a known predictor of both pedophilia and necrophilia.

*Attack paraphilias* tend to be more rare given the risk involved and their correlation with psychopathy, which is also statistically rare. The attack paraphilias relating to the London and area serial murders discussed in this book, both solved and unsolved, include:

- Amokoscisia: A desire or compulsion to slash, disfigure, or mutilate women, sometimes known as Jack the Ripper Syndrome. Correlated with erotophonophilia, necrophilia, and necrosadism.
- Blastolagnia: A fantasy-based fixation on sexually initiating young females, usually teens or preteen virgins, and often by force. Correlated with pedophilia.
- Erotophonophilia: A paraphilia associated with what are known as lust murders, specifically the murdering and mutilating of females, often strangers. Correlated with necrosadism.
- Necrophilia: Arousal through engaging in sexual acts with or being intimately connected to human corpses. Correlated with numerous necrophilic spectrum behaviours, including necrosadism.
- Necrosadism: Arousal or preoccupation with committing indignities to or defiling and/or mutilating and humiliating dead bodies. Correlated with erotophonophilia, odaxelagnia, and cannibalistic behaviours not otherwise classified.
- Odaxelagnia: A sexual fixation on biting or inflicting injuries or markings with one's teeth. Correlated with erotophonophilia and necrosadism.
- Pedophilia: A sexual preference for young children or apparently prepubescent adolescents. Common among what's known as polymorphistic sexual murderers, or sadistic killers who have no preferred victim or gender and who simply require a victim they can easily control for sadistic purposes.
- Sadism: Sexual arousal from inflicting suffering on others or rendering people helpless and eliciting responses that convey fear, panic, or pain in order to gratify the offender. Correlated with all of the other attack paraphilias cited here.

The origins of these and other paraphilias—many of which show up in London before even being formally classified in the clinical and forensic literature—and how and why they take hold to dominate a person's life has been the focus of much debate. Some experts have proposed a combination of environmental and biological explanations. For instance, necrophilia has been affiliated with diminished intelligence and compromised brain development in countless case studies (biological), as well as parental neglect and sexual prohibition in the home during developmental years (environmental). It is also disproportionately represented among persons of both genders who have a paralysing fear of rejection or abandonment, or who were punished as children for viewing erotic material. Other explanations are purely environmental, the most compelling and frequently cited being what's known as the "vandalized love map" theory.

The vandalized love map theory was first proposed by pioneering psychologist Dr. John Money at Johns Hopkins University in the 1980s. In essence, Money's theory would seem to explain two facts about paraphilias. The first is why they tend to be more common among males, and the second is why victims of sexual abuse often become abusers themselves. Money proposed that it is human nature, and the product of our evolutionary biology once we begin to develop a sexual curiosity and awareness of our bodies in childhood or early adolescence, to instinctively form innate interconnections between sex and consent, love and lust, intimacy and respect. If left to his or her own devices, a healthy child in a healthy household will do this on his or her own accord, using his or her parents and other adult role models as exemplars. These ensuing connections are what are collectively known as the love map—a frame of reference for all intimate relationships through each stage in life. However, the child who (during this very sensitive and exploratory, curious, and role-playing stage) is subject to mockery, prevention, prohibition, or punishment will have the routes of reference between sex and consent, love and lust, intimacy and respect all corrupted and re-routed. As the child's love map becomes vandalized and healthy connections are damaged, the child becomes imprinted with ideas of the body and intimate situations that are highly abnormal, even violent and humiliating. Like so many things in life, it all goes back to childhood, and the trauma associated with a vandalized love map will in later years form bizarre sexual preferences that replace people with objects and consenting and reciprocal situations with bizarre and sadistic fantasies left to fester as the child grows older and learns to act on them.

It is male children who are the most common victims of the vandalized love map, or least whose lives show evidence of tampering years later. Dr. Money's explanation for this is that, because male brains are often more visually oriented than those of females—which tend to be more sensory—males will in some cases visually fixate on specific objects that are immediately available as substitutions for people as they learn to compensate in the face of trauma and shame. Sometimes, this happens during the actual process of the love map being vandalized, such as when a specific visual stimulus becomes forever associated with a life-changing traumatic incident. The child, in looking at a pair of women's shoes, the family dog, or a set of soiled clothing on the floor while being physically punished for accessing an erotic image or touching themselves, may in turn develop a visual association between sexual arousal, pain, humiliation, and the image of the item—or the item itself. Over time, the strength of these associations may also expand to take on new stimuli, which also explains why paraphiliacs seldom have only one fetish or fixation. It also explains why many sexually abused males go on to become abusers themselves, in that the trauma of being abused simultaneously vandalizes their own love maps and also prompts them to perpetuate the same pattern of vandalism and cycle of abuse as they grow older and victimize other children.

Of course, not every vandalized love map translates into the development of attack paraphilias. Some never even make it as far as the preparatory stage, while others go on to become debilitating, transforming their hosts into dangerous and incorrigible predators. Either way, the shift from idle, preparatory paraphilias kept behind closed doors to the willingness to take the life of an innocent stranger to indulge one or more attack paraphilias is not without some type of distant early warning. With few exceptions, attack paraphilias are preceded by experimentation with preparatory paraphilias as a type of dress rehearsal for more serious criminal offending. It is therefore important to understand that all sexual offenders—including those who the associated research still refers to as "rapists"—have their own distinct pathways of escalation. This includes whether or not they eventually graduate to sexual murder and by extension serial murder. To understand the crimes outlined in the pages that follow, we must therefore first try to understand the MO of each category of rapist, nearly all of whom are discussed throughout this book.

## RAPIST TYPOLOGIES

During the historical period covered here, it is evident that neither the medical nor legal system placed a great deal of interest in the rights of women, or by extension, children. This indifference no doubt also helped inspire the systemic culture of permissiveness and depravity that consumed London and area during that same era—one later seen throughout Canada as a whole in the 1980s and 1990s, as the national homicide rate reached a historical high. The current movement to (re)educate the public about the myths and realities of sexual assault has unfortunately meant having to try and reprogram many of the collective attitudes about rape as a result of what went on back then, and what has since been passed down through equally offensive traditions and even court decisions. It was a time in history when it seems that sexual consent and sexual submission—or more accurately, sexual surrender—were seen as the same thing. Some of the court decisions that emerged from this period are nothing short of appalling in terms of how suspects, and even convicted killers, were coddled by the Canadian legal system—the denial of sex itself being seen as a form of provocation and a justification for violence, lessening the responsibility of the accused. The one positive legacy of this nadir of common sense is how these cases have since allowed experts to assemble an inventory of rapist characteristics over time, and with each typology of rapist being gauged according to two main motivators: sexuality/fantasy and aggression/rage.

- Type 1 Rapist: High/High - *High* sexuality/fantasy and *high* aggression/rage. This is among the most paraphilic of typologies, with a desire to hurt, humiliate, and dominate, and with the offender placing great erotic value on destructive behaviours, including murder. Often associated with a "park rapist," this typology relies heavily on mental rehearsal and often involves a preferred location or victim type, with the offender scouting attack positions ahead of time.

- Type 2 Rapist: Low/High – *Low* sexuality/fantasy and *high* aggression/rage. Extreme violence in the case of this typology is inevitable, regardless of the age of the victim and even in the case of full submission. The rage is not the result of a sexual impulse, but is a sadistic end in itself, and is used to control, instill fear, or cause pain—any of which may or may not have a paraphilic purpose. Often associated with a "prison rapist," this typology has no preferred victim and may involve the use of weapons or unusual objects used for the purposes of foreign-object penetration.

- Type 3 Rapist: Low/High – *Low* sexuality/fantasy and *high* aggression/rage. This typology is nearly identical to the Type 2 Rapist, other than that there is a specific victim or preferred victim type sought out as the target for the offender's rage. Often associated with a "revenge rapist," victims may be chosen for a vindictive purpose because they can function as stand-ins for a specific individual (estranged spouse, overbearing

mother, etc.) for whom the offender has had a long-standing revenge fantasy involving sexual humiliation or torture.
- Type 4 Rapist: High/Low – *High* sexuality/fantasy and *low* aggression/rage. This typology is associated with non-sadistic but sexually preoccupied offenders, and who typically have a range of paraphilic interests and a poor self-image. Often associated with both a "date rapist" and "child molester," offenders in this group will often use incapacitating agents such as drugs or alcohol, or will simply prey on smaller or more vulnerable victims in order to (initially) minimize violence, overcome resistance, and be able to experiment with different paraphilias uninterrupted.
- Type 5 Rapist: Low/Low – *Low* sexuality/fantasy and *low* aggression/rage. This typology is associated with impulsive, comparatively non-invasive acts of sexual assault, with offenders in this group generally lacking both impulse control and self-awareness, committing assaults in passing, over top of clothing, or post-mortem. Often associated with a "groper," offenders of this typology are for the most part socially and sexually inadequate, the assault being not-so-much paraphilic as it is a matter of either attention-seeking or curiosity that targets a workplace subordinate, a service industry worker, or some other convenient and accessible target.

But beyond merely cataloguing these typologies and the associated behaviours, the London crime saga detailed in this book also provides retrospective insight into how the design of the Forest City—or any city for that matter—might actually enable or even induce an offender to carry out his crimes. Like degenerate junkies who are continuously seeking to recreate the intensity of the first experience, forever chasing the rush of the first high, we historically see two distinct types of interactions between offenders and their surrounding geography emerge in London as their crimes begin to escalate in frequency. This spatial interactivity has significant implications with respect to understanding how victims are selected and acquired, as well as explaining larger patterns in offending. Sometimes known as psychogeography, these spatial models can be affected by factors as simple as access to a vehicle, stable employment, and knowledge of police investigative techniques. The two dominant psychogeographic typologies among serial offenders are what are known as the *marauder offender* and the *commuter offender*.

As the name suggests, like a predator roaming a savannah, the marauder attacks and kills within a specific and comparatively restricted territory, where he is able move freely and exploit a superior knowledge of the terrain. A commuter, on the other hand, exploits his anonymity by offending while away from his traditional home base, travelling in and out of a location without being detected or when able to use occupation, leisure, or some other lawful pretence as the reason for being there—his cover story. London's precarious geographic position and access to the King's 400 series highways made the city a prime candidate for commuter-style offending during the historical period covered here.

The marauder and commuter typologies can actually be broken down even further, according to individuating signatures where killers revert to and rely on certain mental maps before, during, and after a given crime. These four psychogeographic subtypes include:

The Hunter: A marauder-style offender who targets a specific victim or type of victim in the immediate area of his home base (residence, workplace, familiar neighbourhood, etc.), staying within a predetermined zone known as an "action space" where he knows the terrain and is most confident, e.g.: "Grim Sleeper" Lonnie Franklin Jr., "Taco Bell Strangler" Henry Louis Wallace.

The Poacher: A commuter-style offender, with a great degree of mobility, who targets victims—usually a specific type—while away from his home base. The poacher is able to exploit his anonymity as a stranger passing through, as well as exploit police jurisdictional and informational limitations, e.g.: "I-5 Strangler" Roger Kibbe, "Railway Killer" Angel Resindez.

The Troller: An opportunistic and impulsive offender of either the marauder or commuter variety who will attack whenever and wherever opportunity strikes, and while going about his daily business, e.g: "Night Stalker" Richard Ramirez, "Co-Ed Killer" Edmund Kemper.

The Trapper: Often associated with older and more organized offenders, it describes a manipulative scenario in which the victim is lured to a specific location or into a compromising situation. These locations or situations are ones where the offender has a distinct tactical advantage and privacy, often in his own home, e.g.: "Slavemaster" John Edward Robinson, "Killer Clown" John Wayne Gacy.

Whichever subtype a killer falls into, though they are not always exclusive, will determine how they go about acquiring victims and what their relationship is to their victims. The most recent literature, stemming from aggregated victimology data and other studies in preferentially-motivated offending, suggests that there are five types of victims in cases of serial homicide: strangers, targeted strangers (where the offender has stalked and knows who the victim is but not vice-versa), acquaintances, relatives, or those in a client/customer relationship (limited to drug or sexual transactions). While the offender-victim relationship may vary with each case, the method used by the killer will often be contoured by his knowledge of the immediate environment and his own psychogeographic makeup. As a result, there are three separate "contact" processes that describe how offenders and victims are mostly likely to first encounter each other, all of which are reflected in the London case studies:

- The Ruse: A trick, con, bait, promise, inducement, or diversion used to lure the victim into a position in which they are vulnerable. This might range from a trapper-style killer posting an Internet advertisement to a poacher cruising the highway looking for hitchhikers to lure to his vehicle under the pretence of a free ride.
- The Blitz: An immediate, unprovoked, and unannounced attack with no prior warning or interaction, often in an isolated but public location. The blitz is frequently associated with the troller-style offender who acts spontaneously when a suitable victim, usually a stranger, is identified.
- The Surprise: The premeditated use of cunning, stealth, or exploitation of a given situation (power outage, bad weather, mistaken identity, blind corner, etc.) to attack a victim. This would include surreptitious entry into a victim's home or car.

As with both the psychogeographic typologies and offender categories outlined here, these contact methods can vary depending on victim responses or immediate environmental considerations, with killers employing some version of all three as their MO fluctuates; the signature, however, will of course remain unchanged. It has been necessary to outline these terms at this stage to better understand some of the references coming, most of which will be referred to by name only and without further definition. The reader may therefore find it useful to use this chapter as a reference tool moving forward.

Suffice it to say that, after absorbing this preliminary information—this book's version of what's sometimes called a *dramatis personae*, or a type of background on a given story's set of characters—it should by now be evident that the road to follow is a dark one, a veritable Canadian horror story. That story begins not in London but in the neighbouring town of Clinton, Ontario in June of 1959.

# -CHAPTER 2-
# THE TRUSCOTT HANGOVER: 1959-62

hangover [hang-oh-ver]
*noun*

1. The disagreeable physical after effects of drunkenness.
2. Something remaining behind from a former period or state of affairs.
3. Any aftermath or lingering effect from a distressing experience.

# STRANGER DANGER

In the summer of '59, the town of Clinton, Ontario—just under an hour's commute from London and with a population of roughly 3000 people—served as an area headquarters for the Royal Canadian Air Force (RCAF) Station Clinton. For all intents and purposes, the air base *was* Clinton; it was the backbone of the local economy and a place where everyone knew each other. The idea that a stranger could undetectably waltz into such a tight-knit rural community populated by largely God-fearing civil servants and flyboys was all but unconscionable. It turns out that one young boy nearly paid with his life in order for the townspeople to defend the local myth.

By comparison, the London of 1959 was getting wise, or was at least in marginally less denial, about the reality of external predators dropping in and out of the city at their leisure. Exploiting any number of the new King's Highway interchanges that connected the Forest City to the world outside, strangers could make their way to London, troll its streets, and be gone again before anyone took notice. Fifty years before the idea of the commuter killer was first identified by experts working with Scotland Yard, the possibility that London's young and vulnerable might also fall prey to an itinerant sexual psychopath was first realized on the frigid evening of January 6th, 1956.

Just after 8:00 p.m. that evening, five-year-old Susan Cadieux—the quintessence of delicate innocence—left her family home at 665 York Street with her two brothers and an older neighbourhood girl to play on the property of St. Mary's School, located kitty-corner to her house at the intersection of York and Lyle Streets. Shortly after the foursome arrived at the playground, Susan was approached by a man in a drab overcoat and wearing an Ushanka—a wool cap made famous by Soviet Red Army infantry—and was later seen walking away with him hand-in-hand. Her last known words were "This man is going to give me something" as she and the stranger walked off into the night. When her brothers' faces gave away their concern about where she might be headed, the older girl chaperoning the group gave chase, only to slip on the ice and fall face first to the frozen ground. When she got back up, the stranger was seen carrying the now docile Susan in his arms. Neither the girl nor Susan's brothers opted to pursue. Despite initial concerns, because the stranger had apparently dropped the name of a senior priest at the church located on the same property, a small Catholic parish with an equally small congregation, he was assumed to pose no real threat. But when neither Susan nor the stranger returned and the temperature continued to plummet, those initial concerns soon returned and the children ran home where their parents called police.

Over the course of the night and on into the morning of the 7th, Susan's family and neighbours assisted London cops in scouring the area, all the while knowing that time was running out. A public address on local radio by Father O'Rourke, the same priest whose name had been used by the abductor as part of the ruse used to lure young Susan away, included a plea for more searchers to join the effort. At shortly after 10:00 a.m. on January 7th, Susan's tiny, frozen body was found on a set of railway tracks bisecting a construction supply yard on nearby William Street, roughly two blocks west and eight blocks north of the playground where the girl was snatched. Susan had been sexually assaulted, redressed, and then abandoned in the yard sometime in the night. Terrified, traumatized, lost, and all alone, she eventually crumpled to the ground and died of exposure just a few hours before she was found.

Susan's death punctuated a series of unsolved sexual assaults—at least ten—on London children in public places over the preceding year. Armed with a decent composite drawing of the suspect and physical evidence that would eventually include a workable offender DNA profile, the case has appeared—and has been confidently declared—to be solvable at various points in history but still remains cold. There has never been a face to match to the police sketch and never a suspect DNA profile to match to the biological evidence at scene. One thing of which people at the time seemed convinced was that the pedophilic killer was not a local. His manner of dress and the body's proximity to an international rail line suggested a transient, perhaps a labourer from out of province or even a boxcar nomad. The city certainly had a history of both, most notably a one-legged Texan drifter and cop killer named Marion "Peg Leg" Brown, whose ghost is said to still haunt London's old crenulated courthouse and gallows. But then questions inevitably arose. How did the attacker travel so far with the little girl without a car, especially in the snow and against a biting winter headwind? How did he know Father O'Rourke was the priest at St. Mary's Church? Was Susan's killer one of the many offenders who seemed to come to London to prey on its most vulnerable or was he a homegrown "degenerate" as the newspapers called him?

Left: Susan Cadieux's surviving brothers and a neighbouring girl assist renowned *London Free Press* courtroom sketch artist Charlie Bradford create a composite drawing of Susan's killer. Right: The finished product—a rarely seen head-to-toe sketch of the suspect, known in the press as only "The Degenerate." The sketch was circulated in newspapers and across police stations throughout North America over the following years without success and the case remains unsolved—the oldest known case with a workable suspect DNA profile in Canada. Courtesy: Western University Archives.

Back in the town of Clinton, the chillingly similar vanishing of 12-year-old Lynne Harper on June 9th, 1959 led to similar questions about strangers in their midst. Over a half-century and a wrongful conviction later, most of these questions and more remain unanswered. Lynne Harper was over twice Susan Cadieux's age but, like Susan, was also an active young member of her local church and loved the outdoors. It was at both Sunday school and her regular elementary school where she met 14-year-old Steven Truscott. Before long, their names would remain soldered together forever in one of the most infamous crimes, investigations, and miscarriages of justice in national history.

The evening of Tuesday, June 9th was unseasonably hot. On that evening, Truscott had been seen doubling Lynne on the crossbars of his ten-speed bicycle down County Road towards the Bayfield River. Steven would later tell police that he dropped the girl off—unharmed—near the corner of County Road and Highway 8, where he watched her get into an unfamiliar vehicle. When she failed to return later that night, police were called and a massive search undertaken. Two days later, her ravaged and garroted corpse was found in a nearby woodlot. She had been strangled with her own blouse.

The subsequent police investigation, rush to judgement into Lynne Harper's violent death, and wrongful conviction of Truscott for the murder would ultimately and irrevocably change the landscape of Canadian policing—and the nation's already precarious justice system as a whole. A controversy swirled for years before an eventual miscarriage of justice was officially declared. The fiasco would also have a cascading effect on the crucible of agencies policing the province at the time—a ripple effect that would have direct implications on the people of London.

In this iconic 1959 photograph synonymous with Truscott's trial and conviction, the awkward but popular 14-year-old is seen posing with his fateful bicycle shortly before the murder of Lynne Harper that same year. Courtesy: Western University Archives.

As with the case of Susan Cadieux, questions immediately arose as to who, what kind of sadistic stranger, could have come into their little corner of the world and have done this to one of the town's own. In the end, it was ultimately easier to opt a more convenient and timely answer—there was an enemy within.

# INNOCENCE LOST

Cultural anthropologist René Girard, studying the relationship between criminals and victims in the ancient world, wrote about this same phenomenon in his foundational 1979 book, *Violence and the Sacred*. In his examining the role played by violence as both a destructive and reconstructive force in preindustrial societies, Girard noted that communities of different ethnic, religious, and political backgrounds all dealt with criminal violence in similar fashion. Simply put, violence amongst these isolated cultures of antiquity functioned as a force of social cohesion and order and was even elevated at times to something sacred—something that ensured the preservation of community life. More specifically, violence meant, and ultimately demanded, the community select a "surrogate victim" whose death was needed to restore the balance and collective innocence of the group following times of trauma, whether trauma stemming from pestilence, war, famine, or—as with the murder of Lynne Harper—acts of criminal violence. Whether in 1959 BC or 1959 AD, history has shown that death begets death and that otherwise rational people will demand sacrifice to restore a tenuous equilibrium.

The town of Clinton needed, in historically predictable fashion, the blood of another to right this egregious injustice and offence against the entire community. After two OPP officers attended at the body dump site, a narrative was then quickly contoured to fit the scene—a hypothesis attached to the evidence—that would ensure a surrogate victim was easy to find and made to pay. On June 12$^{th}$, 1959, just after 7:00 p.m., Steven Truscott was arrested and within hours charged with capital murder (the earlier equivalent of first degree murder) in the death of Lynne Harper. Even at Truscott's young age, a conviction, if tried as an adult, would similarly mean *capital* punishment—death by hanging.

What endures today is a watershed of police tunnel vision that blurs the line between well-intentioned corner cutting in the interest of time and a clear-cut malicious abuse of process. The case levelled against Truscott—albeit about thirty years before modern defence disclosure rules came into being—ensured a stacked deck for the prosecution. Exculpatory evidence was ignored, statements from witnesses were selected with a jaundiced eye towards police-endorsed and even perjured testimony, and the prosecution wove a masterful tapestry from flimsy threads of circumstantial evidence, all over a two week trial in September of 1959 in the nearby town of Goderich. Several eyewitnesses offered unbiased accounts that seemed to contradict the tight, theory-based time-line relied on by the Crown to inculpate Truscott, but were never called to testify. Parental speculation about Lynne, just prior to her death, having possibly been hitchhiking to a grandmother's house nearly two hours away was later denied despite this same information being sent out on the "wire" that same night—information also contained in the original police teletype message sent to neighbouring law enforcement agencies. Defence lawyers of the day, however, only had access to whatever vetted information from the original police file was actually—and selectively—presented in court by the prosecution.

In the end, Truscott's police statement about an unknown car with an unknown driver was dismissed as little more than an attempt to throw off the police. He was tried as an adult and in short order convicted of capital murder on September 30th, 1959. Despite the jury having asked the judge to show leniency—an unusual request given the brutality of the crime and perhaps indicative of their having nagging doubts about Truscott's actual guilt—the presiding judge, Justice Ronald Ferguson, had no choice but to impose the required death sentence by hanging. While Truscott fully expected to be hanged before his 15th birthday, it turned out that the government had no interest in hanging a boy, and his death sentence was soon commuted to life in prison.

What followed was a predictably bureaucratic, Kafkaesque process in which Truscott's various appeals of his hasty conviction ended up in countless legal logjams while he languished in prison. After a final rejection by the Ontario Court of Appeal in February of 1960 and the appeal route having been fully exhausted, it seemed as though the people of Clinton could go back to business as usual. At last, or so they thought, they could try to return to the perceived state of innocence, or perhaps blissful ignorance, that had existed prior to June of 1959.

With the appeals exhausted, the police also sought to erase the blight that was the Lynne Harper murder by disposing of most of the exhibits in the case. In fairness, this would actually not have been out of the ordinary for any case at the time. Even today police agencies have fairly regimented "retention policies" with respect to exhibits and evidence and the space they occupy in storage—dated exhibits that require purging in order to make room for new property and evidence coming in on fresh cases. However, major crimes such as homicides are typically looked at with greater discretion in terms what is and is not kept for the future, precisely for situations such as this one. In the fall of '59, lead investigators could likely have never imagined a time when these items might have renewed relevance. Instead, the baby went out with the bath water and, like the police, the locals followed suit. Photos of Truscott were burned and the name was verboten from being spoken in public. *It* never happened; *he* never existed.

## "A MISCARRIAGE OF JUSTICE"

The reality is that it did happen, and that Truscott's story was far from over and the Lynne Harper murder case far from closed. Following the commutation of his sentence from death by hanging to life in prison, Truscott was transferred into the federal penitentiary system. Despite the undercurrent of murmurings that had existed since the trial, seven years later in 1966, journalist Isabel LeBourdais's book *The Trial of Steven Truscott* raised the argument, publicly for the first time, that Truscott had been wrongfully convicted. The book quickly ignited the already simmering fire into a raging national debate about the mishandling of the original investigation and trial alike. As an indication of the unaccountable hubris with which the Canadian justice system operated at the time, Justice Ronald Ferguson—who had presided over Truscott's trial—went so far as to petition the Ontario Attorney General and even Prime Minister Pierre Trudeau to have LeBourdais jailed for public mischief. It was one step short of demanding a public book burning in the tradition of the Third Reich. Justice Ferguson contended that grounds for criminal charges existed as a result of her book, as one of the judge's angry letters stated, having "disturbed the emotions … throughout the Anglo-Saxon world." Needless to say, no charges were ever brought in one of the few decisions from the day in which wisdom prevailed.

LeBourdais's polemical book—which only put into print what many Canadians already knew—also caught the attention of the federal government, and later that same year the case was referred to the Supreme Court of Canada for review. Still, citing "many incredibilities" among the witnesses, some old and some new, the highest court in the land rejected the possibility of a new trial in spite of exculpatory evidence, and Truscott was sent back to prison to serve the remainder of his life sentence. Two years later, Truscott was released on parole before blending back into society and rebuilding his life as a free man with a wife and three children. Although no longer Canada's most high profile prisoner and his Scarlet Letter #6730 inmate number having been removed, Truscott's stature as a poster child for police and prosecutorial reform would remain alive in the collective public conscience. Truscott and his family later emerged from obscurity in 1997, by which time investigative journalism in Canada had come a long way.

Then, in 2000, the Canadian Broadcasting Corporation's long-running investigative series *the fifth estate* aired an in-depth television documentary detailing the circumstances of Truscott's arrest and conviction that shocked Canadians. The episode was followed in 2001 by Julian Sher's book *Until You Are Dead*, a text that prevails as the definitive account of the whole affair, including an intrepid re-investigation of the original investigation that is unrivalled in its sourcing and detail. Ahead of the renewed publicity, Truscott's case had also gained the attention of notable Canadian lawyer James Lockyer, the founding director of the Association in Defence of the Wrongfully Convicted, and who took up the cause in the Ontario Court of Appeal. Meteoric advances in forensic science had meant that there was new evidence that cast even more doubt on the soundness of the original conviction. Some of that crucial new evidence now demonstrably showed that Lynne Harper died much later than initially maintained by the police and prosecution. The time-line used by the Crown, which had placed Truscott at or near the scene, it turns out, had been nothing more than an unsubstantiated guess.

On August 27th, 2008, almost forty-nine years to the day from when he was convicted by a jury of his peers, Truscott was officially acquitted in what was condemned by the Court of Appeal as "a miscarriage of justice that must be quashed." Following the unanimous ruling, Attorney General Michael Bryant humbly apologized for Truscott's ordeal, stating that he was "truly sorry" for the debacle that had spanned decades, and that the Crown would not be appealing the decision. But with Truscott's acquittal, the court's admonition and Bryant's apology, it was June 10th, 1959 all over again. The murder of Lynne Harper was officially now an unsolved historical homicide—long since cold.

# A WOLF IN ASS'S CLOTHING

The compounding effect of wrongful convictions is that with one injustice ostensibly being remedied, though not necessarily undone, a new one is immediately unveiled. Much has been written about the Truscott affair and it is well beyond the scope of this book to connect the dots and offer a single proposed solution. This chapter is principally about how the aftermath of the mistakes made in the Truscott case—the Truscott hangover—had a chilling effect on and created a defeatist undercurrent within the OPP and other police agencies in Ontario as early as 1960. The soundness of the original investigation, even before LeBourdais's book sparked national controversy, had its doubters and seemed to have helped create a climate of investigatory reticence and tentativeness within the upper police ranks. It was a tentativeness that had serious consequences when London—in the eye of the storm—later became besieged by serial murderers beginning in 1963.

In looking back at the Lynne Harper murder, the Truscott (mis)investigation and the implications of both in the London CMA, we can today better understand how there were a number of other viable suspects who should have been more closely examined—suspects who are either known or suspected to have also been operating and preying in the Forest City as far back as the early 1950s. With the benefit of hindsight and improved research on sex killers and pedophiles, these individuals' activities before and after the Harper murder can today be used to at least help narrow the search for the real killer fifty years on. For instance, one area of criminal behavioural analysis that has made significant advances in recent decades, and which is referenced routinely throughout this book is how certain primary paraphilias serve as gateway behaviours for attack paraphilias and more serious forms of offending.

The Teten profiling system, named after pioneering FBI investigator and "mind hunter" Howard Teten, is just one example of how to apply criminal behavioural analysis to a crime scene in the context of paraphilias. The Teten system is neither clairvoyance nor rocket science. It simply reflects good intuition and deductive reasoning, or the ability to draw specific conclusions by looking at generalities. In other words, using both the scientific method and basic common sense. While named for Teten, this system, and the ability to draw conclusions with respect to specificities of a current case by drawing on generalities of other earlier cases, dates back to what was likely the first criminal profile ever developed. Dr. Thomas Bond, the forensic pathologist who performed autopsies on a number of the Whitechapel victims in 1888, women killed by someone who was thought to be Jack the Ripper, provided Scotland Yard with a behavioural profile deduced from the nature of the wounds inflicted on the victims. Dr. James Brussel, a New York psychiatrist, was similarly recruited to provide a behavioural profile of the "Mad Bomber" George Metesky who terrorized Manhattan for sixteen years, bombing landmarks like Penn Station and Radio City Music Hall before being arrested in January of 1957. Since then, this same profiling method has become one of the FBI's flagship training programs, and has been rebranded as the more official-sounding Criminal Investigative Analysis Program (CIAP), colloquially still known as the Teten system.

In applying the Teten system retrospectively and overlaying it onto London and Southwestern Ontario in the late 1950s, it would certainly seem that there are persons whose documented behaviours and paraphilias should have made them far more suitable suspects than Truscott, but who went undetected both in the summer of '59 and afterwards. Three weeks after Lynne Harper's murder, and just over two weeks after Truscott had been arrested and charged with the crime, a washout RCAF Sergeant stationed in nearby Aylmer was admitted to a psychiatric hospital in London suffering from debilitating "depression and guilt" of an unspecified nature. The man's name was Alexander Kalichuk, generally known as the base drunk at RCAF Station Aylmer, about a half hour's drive east of London on Highway 401. The base drunk was also his reputation at his previous posting at RCAF Trenton, a military community several hours north, where he had been stationed as a supply man, like Lynne Harper's father, between 1950 and 1957. A stodgy day drinker loathed by his stepchildren and languishing in a pointless marriage, Kalichuk made several attempts to transition to civilian life after the Second World War without success, continually crawling back to military life in various support positions with the RCAF. While stationed at Trenton, he was also arrested and charged for various acts of exhibitionism. Following his conviction for these offences, he was transferred to Station Aylmer in 1957. What was unusual, even for a hard-drinking recluse like Kalichuk, was that in spite of his using the structure of military life as a crutch, he generally shunned the military community and never lived on or near the bases where he was stationed. By late 1957, he was stationed at Aylmer but was living almost an hour north in Huron County, just twenty minutes from RCAF Station Clinton. Kalichuk was also a frequent visitor to the air base at Clinton, and by all accounts knew Leslie Harper, Lynne's father.

Heavy drinking was not Kalichuk's only vice. While still on probation for the indecent acts committed in Trenton, on the same day Lynne Harper vanished, Kalichuk's probation officer notified his superiors that Kalichuk had been reported in previous weeks to have again committed acts of exhibitionism, this time in the town of Seaforth, near Clinton. What the probation officer failed to mention was an even more alarming incident. Roughly three weeks before the Harper murder, Kalichuk had been arrested and charged by OPP officers in St. Thomas—a town equidistant between London and Aylmer—after luring a ten-year-old girl into his car and showing her a bag of women's panties collected from places unknown. Despite being on probation for a similar sexual offence at the time, a two-bit St. Thomas judge carelessly dismissed the charge of contributing to the delinquency of a minor at Kalichuk's first court appearance, giving him a verbal warning and sending him on his way after he paid a small fine for having an open container of liquor in his car when arrested. No further evidence on the origin of the women's undergarments, his intentions with the 10-year-old, or Kalichuk's reason for being in the area that day was ever entered on the record. He then walked out of St. Thomas court Scot-free less than two weeks before twelve-year-old Lynne Harper would also apparently be lured to a vehicle, raped, and murdered.

Whether Kalichuk had any cause to be in London between 1955 and 1956, when children were being molested at random and Susan Cadieux was killed, remains uncertain. What is certain is that by 1959, Kalichuk was a convicted sex offender living just outside of Clinton and repeat offending over a wide area. This included Aylmer to the east, Seaforth to the north, and St. Thomas, just ten minutes outside the London city limits to the southwest. In addition to the roadside luring incident in May 1959, there had been other reports of a suspicious male trying to lure females to his vehicle throughout rural towns at all points in between—incidents that prompted community warnings to be on the lookout for strange vehicles and a caution to keep an eye on young children playing near the road. The areas in which the warnings were issued included London.

During his time with the RCAF, Kalichuk was never so much as looked at as a suspect in the Harper murder. The police were confident that they had arrested and charged the real killer and the case was closed. They had their man—or boy—and that was that. In reality, many cops knew better, but dared not say it. In the 1950s, Kalichuk had a couple of logistical advantages that had allowed him to keep a low profile. Ironically, he had learned to fly under the radar and stay off the grid in a town that then claimed to be the "home" of Canada's radar system. In his moving from Trenton to Aylmer to Clinton to Centralia and then back to Clinton, and living and offending in a random assortment of places across the entire region, Kalichuk knew that information between police departments—even between OPP detachments—moved at a glacial pace, if it moved at all. Aside from criminal convictions that were a matter of federal warehousing and that only his probation officer would ever know about, the isolated, discrete incidents for which Kalichuk was warned, suspected, or charged but not convicted would remain static in file drawers and banker's boxes at lone police detachments and never find a larger readership. Further, the fact that Kalichuk lived off the base and opted out of military social circles limited the ability for his colleagues to pick up on his perversions. His being dismissed as the innocuous base drunk was in fact the perfect cover for his truly predatory nature—a wolf in an ass's clothing. As subsequent chapters will show, however, Kalichuk was the first of many repeat offenders to exploit the London region's unique geography and awkward assemblage of urban-rural communities, as well as its equally awkward cobbling of different law enforcement agencies, all of whom were wearing blinders for the better part of a quarter-century.

In and out of hospitals and psychiatric facilities during the final years of his life, Kalichuk literally drank himself to death in an asylum in 1975. While Kalichuk took what he knew about Lynne Harper's murder to his grave with him, and while the OPP remain circumspect whether he, at any time, had been considered a suspect in the Lynne Harper murder, there is little question that the base drunk was a highly active predator with well-established criminal paraphilias (exhibitionism and pedophilia for starters), although he was not the only one. In fact, beyond Kalichuk, one finds other potential suspects and paraphiliacs who, it would seem, were never even given a second glance.

The abrupt departure, for instance, of Station Clinton's electrician, Clayton Dennis, in the fall of '59, might not have otherwise been suspicious were Dennis not also a convicted rapist with a predilection for young girls. On the other hand, Matthew Meron, a junior airmen at the base, was only nineteen, but had access to a car and would have spent time with Lynne at the local pool where he was a lifeguard and Lynne was a regular swimmer. Meron also abruptly transferred from Clinton in the wake of the murder, eventually being dishonourably discharged from the air force, but not before trying to rape and strangle his own daughter in a wood lot in following years. Were Meron not interrupted by a group of hunters, the girl's otherwise inevitable death might have triggered the interest of OPP homicide investigators to take a second look at Meron in the Harper murder. As it stands, neither Dennis nor Meron was ever questioned by police about their activities on June 9$^{th}$, 1959. Not then; not ever.

Then there was Dr. David Hall Brooks, the chief medical examiner at Station Clinton. He, along with pathologist Dr. John Penistan and OPP Forensic Identification Officer John Erskine, was one of the prosecution's star witnesses with respect to the contaminated physical evidence at the scene and on Truscott's body. By 1968, while practising in New Brunswick, Brooks had been accused of exposing himself to his patients, just like Kalichuk. In the following years, Brooks quit medicine altogether and moved to New Jersey amidst an investigation by the RCMP into sex offences committed across the country during the course of his blemished medical career. One can only be confounded by the fact that an exhibitionist and blatant paraphiliac could be so closely connected to the Truscott case and be permitted to obtain a position of trust and authority with respect to the investigation. Moreover, did Brooks—as clearly the most eager of the forensic witnesses to depose what we now know to be questionable, perhaps even perjured testimony against Truscott—stand to gain some direct advantage by ensuring his conviction and execution? Again, more questions than answers.

Beyond the cabal of sexual deviants indigenous to the Clinton area and working the Truscott case from the inside, there is of course the London factor to consider. With Sgt. Kalichuk offending near London and being institutionalized in London in the late 1950s, and with a string of still unsolved sexual attacks against children in London and area during that same period, the Forest City found itself in the cross-hairs of sexual psychopaths from across the region. The city was smack-dab in the middle of a proverbial spider's web of rural routes that connected it to towns like Clinton and Goderich to the north, and the King's Highway system that connected it to all points east and west. As a type of atoll that circumscribed London, this chain of roads, both old and new, rendered the Forest City equidistant to any number of criminal staging areas ideal for circumnavigation by motivated and commuter-style predators. It also made it the ideal place to hide in plain sight, or perhaps like Cadieux's killer, pass through on seemingly legitimate business.

The nefarious presence of Kalichuk at London's boundary in 1959 would all but confirm that the concept of a "local" crime problem was by the dawn of the next decade a total misnomer. As the landscape surrounding the London CMA in all directions was changing and the automobile was altering the landscape of crime across the entire continent, the fiasco that was the Truscott investigation would serve as a cautionary tale about the newfound vulnerability of traditionally "closed" communities like London. At the same time, it created a climate of uncertainty among police investigators faced with new challenges and a seemingly new breed of mobile killer. Lastly, it created a climate of uncertainty about established and once time-honoured methods and instincts. No longer would shaking down the usual suspects wash as an investigative tactic, either in theory or in practise. Times had changed; the police had not. Moving forward, the only remedy for the whole affair and to prevent a repeat occurrence—the OPP equivalent of an ounce of prevention—was to play it safe and avoid another Truscott at all costs. There would be no getting fooled again.

## THE BIG CHILL

Weighing the toll and chilling effect that the botched Truscott case had on the institutional culture of the police in Ontario—the OPP in particular—is difficult to officially quantify. In the grand scheme of things, the police emerged smelling half-decent when the whole affair was revealed as a miscarriage of justice in 2008. Although Attorney General Michael Bryant ended up taking much of the heat on behalf of his Crown predecessors, the reality is that the whole injustice began with a few people making some key decisions on the fly on a humid afternoon nearly a full half-century earlier. All of these initial investigators are now dead, and they were never held to public account for laying the groundwork that led to Truscott's vigorous and slanted prosecution while the real killer walked free.

The lead investigator, OPP Inspector Harold Graham, was an old school cop who got promoted to the upper ranks, it would seem, in spite of himself. He for the most part began as a well-intentioned but simple man who, like most cops promoted beyond their IQ score, later transmutated into something of an egomaniacal martinet under the pressures of being in the public eye. All the while, he remained a tireless believer in justice—at least his narrow definition of it. He would frequently ask his officers the tough questions about their work, not as a matter of meddling micromanagement as might be the case today but as a matter of moral obligation. Well ahead of precedent-setting court decisions that have scrutinized derailed police investigations and wrongful convictions, Inspector Graham tried to hammer home to his detectives that it is a *crime* and not a *person* that the police are tasked with investigating. He stressed that investigations only stop at a particular person when they are the only one left standing and cannot be eliminated as a suspect. Inspector Graham might have been in charge, but he was certainly in the minority in terms of how he looked at murder investigations.

In time, the Inspector's moral maxims not surprisingly proved difficult to live up to, not just for his men but also for himself. The term "interrogation" was not yet in regular use in 1959, but during a *voir dire* at the trial and in the absence of the jury, Graham was nonetheless questioned at length by defence counsel about his so-called "examination" of Truscott following his arrest. While today interviews at police facilities are required to be audio-video recorded—or make full use of whatever technologies are reasonably available—no efforts were made at the time to document the precise questions and answers resulting from Graham and Truscott's exchanges. All Graham had to account for his time spent with Truscott was some paltry notes scribbled on a single piece of paper. Although the statement was eventually and rightfully ruled inadmissible, the jury would never hear of the dubious interview and no one was held to publicly account for how the boy was treated. Behind closed doors, however, some cops had questions of their own about what really went on in the room that night.

Although there was still a long road to be travelled by Truscott during his journey to exoneration, as early as the mid-1960s, already-growing dissent in the ranks about how the case had been handled and evidence processed meant that these questions were beginning to surface in mixed company. It seemed as if Inspector Graham had indulged in some serious reverse engineering of evidence to justify a charge of capital murder, and in the years after the trial he earned a reputation as a man not to be provoked. This meant that talk about the investigation and what (even in that era) were considered to be egregious procedural missteps were quickly suppressed and driven underground—lest Graham or his papier-mâché sponsors higher-up get wind of such mutinous comments. Before long it was obvious that Graham—at one time something of a matinée idol among the OPP rank and file—and a number of other investigators involved in the Truscott affair were having an overdue falling out. This included the lead forensic technician, Identification Officer Erskine, who went to great lengths to distance himself from Graham in future assignments. Just as Truscott's conviction and death sentence had failed to return life to normal at RCAF Station Clinton, and just as Truscott's name was not to be mentioned in public, so too did the OPP investigative units across Ontario find themselves forever changed by the case—Mayberry interrupted. What happened in Clinton that summer would trigger a significant sea change in the organizational culture of the OPP, especially among senior brass who advocated (and in some cases enforced) a new tradition of plodding and pussyfooting when it mattered most. However, it would not surprisingly be the public rather than the police who would end up paying for the change.

Despite the eventual court finding and the Attorney General apology, it would be fair to say that for many years there were still investigators who stood fast and maintained an unwavering belief that the right man had been arrested and incarcerated for Lynne Harper's murder the first time around. It was not a universally held sentiment. Alliances were splintered, and rumours and disloyalty abounded; then, once LeBourdais's book was released in 1966 and so aggressively challenged official history for the first time, things became even tenser. Even the true believers who had kept their heads buried in the sand between 1959 and 1966 knew from the history books—cases like those of Adolph Beck or Alfred Dreyfus—that more trouble was afoot in the years to come. It was time to batten down the hatches.

The timing of LeBourdais's investigative exposition of the whole Truscott affair could not have been more significant. In other words, for the OPP, it couldn't have been worse. Seven years had elapsed since the Harper murder and the tide had washed over. Commanding officers had come and gone and many people had been promoted or transferred, retired, and died. Eventually the institutional memory of the Truscott case within the OPP was open to official reinterpretation for the first time. Of those junior investigators on the sidelines or serving as errand boys in 1959, by 1966 many were senior or supervising investigators. Those men included one Dennis Alsop.

The increased scrutiny of the police in the socially liberal and libertarian 1960s, coupled with the lingering distaste of how Truscott was investigated, would make all cops very wary of jumping in with both feet, as Inspector Graham had, in major investigations from that point forward. In London and region in particular, OPP detectives would be manacled to either a desk or a rule book—sometimes both—for years to come with no exceptions. Truscott's statement had been thrown out of court, the police rebuked by the trial judge, and the jury had put a caveat in their guilty verdict, perhaps sensing that the investigation didn't seem quite right and the police hadn't been on the up and up. Academics and journalists were now openly challenging the methods and the integrity of once sacrosanct police tactics—a tradition that continues today without relent. By the end of 1966, people were pulling on the individual threads of the OPP's sweater, one at a time, and slowly the whole Truscott case and the entire OPP frame of reference was unravelling. Moving forward, those running murder investigations would need an *admissible* statement or confession complete with detailed notes that at that time was simply not the way things were done. They would need ironclad forensic evidence and indisputable time-lines. Most importantly, they would need an obvious motive, or better yet, wall-to-wall eye witnesses who, unlike in the Truscott trial, were solely of service to the police. A smoking gun—better yet two smoking guns just to be safe—would have also been nice. It was an impossible and fantastical wish list, but the odds, they thought, were slight at best that there would be another sex slaying in rural Ontario on the scale of the Harper murder. They had no idea about the torrent of horrific violence and trail of bodies that was in the offing.

Soon, a perfect storm emerged. As a culture of risk aversion came to define OPP investigative tactics, the autonomy of individual investigators was curtailed wholesale by bureaucrats in Toronto where the criticism about the handling of Truscott's case seemed the sharpest. By the mid-1960s, even before the publication of LeBourdais's monograph and the Truscott hangover set in, the rural areas under OPP control surrounding London would be the unfortunate inheritors of the lion's share of the Forest City's serial sex murders, but with little interest, risk tolerance, or wherewithal to tackle them. London's frontier town design at the time made the rural outskirts the perfect fluid space through which killers could slip in and out of the city, and the ideal environment for disposing of their mostly young victims. While the London Police would certainly absorb their fair share of cases from the 1960s onward, it was the newly raw OPP, still licking their wounds, that bore the brunt of the storm. While London called itself the Forest City at the time, the reality is that it was the forests outside the city—all in OPP jurisdiction—that made for better body dump sites. So did the countless lakes, marshes, woodlots, and ravines that dotted the greater London area. While today joint-force operations or interagency task forces, comprised of several police departments having a vested interest in a murder or series of murders, will collaboratively undertake an investigation in unison—what is known as the multi-jurisdictional major case management model—in earlier years a more simplistic policy prevailed: the department that has jurisdiction over where the body is found, keeps it.

This was at least the understanding and standing agreement between London Police and the OPP during the city's darkest age, and one that would fundamentally change the outcome of the investigations that followed. Even if a victim lived in London, went to school in London, and was kidnapped and killed in London, if the body was dumped or otherwise moved beyond the city limits, the OPP inherited the case hook, line, sinker. It was an exercise in territoriality that would be lambasted in future public inquiries, most notably in the Campbell Commission report published in 1996. The report, officially known as the Bernardo Investigation Review, resulted in both the then Toronto Metropolitan Police and Niagara Regional Police taking serious flack for hoarding information and files with respect to the rapes and murders of Paul Bernardo, simultaneously a serial killer in the Niagara area and a serial rapist in the Toronto area between 1987 and 1992. That report, tabled by renowned Justice Archie Campbell, led to a now centralized case-management system that allows for the inter-agency sharing of homicide data between various police services across Ontario, ideally between neighbouring law enforcement agencies. A similar system is also commonplace across other provinces using specialized file-sharing software programs such as Powercase, E&R, and X-FIRE. But in the 1960s, 1970s, and 1980s, there was no such system, no such logic, no such anything. With the OPP in the London area living the legacy of the soon-to-be notorious Truscott investigation, the perfectly gift-wrapped investigations they longed for to wash the taste of the Harper murder away simply would not come. The onslaught of slayings that they soon faced would ensure that many cases never even got off the ground before a new victim turned up in their territory. As with many of the victims from the London area they inherited, the descendants of the Truscott affair would soon be drowning—the weight of the Truscott legacy having made it impossible to come up for air. Dennis Alsop would try, but as happens to many drowning men, those around him eventually managed to pull him under.

## - CHAPTER 3 -
# FLASHPOINT: 1963-67

"Confusion now hath made his masterpiece."
-Shakespeare, *Macbeth*

# 14 KING

Back in London and area, the turbulent 1960s, even in the wake of the Lynne Harper murder, began somewhat innocently. After all, Truscott was safely locked away and while young Susan Cadieux's killer had yet to be caught, he seemed by that point to be long gone, and now some other city's problem. In fact, by 1960, all signs pointed to the region turning a corner and mobilizing towards a time of prosperity and social harmony. Things couldn't have been farther off the mark.

On New Year's Day 1961, London began the process of annexing various areas that surrounded it and drawing them into the larger matrix of the corporate municipality as the city relentlessly expanded. At 12:00 a.m. on January 1$^{st}$, the first two quasi-towns to get swallowed up were selectively severed portions of London Township and Westminster Township to the south of the city's boundary. At the same time, the London Police absorbed the thirty-three officer, Barney Fife-like department that policed London Township, bringing the force's complement to just over 200 officers, all of whom would soon be sandwiched together in its vintage 1930 headquarters at 14 King Street in the city's core. It was a station house, now demolished, that would see more horror, tragedy, and bewilderment than anyone had bargained for when it was selected as an ad hoc replacement to the crumbling old headquarters on nearby Carling Street, a building that dated almost back to the department's founding in 1855.

As the calendar turned from 1960 to 1961, London quadrupled its size in land mass and added over one hundred thousand residents overnight. These figures actually exaggerated the actual state of the city and amounted to what, in economics, is known as hyperinflation, or when a commodity increases in size or value so quickly that it is neither sustainable nor truly representative of its actual value. In reality, the city's cultural makeup and day-to-day affairs changed very little, with this "growth" being little more than the signing of some documents and redrawing of some lines on a map. The much celebrated expansion was certainly not reflected on the streets of the city proper, which remained largely as it was.

By 1962, the London Police Department, already stretched for space at 14 King, was beginning to look like a comparatively progressive department with the hiring of its first two sworn female officers that same year. Assigned to the Morality Division and tasked almost exclusively with touring newsstands and convenience stores in search of obscene material likely to offend the city's proudly conservative citizenry, within three years, one of the two officers would be dead, and the other would have resigned. But the department soldiered on in the same spirit of expansion that defined the city as a whole. The year 1963 in particular was a momentous one. London's new Chief of Police, Finlay Carroll, was sworn in as top cop on New Year's Day, and within a week's time, the new Ontario Police College (OPC) in Aylmer would welcome its first class of recruits. Ironically—or not—the OPC was established in 1962 on the heels of the Truscott trial at the former RCAF Station Aylmer installation where Sgt. Kalichuk had once been stationed in between his attempts to lure children into his car near London. The hope was that with a centralized provincial training academy, the profound differences in terms of competence and performance among the array of police departments scattered across Ontario could be improved through a standardized basic constable training curriculum. In what was at the time—and still is—the longest unchanged and unreformed institutional model in the free world, dating to Sir Robert's Peel's *Metropolitan Police Act* of 1829, such a progressive idea was certainly bold and disruptively innovative by the standards of the day.

# VICTIMS: MARGARET SHEELER, AGE 20 & UNBORN CHILD

Fast forward to Christmas of 1963. At the time, 20-year-old Margaret Sheeler and her husband were newlyweds living in a recently completed townhouse complex on a street known as the Bridle Path. In the early 1960s—borrowing on the prestige of the Bridle Path in what was then North York, and which prevails as one of the tonier neighbourhoods in Greater Toronto—Margaret's home was considered a prestigious enclave for young couples starting life together. Her husband Philip, an up-and-comer in the regional management division of the now defunct Dominion chain of national supermarkets, was, despite his modest middle-management success, generally disliked by Margaret's parents. Hard drinking and abrasive, Philip had met Margaret in their native Essex County when she was still in high school and the two exchanged nuptials somewhat haphazardly, which was not necessarily uncommon at the time, especially in the case of a premarital pregnancy. That pregnancy, in early July of 1963, brought an October shotgun marriage with the couple soon relocating to London.

But by December of that year, things had reached a flashpoint for Margaret, just as they had for the new city she called home. Now over 5 ½ months pregnant, Margaret had two problems. First, her new husband was clearly unravelling. Off work for the Christmas holidays, boredom and anxiety brought on the thirst, and Philip turned to day drinking to quell his idle hands. Increasingly disinhibited, he began making a number of statements suggesting that he regretted marrying his wife. Secondly, Margaret had been followed to the city by a former lover, one who seemed intent on keeping the flame alive. He also seemed even more intent on reclaiming Margaret in spite of her recent vows, flashy new residence, and newborn in the offing.

On the evening of December 27th, a Friday, the Sheelers were hosting a dinner party for friends, who by all accounts, were looking forward to being entertained in one of the city's newer neighbourhoods. But as it turned out, the night was not ideal for doing much of anything. A stereotypically event-spoiling London lake-effect snowstorm had moved in quickly at around 7:00 p.m. Still, the visitors to 21 Bridle Path pushed on and made it to the townhouse shortly after 8:00 p.m., about an hour later than expected. What they found when they arrived was entirely unexpected. Margaret's husband answered the door, glass of hooch in hand, and began pacing maniacally. The visitors, it seemed, had just fallen backwards into the awkward aftermath of what looked like a heated domestic dispute, except there was one missing link: Margaret was gone.

As the evening progressed, and unreciprocated pleasantries hung in the air, Margaret's new husband cranked highballs while fidgeting and performing profane soliloquies under his breath. The couple's attention soon turned to the burning roast in the oven and the half prepared hors d'oeuvres lingering on the counter of the galley kitchen. With further prompting, the inebriated host confessed that he and his wife had had an argument, and she had walked out literally minutes before their guests' arrival. She had supposedly declared that she was going back to her parents' house, which was over an hour's drive from London in *good* weather. Of course, none of the usual follow-up questions were asked about how Margaret, at nearly six-months pregnant, planned to get there in the midst of a December snowstorm while the lone family car remained parked the driveway. After all, the visitors were his friends.

The next evening, in the absence of drink or the watchful eyes of meddling dinner guests, Margaret's husband finally called the front desk at 14 King. It seemed Philip was very familiar with the London Police policy at the time, that a person—child, adult, pregnant woman or otherwise—needed to be missing a full 24 hours before a report would be filed and taken seriously, regardless of extenuating circumstances. Providing a dry recitation of what he had told his guests on the previous evening, a now composed and comparatively sober Philip explained that his wife had abruptly stormed out of the house about an argument over empty liquor bottles at 8:00 p.m. on the previous night. He explained that he figured Margaret's departure was a plea for attention, as though she were some child threatening to runaway to join the circus and whose bluff needed to be called. So call her bluff he did, and never went looking.

Over the following days and weeks, various people known to Margaret were interviewed and perfunctory calls placed to other police agencies providing descriptions and details about the missing mother-to-be (the London Police didn't join the provincial teletype network until 1965), but to no avail. Incredibly, no one actually set out to look for Margaret in what was then a newly developed subdivision encroaching into undeveloped farmland. If a thorough search had been undertaken, considering Margaret was said to have ventured into near whiteout conditions, one might have assumed she had become disoriented and wouldn't have made it very far. Sadly, it wasn't until two young neighbourhood boys, searching for nothing in particular on the afternoon of January 24th, stumbled across the frozen corpse of Margaret Sheeler. Laying in a supine position and having defied the decomposition process by virtue of the winter elements, her abdomen containing her late second trimester child was found pointed toward the sky as she lay forgotten in a vacant lot primed for residential development only a few hundred metres from her home.

# SHADOW PLAY

The strange part is that Margaret didn't die from exposure as expected. Margaret was found positioned on her back among some tall, ice-coated weeds after being stripped fully naked and her clothes left strewn in a circle covering a massive thirty-foot perimeter around the body. She had been beaten severely about the face and head and was ultimately killed by blunt-force trauma. More importantly, the attending pathologist concluded that she had been killed elsewhere and then transported to the location—accessible only on foot at the time—and that these actions took place in immediate succession.

Margaret had been beaten to death, stripped nude, and then left on her back out in the open. This odd sequence of events was determined to have occurred in part by process of elimination, as in spite of the disrobing of the body—a sexual homicide by definition—both the coroner and the attending pathologist ruled that there was no sign of an actual rape. Stranger still is that her winter coat was not among the clothing items found circumscribing the body at the scene, suggesting that the killer either took it with him or that she left without wearing a coat, while pregnant, and walking head-on into a brutal December storm. Neither scenario seemed any likelier then than it does now. What does seem clear, however, is that Margaret's murder was the first of innumerable London cases to show evidence of significant crime scene staging—pure subterfuge designed to throw off police—after the transportation of the body from the primary crime scene. The absence of sexual intrusion but the removal of the clothing to artificially suggest a sexual motive indicates that whoever murdered Margaret that wintry night wanted the police to think she had been attacked for a sexual purpose and her clothes torn off during some kind of frenzied snowstorm rape—only he forgot her coat in order to complete the tableau. It was the first of countless investigative and forensic countermeasures used by London killers in the decades to come to cover their tracks and occlude their true motives—measures that for the most part seem to have been carried out successfully.

In short order, Philip, Margaret's husband, and her former boyfriend who had tailed her to the Forest City, were both in the wind. While the early police investigation and local rumour mill had fingers pointing at the husband more than the former beau, little it seems was done to follow up and track his movements after his hastily leaving London. If, as the police initially thought, it might have been possible for Margaret to have walked out of the house and into a snowstorm in the heat of the moment, only to be snatched by her obsessed former lover, it doesn't explain why Philip would climb inside a bottle to muster the liquid courage to lie to his dinner guests, not at least while he might have been out looking for the mother of his child-to-be. The absence of a winter coat amongst the items strewn at the scene, coupled with the roast left in the oven and half-prepared food left on the counter suggest that Margaret's departure from the house had been neither expected nor planned. Someone took her from the home and through a blizzard—whether alive or dead—to the vacant lot where she and her unborn child were found frozen to the ground weeks later. Today, we also know that concealing a victim at or near the primary crime scene, especially on land, is the least common "disposal pathway" used by killers, statistically speaking. Its primary purpose is to *delay* rather than necessarily *prevent* discovery of the body—to put time and space between the killer and the victim. It seems that, in this case, a month was more than enough time.

## VICTIM: VICTORIA MAYO, AGE 32

While Margaret Sheeler's body was discovered outdoors amid the darkness of a typical London winter, the Forest City's next unsolved murder occurred indoors during the dog days of summer. But that's not where the differences end. Summertime in the city has always meant Londoners seeking relief from tortuous temperatures wrought by the region's humid continental climate by leaving their windows ajar, even when they should know better. With only a flimsy screen serving as a protective membrane between their bedrooms and those lurking the streets outside, many locals played and continue to play the odds that the small chance of their home being invaded is worth the risk for a brief respite from the heat. Victoria Mayo, a recently divorced 32-year-old single mother living in the lower unit of a three-story walk-up apartment on Sydenham Street was no such risk taker. This is, in part, what makes her murder remain so baffling.

On the morning of August 6th, 1964, Victoria's young son wandered into her bedroom at 194 Sydenham, confused as to why his mother hadn't woken up to prepare him breakfast as usual. The young boy also wasn't sure what exactly he was looking at when he walked in the room, or why his mother wasn't moving. It would seem that neighbours, later hearing the boy's cries for help, called police who attended to find the main door locked from the inside. With the boy being too short to reach the latch, the first uniformed officers to arrive gained access to the unit with the building superintendent's key, rushing to Victoria's bedroom to find a horrific scene. The victim was found, like Sheeler before her, on her back, but had apparently been attacked while sleeping. Laying in a pool of blood and still dressed in her nightgown, Victoria had not been sexually assaulted by her attacker. Like other erotophonophilic killers—the "Rostov Ripper" Andrei Chikatilo arguably being the most infamous of the modern age—it seemed he was sexually satiated simply by inflicting repeated stab wounds. The nature of the wounds suggested a mixed level of offender organization—the entry was methodical and controlled, but the murder entirely uncontrolled. Each plunge of the blade had been carried out feverishly, in a thrashing frenzy as though her killer was in the throes of a psychotic state, or was simply overcome with excitement—a textbook lust killing where the "lust" refers to blood lust and the mutilations are in themselves what sexually gratify the killer.

The surprise attack in the Mayo case is especially notable since her slaying would be the first of several nighttime home invasion murders to follow in London, and the first in the city's history not accompanied by some other secondary crime, such as sexual assault or robbery. What investigators lacked in training (or available knowledge at the time) to recognize was that an atrocious and over-the-top murder of this nature, occurring in the victim's home but also lacking a distinct signature is—in the tradition of the Teten system developed roughly a decade later—a strong indicator of an offender's day to day behaviours. In the Mayo murder, we see an almost schizophrenic struggle between organized and disorganized elements, as well as a weapon (knife) that, second only to strangulation, has proven to be amongst the most variable and discretionary of killing methods used by both serial and sexual murderers.

Stabbed over a dozen times while her son slept in the next room, Victoria's killer had stealthily forced entry via the centre window of three vertically-sliding panes that looked down into her living room from the building's parking lot, the young divorcée's apartment being in the lower level of the building. From the inside looking out, the windows provided an unobstructed view south towards what was then, and now, a densely populated mix of upscale historic homes and student rental tenements. For all intents and purposes it was a high-risk target for the killer and the first of several London apartment murders that seemed to defy conventional logic, and in some cases, even gravity. Exactly how and why the killer targeted Victoria, leaving her son unharmed, and was able to enter and exit without leaving any patent or latent evidence remains unclear. There was not so much as a fingerprint on the window or a footprint on the wall, upon which the killer would have needed to brace himself when climbing into the lower level unit. Despite explosive violence shown inside, the fact that Victoria's killer could compose himself and leave just as stealthily as he entered all but confirms that he had experience with a crime of this type sometime prior to the summer of '64, and that it was a crime he was likely to repeat in future.

The one question that London detectives were able to answer early on was the killer's blood type—a lucky find stemming from the one mistake he did make. It turned out that Victoria's killer had cut himself on his own knife while brutally attacking her in the darkness of her subterranean bedroom, a not uncommon offender injury in any attack using an edged weapon. But it would be another thirty years before DNA technology would be able confirm exactly whose blood was mixed with Victoria's gore, matted on the bed and on the wall. In the meantime, no one is certain how many others her assailant may have killed. In looking back, it would seem that in London alone, the answer is at least one.

## WHILE THE CITY SLEEPS

Following Howard Teten's first successful offender profile created for the FBI—the case of David Meirhofer in 1974—we have since then also learned a great deal with respect to identifying recurring patterns between murders committed indoors versus outdoors, as well as how and where a murderer disposes of the bodies of his victims. For instance, a 2012 study in Hong Kong—one of the most densely populated places on the planet—as well as separate 2014 data from the United States which has the highest murder rate in the world, both published in the leading peer-reviewed journal *Homicide Studies*, independently confirm that the relationship of victims to their killers tends to reflect one of two extremes when the body is left at the scene without additional staging: the victim is likely to be either an intimate partner or a targeted stranger. The majority of the victims are also female and found, as was Victoria, fully or at least partially clothed. More concerning is data obtained by the FBI, which confirms that nearly half of offenders who use this method in targeted stranger murders go on to kill at least three other victims, all in similar fashion.

In the Mayo slaying, we have a young mother murdered in her sleep while in an apparently secure apartment unit located in a perceived safe neighbourhood. The murder being committed indoors in itself means that, as with Richard Ramirez's crimes equally showing a mixed level of organization, the entry in the Mayo case was subject to some degree of planning and was also skilful in spite of the madness that followed. The preferential targeting of Victoria also suggests that her nocturnal intruder had some degree of control over his actions and possibly even knew the whereabouts of the victim's room—as though he might have previously been watching through the same window he later entered. Since Teten's foundational success story and the subsequent work of Robert Keppel, whose profiling methods helped catch the DC Snipers in 2002, it is now generally accepted that murderers whose preparatory paraphilias consist of scopophilia or crytoscopophilia—including Peeping Tom activities—will similarly tend to commit murders indoors once they escalate to the associated attack paraphilias. On the other hand, offenders who commit murders outdoors or move or dispose of bodies in the open, in many cases, have a history of exhibitionism or preparatory paraphilias that similarly require an outdoor public venue as part of their preliminary fantasy development. The correlation between attack, murder, and disposal sites and what is often years' worth of experimentation and rehearsal during the preparatory stage should not seem surprising.

Even the most fearless and sadistic of psychopaths will not generally wake up one day and decide to start entering occupied homes at random in order to claim his victims, not without first knowing how to do it well and evade capture. But the Peeping Tom or crytoscopophilic stalker, who escalates to attack paraphilias, is not just accustomed to approaching homes at night and identifying security vulnerabilities in windows and doors; by the time he moves to the next stage, he is also bored with it. Similarly, the exhibitionist who has been pushing the limits of sexually aberrant public behaviour, for years in some cases, may later become entirely disinhibited from committing more serious crimes out in the open. Many other offenders would be fearful that witnesses could be watching from a distance, that they might be recorded going to or from the crime scene on a concealed CCTV camera, or that they might be interrupted or even caught red-handed by the police or an intervening citizen. The exhibitionist, on the other hand, knows how to account for these risks and is at home offending in the outdoors. Beyond that, he is aroused by risks associated with being in the public sphere, up to and including the ability to kidnap, kill, and dispose of victims in parks, streams, forests, and parking lots without a second thought. By the time an exhibitionist escalates to acts of sexual murder, the outdoors is all he knows.

But in August 1964, just as with the murder of Margaret Sheeler the previous December, London cops were baffled by the slaying of Victoria Mayo at the hands of an elusive nighttime intruder. Then, three years later, in October of 1967, there was a break in the case. Actually, it wasn't a break as much as a gift—the killer offering himself up to police on a platter. At a downtown division of the Toronto Metropolitan "Metro" Police, an unemployed Hungarian transient and former dishwasher walked into the station lobby and spontaneously confessed to the desk sergeant that he had stabbed a woman to death—at least one—in her apartment in London a few years earlier. He was sketchy on the details, but after further questioning and Metro cops liaising with London detectives back at 14 King, the location of the crime was ultimately determined to be 194 Sydenham Street, the victim Victoria Mayo.

The killer's name was Sandor Fulep and he hadn't ever been on the radar of the London Police. Not even close. His movements in and around the time of the Mayo murder and what exactly he was doing in London in the summer of '64 are still unaccounted for. Between August of that year and his turning himself in to police in late '67, it remains unclear where Fulep was and what he had been up to—those details he conveniently left out of his spontaneous confession. After being sent to the Oak Ridge Institute in Penetanguishene, affectionately known as the "Criminal Insane Building" at the time, murder charges were stayed against Fulep when it was decided that he was effectively out of his mind when he walked into the police station in Toronto. His unsolicited confession—however accurate—was subsequently considered inadmissible. No one contested that he hadn't actually committed the murder, just that his admission was unreliable and the words of a mad man. Incredibly, the Crown did an about-face within the year and later opted to re-initiate the prosecution, only to then withdraw the charges for a second and final time. The reason the second time around was purportedly a lack of evidence, while again proclaiming that Fulep was mentally ill. Even after walking into a police station and confessing of his own free will, Fulep would never be held accountable for the death of Mayo or any of his other possible victims, and the Sydenham Street stabbing would remain officially unsolved for another three decades. Within a few months, Fulep was apparently deemed cured of whatever was making him ill, and was back out walking the streets without supervision.

The procedural snafu surrounding Fulep's aborted prosecution, and his release into society after being deemed "cured" of the same "insanity" that led him to murder Victoria Mayo in the first place, is unfortunately, not unique in the country's blemished history of forensic mental health decisions. In fact, as seen in countless murders in the London area over this period, the understanding of psychosis and criminal responsibility was at the time still rooted in the outmoded Victorian Era culture of the asylum and the collective misunderstandings of mental health. Terms like "sociopath" and "pervert" were used interchangeably and routinely thrown around by police investigators and court officials without any real qualification or clarification. The prevalence of criminal signatures and attack paraphilias was deemed to be representative of sexual offenders being insane, without regard to their level of organization or ability to maintain day to day occupational and social functioning during the cooling-off periods between their crimes. After all, what sane person—or so the thinking went—would break into an occupied apartment in the middle of the night, horrifically mutilate a complete stranger, and then disappear for several years, only to later resurface to confess to a single crime of what was likely many?

Such questions were confronted in the contemporaneously published 1962 novel *One Flew Over the Cuckoo's Nest* by Ken Kesey, later made into an Academy Award winning film in 1975. As a great example of how books and films inform and inspire wider public debate on crime and punishment, and can become vehicles for both legislative and procedural reform—what I've referred to in other works as *literary criminology*—the novel depicts a recidivist criminal (repeat offender) who is able to secure a cushy sentence in a psychiatric hospital after faking insanity on assault and illegal gambling charges. The novel is less a commentary on how easily the medico-legal system was exploited by motivated offenders during that period—which it certainly was—as much as it is an exposé of the fact that definitions of insanity and mental illness were, at the time, little more than guesswork based on a mash-up of outdated models of behavioural modification. The timing of Kesey's novel, as well as many of the insanity defences raised in London and elsewhere in Canada during this period, is also a direct reflection of failed attempts at adopting what was known as the Durham Rule in the assessment of an offender's mental state. Specifically, this is the notion that "temporary insanity" could be equated with a person having an "irresistible impulse" to offend.

Unlike the M'Naughten Rule that had been in place since the first successful common law system insanity defence in 1843, the Durham Rule crept up in late 1950s America, beginning with the eponymous 1954 case of *Durham v. United States*. While never officially a binding rule with respect to sentencing in Canada, the paradigm shift stateside had, by the 1960s, come to be hugely influential in terms of how criminal responsibility was adjudicated and defined across the continent. By the 1970s, both in Canada and the U.S., the Durham Rule and its controversial irresistible-impulse clause was scrapped as it was seen as giving too much power to psychiatrists and other mental health "experts" in determining mental competence at trial. It had also quite ridiculously equated everything from explosive tempers to paraphilic impulses, and by extension, what we now know to be psychopathy, with insanity. In other words, the Durham Rule suggested that the willingness to indulge bizarre or sadistic fetishes that other rational people would not was in itself a sign of insanity—temporary or otherwise. In the meantime, before the unequivocal reclaiming of the M'Naughten Rule and a similar set of guidelines in the U.S. known as the Brawner Rule, considerable damage was done. It was cities such as London and its citizens that were ultimately made to pay, as offenders, their lawyers, and junk-science doctors played the system like a fiddle during the Durham years.

While Kesey's novel, which was written during the same period as the Fulep case, is set in the state of Oregon, London embodied in real life the scenario depicted—except in London, it would seem, the more sadistic and depraved a murderer, the greater the chance of his being declared insane and eluding prosecution. Fulep would not be the last of London's killers to be treated with kid gloves under the loosey-goosey standards of the time, nor would he be the last who received a pass on any possible previous misdeeds, including murders, all under the auspices of his being declared not criminally responsible (NCR) when it suited him. In recent years, NCR classifications have once again enraged Canadians, most notably in the case of Vincent Li, the Chinese immigrant who, in 2008, murdered, beheaded, and cannibalized fellow Greyhound Bus passenger Tim McLean while he slept in his seat en route to Winnipeg. At his trial the following year, the judge accepted that Li was psychotic at the time of the murder, attacking a defenceless McLean because he thought he was following the orders of God. No one of course was able to explain why he only targeted the most vulnerable of the coach's passengers—asleep at the time—to act on God's commands, why he consumed McLean's eye balls and flayed the corpse, or whether God also told him to taunt the RCMP officers on scene, one of whom later committed suicide after suffering from Post-Traumatic Stress Disorder as a result of the horrific incident. With a young man and a veteran cop now dead, Li is already out on unescorted day passes from his forensic mental health facility, and back to living life. Decades earlier and back in London and area, one has to question how the publicized accounts of confessed murderers similarly getting away with it—getting away with *everything* for that matter—might have inspired and disinhibited other would-be predators under a much more liberal NCR system than the one we have in place today. All evidence points to it creating a culture of permissiveness and inspiring a new form of extreme killing, where the more paraphilic and brutal a murder the better the chances of being declared NCR. This is assuming the killer was apprehended in the first place, which was seldom—if ever.

# MICHAEL ARNTFIELD

# VICTIM: GEORGIA JACKSON, AGE 20

It wasn't long before the type of extraordinary brutality, once hoped to be contained to isolated incidents such as the Mayo murder and limited to the likes of insane night stalkers like Sandor Fulep, returned to the London area with a vengeance. Soon the police and public alike would be forced to reframe their perspectives on violent crime, and come to terms with new forms of depravity and psychopathy that had never before been seen in the area, but which were now there to stay.

In February of 1966, 20-year-old Georgia Jackson was a kindly young woman active in the local Jehovah's Witnesses community and working part-time at the Aylmer Dairy Bar, a throwback to 1950s drug stores that served milkshakes and short-order items at a snack counter, and located just off the Highway 73 exit on Highway 401, about thirty minutes southeast of London.

Georgia lived at home with her family on Pine Street, roughly a three-iron shot from the Aylmer Arena where most of the townspeople could be found on any given night in the wintertime.

Georgia was by definition a very low-risk victim in terms of lifestyle indicators. Aside from her being a waitress—a statistically overrepresented occupational group when it comes to violent crime involving acquaintance and targeted stranger attacks—she was like so many of the London and area's victims, a truly innocent and unlikely target. A chaste young woman committed to the Jehovah's Witnesses community and local Kingdom Hall, she had very limited access to outsiders, other than brief transactions and exchanges of friendly smiles during the course of her table-waiting at work. The Aylmer Dairy Bar was, at the time, a favourite amongst truckers and highwaymen, travelling salesmen, staff at the fledgling Ontario Police College, and local farm hands, not to mention the labourers at the Canadian National Railway yard in nearby Ingersoll. On the afternoon of February 18th, one of Georgia's regular customers was in the restaurant and somehow became aware that she was working the closing shift, ending at 6:00 p.m. But in February of 1966, in small town Aylmer, 6:00 p.m. might as well have been midnight. After closing up shop with the owner, Georgia made her way into a darkened and utterly deserted John Street to begin the quick but cold walk home to Pine Street, located only about two blocks south.

When 7:00 p.m. came and went and Georgia still hadn't arrived home for dinner, her parents began to fret. It could not have been more out of character for the girl. Georgia's brother and sister were dispatched by their mother to venture out as a pair to look for her along the route she would normally have taken home. Their trek took them to the Aylmer Arena, a business that was still open in order to accommodate nighttime hockey practises. In canvassing the employees and players there, Georgia's increasingly worried siblings found that no one had seen her.

Shortly after 8:00 p.m., Georgia's brother and sister returned home to their panic-stricken parents who realized at that time that something was definitely wrong. They called the Aylmer Police who were apparently not at all concerned, assuring Georgia's father George that his daughter must have run away, that foul play could immediately be ruled out—that it *must* be ruled out. Foul play simply didn't exist in that neck of the woods, her parents were assured. It was a baseless and negligent conclusion, but one that would be catastrophically repeated over the coming years as women and children in London and its surrounding towns began to vanish. Nonetheless, a basic report was taken, with the Jacksons being told to call "when" (not if) she returned home.

Then, 48 hours later, the phone rang at the Jackson home. Georgia's mother picked up the receiver to hear silence on the other end, other than some background noise. It gave the impression that the caller was outside at a pay telephone beside a roadway, with the door to the booth open. "Hello?" she stated repeatedly, only to get no answer. *"Wrong number,"* she thought. But before she could hang up, a muffled and muted voice chimed in on the other end. It sounded like someone—a man in fact—disguising his voice, pretending to be her daughter: "I'm downtown and some men have me." Then the line went dead. Georgia's mother would later say that the voice was "maybe" that of her daughter, although she couldn't be sure. Perhaps it was Georgia being forced to make the call, to pre-emptively throw off authorities with "some men" and "downtown." Or perhaps it was just a cruel crank call. Then again, perhaps it was her abductor, and killer, disguising his voice as part of some sadistic game—a ruse to buy himself time and throw the police a red herring before the investigation even got started. Perhaps it was the killer hoping that the investigation finally would *get* started, and that police would find the series of taunting clues that he had strategically left for them. Sure enough, the call was enough to cast doubt on the theory that Georgia, as a 20-year-old homebody, had randomly run away. A small town investigation slowly lurched to a start.

The following few weeks were filled with unspeakable anguish for Georgia's family as the Jehovah's Witnesses community and local residents banded together to search for what they had resigned themselves would inevitably be the corpse of the wholesome young girl. In time, two ominous clues, including Georgia's personal items, turned up—as though deliberately left by the killer to deride the authorities and townspeople alike. The first item was the scarf Georgia was wearing the night of her disappearance. It was discovered along Highway 73, known as Elgin Road, seemingly tossed from a moving car. The second item, Georgia's winter coat, covered in blood, was located behind a tree in a field off of a local county road known as the Glencolin Line. In keeping with Jehovah's Witnesses' practises, the Jacksons had never had Georgia blood-typed, making it impossible to determine if the blood on the coat was hers. Either way, things were beginning to look grim.

## MURDER CITY

Following the discovery of the girl's clothes at separate locations, the Aylmer Police, now taking the disappearance seriously nearly two weeks after the fact, posted a $500 reward for anyone who located the girl, dead or alive, in the hope that what was then a large sum of money would entice people with useful information to come forward. As with most rewards, it also had the effect of luring opportunists and nutcases to come out of the woodwork. The search continued on in vain as each reported sighting and bogus tip yielded one dashed hope after another. This whole time there had of course also been the nagging question of that mysterious pay phone call to the Jackson home within the window of time when Georgia might still have been alive. Maybe it offered faint hope that she still was, even weeks later. After all, if she was allowed to place a call or was able to momentarily escape to phone home, perhaps the intention was not to hurt her but to hold her. Perhaps he, or they, were still holding her. The Aylmer Police had by this point publicly stated that Georgia would never have entered a car with—or have been seen in the company of—anyone she didn't know and trust implicitly. It seemed that this time they were right.

# BOXTOWN

The afternoon before St. Patrick's Day, on March 16$^{th}$, roughly a full month after Georgia was last seen leaving the Aylmer Dairy Bar but only days after the reward was announced, a local farmer would collect the $500 reward for locating the girl's body. The man, in checking on the status of thawing soil, had reportedly stumbled across the semi-clothed and mutilated body of the young waitress. The body was found in a secluded bush lot off Springfield Road between the Glencolin Line and Dingle Line, just a few dozen metres from where her peacoat had been located. Either the police and citizen search parties had both missed seeing the body when the coat was previously recovered, or the body had only been recently moved to the place it was discovered. The only thing more shocking than what had been done to the girl's body was the nature of the location where it was found. If, as had been stated, Georgia would never have entered a car with someone she didn't know, it made no sense that such a person—her killer—would have known about the location where her body was left. No one Georgia knew, or thought she knew, would have ever ventured into that area or have even known where to find it.

Every town, even one as small as Aylmer, has a proverbial wrong side of the tracks. The placement of Georgia's corpse suggested that the killer had prior knowledge of a location that was off limits to those in the girl's peaceful little world. It was the first of several paradoxes, overwhelming contradictions in the case that would take years to decrypt. It was one of several sadistic cat-and-mouse games played by the killer with local and regional lawmen—games that until now have not been seen for what they really were.

The intersection where the bloodied remains of 20-year-old Georgia Jackson were found was smack-dab in a rustic, Ozark-like area on the outskirts of Aylmer nicknamed Boxtown—a darkened recess of rural Gothic that at the time was carpeted in shanty houses, dilapidated farms, and overgrown patches of land. On weekend nights—or in the summer on just about any night of the week—there existed an unmarked drive of unknown ownership adjacent to where Georgia was found. Customarily used as a lovers' lane—what in a contemporary profiling context would be cited as a "known vice location" and an attractive stakeout spot for both scopophiliacs and exhibitionists—such locations when used as body disposal sites can make strong statements about a killer's propensity for voyeuristic activities and his preparatory paraphilias. Whoever took Georgia to that spot knew it well, and returning there with her was part of a larger, longstanding fantasy. But beyond the laneway itself, the surrounding area of Boxtown was also known to be a rough neck of the woods. It was the kind of place where you probably wouldn't stop to ask for directions and risk crossing any number of the local ne'er-do-wells who called it home in 1966, and most of whom had a certain disdain for passers through. To travel there at night with a young captive girl, perhaps already dead, suggested someone who either didn't know Georgia or who wasn't whom she thought he was. Or perhaps it was someone who was just fearless and cunning—someone who knew the ill-equipped local police, as soon as the body was found, would train in on that neighbourhood and its petty criminal element as their one best lead.

Like clockwork, and in almost tragicomic fashion, the Aylmer Police took the bait and dropped the hammer down hard on the Boxtown boys. After the Jackson girl's body turned up there, her purse and modest jewellery still missing, shakedowns, beat downs, and vexatious stop-and-frisks were the order of the day as the cops tried to flush out the killer, in the process creating friction and dissension among those who either lived in or frequented the area. It was no use. The people who lived there or routinely hid out there to toke up and fornicate among its overgrown paths knew nothing of the case and had nothing to do with it. While the police braced the local residents and questioned all males about their whereabouts on the night of February 18th, the forensic pathologist conducting the autopsy of Georgia Jackson's partially decomposed body had some questions of his own. The girl had clearly been struck in the head with a blunt object, but that's not what killed her. The petechial haemorrhaging in and around the eyes coupled with a lack of ligature marks confirmed that she had been slowly asphyxiated—likely suffocating by being smothered after first being incapacitated by two blows to the back of the skull.

Beyond the ante-mortem injuries (inflicted prior to death) and peri-mortem trauma (inflicted at or near the time of death), there were also a number of post-mortem injuries to the body that, at the time, defied explanation and lacked any real context. The fact was that the police and attending pathologist had no real idea of the enormity of events they were dealing with—no local, regional, or even national comparator to help them understand the horror that had unfolded and the true nature of the monster still in their midst. Aside from having been brutally raped, Georgia's left ear was completely absent. It had been cleanly sheared-off, but was the only appendage missing from the body. More strangely, Georgia's left arm, while still intact, had a length of flesh spanning its entire length, from the armpit to the wrist, where the skin had been taken down, likely by carving, all the way to the bone.

Beyond the missing ear and missing length of flesh along the left arm, the body otherwise showed absolutely no sign of animal scavenging or interference by vermin or carnivores. While the ear appeared to have been removed with near-surgical precision, the damage to the arm disturbingly showed evidence of teeth marks on either end of the missing flesh. Neither the pathologist nor any other expert at the time sought to determine whether the teeth marks were human—perhaps an act of what we now know to be odaxelagnia—or were more consistent with any known animal scavenger. We know today, as they probably did then but chose not to address, that animals in the wild, in locating a partially naked corpse, would not have caused these types of injuries. Scavengers use human and animal remains in the wild, especially in the winter, as sources of food, and not for the type of tentative and experimental mutilation seen on Georgia's body. Further, with an open head wound, bloodied face, and sex organs exposed, no animal would take only one ear, which is essentially useless as a food source. It has, however, been known to be a preferred trophy among homicidal partialists. Animals in the wild also lack the ability to amputate body parts with such accuracy without causing collateral damage to the face or head—both found intact in this case. Blaming animals ultimately turned out to be easier than facing the stark reality of the alternate explanation. As a result, the autopsy was written up to reflect the presence of "apparent" scavenger activity as having interfered with Georgia's remains and having been the underlying cause of the mutilations. In reality, the police were dealing with a type of animal in this case, as well as others to come—one of a breed that had no known origin or pedigree.

# CODEBREAKER

Back in the summer of '59, OPP Forensic Identification Officer Erskine, the lead crime scene technician tasked with the analysis of Lynne Harper's body and the surrounding dump-site, had a young assistant shadowing him—Corporal Dennis Alsop. Following Truscott's arrest, Dennis had been tasked by Erskine to look into the various footwear impressions that had been found in the mud near the body. He was also to manage the day to day administrative duties that come with cataloguing exhibits—in other words, the Joe jobs that Erskine, as the senior forensic tech, could delegate. The shoe print casts were largely useless, as a result of the scene having been trampled by RCAF base police and volunteer searchers, but Erskine wanted to keep the major items for himself as plum career makers. So, for much of the Truscott fiasco, an uncomplaining Dennis was little more than an errand boy, a circumstance—luckily for him—that would mean he was well outside the blast radius when the whole thing exploded in later years. His hands would remain clean while working his first homicide since joining the OPP and establishing himself as a case man. He was kept on the outside looking in, until the Truscott hangover led to the deck being shuffled in terms of detective assignments across the province and who was assigned where. Dennis ended up being shunted into the London-Middlesex County OPP detachment as part of that shuffle. Before long, the deck would be stacked against him.

Dennis had learned from the mistakes of others by riding the pine and watching the machinations of a poor investigation unravel. By the spring thaw of '66, when Georgia Jackson's body turned up in a similar fashion to Lynne Harper's and history seemed to be repeating itself, Corporal Alsop was now Detective Sergeant Alsop. He had been bumped a rank in January of 1963, and this time he was running the show, at least when it came to homicide investigations in the counties surrounding London. By that time, he and his family were also living in London proper—in the eye of the storm. He had been a minor player in the OPP's forensic branch a decade earlier, but there was no more sitting on the sidelines with his mouth shut. He was by now a tried and tested "murder police" as they say.

Going back even before 1959 and the Truscott affair, Dennis had found his way into policing with his eyes closed. Since it had always been something of a calling for him, it was just a matter of where and when it would happen—not if. In the years before policing in Ontario came to be seen by many as a cushy civil service sinecure, Dennis was more the type of gritty investigator you might find in a hardboiled detective novel or a film noir of the 1930s. Graduating at the top of his academy class in 1946, immediately after the Second World War, Dennis went on to become the embodiment of what Raymond Chandler, in describing a natural-born detective in his novel *The Simple Art of Murder*, calls "a common man and yet an usual man … he will take no man's money dishonestly and no man's insolence without due and dispassionate revenge." He was also a lone wolf, learning from the Truscott case that many hands can make light work but also big trouble. By the time he made Detective Sergeant, he was working most files solo—the buck stopping with him as he took sole ownership of his investigations—one part Sam Spade, one part Lieutenant Columbo. While his colleagues of equal rank liked to delegate and manage from behind the safety of a desk, Dennis was out in the field, knocking on doors and rattling chains, always straddling the blurred line between one-man efficiency and personal obsession. When the Jackson file landed on his desk, on St. Patrick's Day 1966, he took one look at the crime scene photos and knew that whoever did this would do it again.

During the war, Dennis was an intelligence officer with the Canadian Army stationed in Holland—his specialty being the physical and technical surveillance of Nazi sympathizers, collaborators, and suspected turncoats. It was an assignment that also frequently required the deciphering of coded enemy messages. After intercepting Axis ciphers, he would—much like his British colleagues at the famed Bletchley Park, who deciphered the code used against them by the Nazis' Enigma Machine—spend hours analyzing messages and looking for repeating patterns that would uncover the hidden truths that lay beneath. By the end of the war, Dennis returned to civilian life only briefly before enlisting with the OPP in 1946 and trading the infiltration of foreign enemies for domestic ones—criminal psychopaths.

A newly promoted Corporal Dennis Alsop while assigned to the OPP's fledgling forensic identification branch. He is seen here standing proudly beside the region's first unmarked crime scene vehicle, c. 1954. Courtesy: Dennis Alsop Jr.

By the time he was working homicide files as the lead detective in the greater London area, and based on his years of code-breaking, cryptography, and military intelligence work, Dennis had learned to look at information much differently than his peers. He was able to see and anticipate patterns and a bigger picture for which many others simply didn't have the training, interest, or natural intuition to see. In looking over the Jackson case, he saw that what the killer had done to her was a type of transmission all of its own—a lurid communiqué being transmitted to effect a very specific message about how the killer saw himself in the bigger narrative he was creating, and in which Dennis was now a player. He was especially troubled by a number of key elements: the mutilation and apparent biting, or eating, of the girl's left arm; the amputation of the left ear as a trophy-taking ritual; the keeping of Georgia's purse and personal effects as keepsakes and twisted souvenirs to relive the crime; the fatuous scattering of her blood-stained clothing to toy with investigators; and the placement of the phone call to taunt the girl's grieving family. Dennis added it all up and knew that none of these events were random. In fact, they were so specific and so methodical in their sequencing—the killer carrying on with these antics well after the murder and when he should have been laying low—that it seemed his fantasy went back a very long way. It had all played out so perfectly that the killer would be unable to stop himself from trying again, perhaps with some new twists. The sequence of events surrounding the end of the Jackson girl's life amounted to a coded message that Dennis had yet to fully decrypt; it was a message which told him in a roundabout way that there was more to come, and new locations and characters to soon follow. As his OPP colleagues plodded along, business-as-usual, Dennis was bracing for impact—for enemy contact. Within the year, he would be forced to revisit another lesson learned hard in combat: you can't win a war fought on multiple fronts, at least not alone. For a while, however, it seemed that he would try.

## VICTIM: GLENDA TEDBALL, AGE 16

In October of 1967, as Dennis Alsop was waiting for the other shoe to drop, Glenda Tedball was 16 years old and never in a million years would have thought that she too would become a name in one of his case files. While living just outside London's metropolitan area, in the small village of Thedford, her family's farm was located about a thirty-minute drive from the city's northwest boundary. Sometime on Halloween afternoon of that same year, while home sick from nearby North Middlesex District High School, Glenda was last seen walking towards the woods at the back of her family's large 50-hectare property. Why she was wandering off into the woods, dried autumn leaves rustling under her feet, was never determined. Regardless of where she was going, or perhaps thought she was going, Glenda would never be seen again.

Not surprisingly, the villagers, all used to leaving their doors unlocked and letting their children run free in the surrounding woods, were horrified by the girl's disappearance. Equally troubling was that, unlike in Georgia Jackson's case a year prior, local police came to the immediate and accurate conclusion that the disappearance was suspicious and indicated foul play. The girl was in imminent danger and the clock was ticking.

Glenda had no history of running away, truancy, or any other type of defiant behaviour. In fact, by all accounts, the young and chubby-cheeked brunette was shy and reclusive, not the type of person to accompany a stranger or to get into a car with someone she didn't know. But Glenda was also the type of girl who would do as she was told if she felt threatened, perhaps by someone lying in wait in the woods behind her house. The fact that she had disappeared in a forest on Halloween only added to public panic, and ignited macabre interest in the case back in London and beyond. Absurd rumours of forest people lurking in the tree line behind farm houses quickly circulated—Glenda's abduction supposedly being part of some secret village society, a pagan ritual to commemorate All Hallows Eve or Samhain on November 1st, the so-called Day of the Dead.

Public pleas for information and the safe return of Glenda went unheeded as these provocative theories and rumours about a regional occult scene soon began to eclipse genuine concern for Glenda's safety. As with every piece of local folklore, in a matter of months, every time the story was repeated, there was some new sordid detail. Somebody was frequently said to know someone who had seen something or who had supposedly been passed inside information from the police, village headman, local Member of Parliament, or someone else in the know. But as volunteers and police teams searched the vast expanses of forest and farmland across the area, not only was there no trace of Glenda, but—of course—no forest people, twig sculptures, or any other evidence to support nonsensical scuttlebutt about an occult ritual having taken place. In time, when stories of the uncanny subsided, Glenda's name was spoken less and less frequently. Newspaper coverage later became non-existent, and before long the whole thing became a dirty village secret that some believed might not have ever happened—the rural legend of the Halloween vanishing.

## COMBING THE JANE DOES

On an unknown date, sometime after the public panic surrounding Glenda's disappearance began to wane, there was yet another disappearance. But this time it wasn't a person, it was Glenda's family home. The farmstead owned by Glenda's mother, Norma Poore, mysteriously burned to the ground on an unknown date sometime after the winter of '68. With that, the plot of land where the house once stood sold rather quickly and the family moved out of town and into obscurity. In the years to come, there were no vigils, no markings of Glenda's birthday, and no competition with Halloween festivities by a commemoration of the anniversary of Glenda's disappearance. It seemed everyone had resigned themselves to the fact that Glenda would never be found and that whoever took her was going to make sure of it.

Over the coming years, as old bones and unidentified human remains turned up around London, the province, and across the entire country, investigators would dutifully compare them to the biometric data and dental records on file for Glenda, but no match was ever made. In fact, unidentified found remains of females (Jane Does) do not typically stay unidentified for long and are vastly outnumbered by unidentified male remains (John Does) by about four to one across North America. The province of Ontario, for instance, currently has only about fourteen Jane Does still on file and awaiting positive identification. Considering how onerous it can be to cross-reference the comparatively small number of found remains to the vast number of open missing persons cases from across a given region or nation—or continent—a total of only fourteen still left unidentified is actually quite impressive and speaks to the recent advances in biological and forensic anthropology, such advances significantly assisting in police investigations.

Of course, DNA (whenever available) can also help expedite and certify matches made between skeletons and missing persons, although even with genetic profiling, some matches seem unlikely if not impossible to make. One example of this would be the unidentified remains of the so-called "Woman in the Well," generally believed to be Saskatchewan's first homicide and one of Canada's oldest unsolved murders. In June of 2006, a construction crew found the partially dismembered remains of a 25-35-year-old woman stuffed into a barrel beneath a Saskatoon gas station. The station, as it turns out, had been built over top of an old livery, and the barrel containing the corpse had been thrown down what was then—approximately one hundred and six years earlier—a well used to water the horses. With no missing persons reports to go on, and a shortage of reliable birth and death records from Saskatchewan at the time, the identity of the victim remains unknown, even though her DNA is now on file.

In Glenda's case, the availability of detailed biographical information and biological data, along with the missing persons report filed by her mother, should in theory have made the process of combing through the list of Jane Does across the continent more straightforward than in other cases. Each time a new set of mystery remains is discovered or unearthed, the same process is repeated and Glenda is one of thousands of missing women whose information is offered for comparison. To this day, no match has been made, and twenty-five years after she vanished, Glenda was officially declared dead. For some it might have signalled the end. In reality, it was a new beginning. With the issuance of Glenda's death certificate in 1992 a new chapter was written, and the case was destined to soon be solved.

## TIP OF THE ICEBERG

By the close of 1967, the bizarre and brutal murders of Margaret Sheeler and Victoria Mayo, as well as the grotesquely sadistic sex slaying of Georgia Jackson, were all unsolved—three homicide investigations going nowhere fast. Glenda Tedball, declared as "endangered missing," also showed no signs of resurfacing. Her file saw little in the way of action, other than when female skeletons would occasionally turn up and could be compared to Glenda's information. Dennis Alsop had caught the Jackson case and would eventually inherit the Tedball disappearance. The others were London city cases.

At the time, the police—both London city cops and the OPP—operated under the assumption that they had two and possibly three sex killers on the loose in the area. Dennis Alsop knew it, and in time a handful of others seemed willing to listen—at least for a while. In reality, even when excluding the Tedball case from the series, the Sheeler, Mayo, and Jackson murders would today have been enough to justify a full-blown task force. In 1967, the closest thing to a task force was Dennis Alsop, alone in the wilderness, and for the most part alone in his suspicion that serial murder—until then thought to be an American problem and the term not even yet in use in Canada—had come to London. Whether it was the kidnapping, murder, and mutilation of a young woman, the slaying and posing of a soon-to-be mother, or a random knife attack on a stranger asleep in her own bed, by year's end all of these men were still at large and the authorities unsure of when they might strike again.

Dennis at least had a good idea on *where* they would strike: London and its surrounding area.

Today, under these same conditions, citizens would be calling for wall-to-wall police on every street corner, the declaration of martial law, and the invocation of the *Emergency Measures Act*. People would be outraged and descending with torches and pitchforks on police headquarters, London City Hall, and the offices of their MPs, demanding a pound of flesh as the city waxed apocalyptic. There would be a public inquiry to help sow the seeds of future lawsuits, inquests, and even more inquiries, as well as news documentaries and exposés galore. There would be Facebook groups and online petitions demanding everything from nightly curfews to the reinstatement of capital punishment. But by the end of 1967, there was nothing. People in London, remembering full well the boogeyman story of Victoria Mayo's murder, knew nothing of the Georgia Jackson murder. People who knew of the Jackson slaying—not many—likely had no idea that Glenda Tedball had vanished, seemingly snatched by someone lurking in the woods on her farm. By 1967, nobody anywhere seemed to know the name Margaret Sheeler at all. It was a different era, and as diligently as the media tried to report on these cases, they could only report what the police told them. Factor in the limited distribution of print newspapers and the fact that television stations signed off after the late night news—with family room TV screens dissolving into nothing but white noise and test patterns—and the result was a public left largely in the dark.

If the citizens of London and its surrounding and largely rural metropolitan area were unable to connect the dots and stand back to see what lay before them, the police were no further ahead. The lack of a central police database prevented the flow of any key information not otherwise carried in an oral, anecdotal version—stories swapped between officers running into colleagues or at rare briefings that put both the London PD and OPP under one roof. Predictable police factionalism, egos, and bureaucracy took care of the rest, as did the cumbersome nature and non-portability of paper case files accumulating in banker's boxes and filing drawers. The crude mediums used to document these cases—mechanical typewriters, handwritten notes on legal-sized paper with carbon-paper backing—amounted to investigative handicaps that few cops today can imagine. Had someone been able to consolidate all of these disparate pieces of information in one place, it might have helped forecast what 1968 would have in store for the Forest City.

At the twilight of 1967, London's trend of sexual homicides was a proverbial iceberg that no one but Dennis Alsop, it seems, was prepared to acknowledge. As with every iceberg, by the time trouble is spotted on the horizon, it's usually too late. With 90 percent of its mass located below the surface of the water and out of immediate view, even if one is able to temporarily evade or even ignore the immediate threat, it is what lies beneath—the insidious and unseen threat—that is ultimately the real danger, and which causes the greatest devastation. As the age of the serial killer in London and area had dawned, the cases in full view were, in their own right, cause for alarm. But beneath the surface and out of view was a problem much larger than anyone at the time could have fathomed, and one that today endures as a social and criminological phenomenon that defies explanation and precedent across Canada. The year 1967 had certainly not been the city's finest hour. Sadly, the worst was yet to come.

# -CHAPTER 4-
# THE TISSUE SLAYINGS: 1968

"All absurdity of conduct arises from the imitation of those whom we cannot resemble."
-Samuel Johnson, *The Rambler*

# DEAD OF WINTER

As 1967 drew to a close, Londoners hoped their city might be out of the woods when it came to the spate of bizarre slayings that had been gripping the region over the previous two years. The winter of '68 was met with renewed but cautious optimism amidst the usual seasonal gloom, as Londoners sought to put the previous year's uncertainty and scariness to bed. They wilfully distracted themselves with the usual unrealistic new year's resolutions, ones that remain largely unchanged today: going back to school, exercising more, smoking less, drinking less, philandering less, and abstaining from any and all things that generally make life tolerable in London in the wintertime. They chose to opiate themselves with novelties like the annual winter ice skating at Wonderland Gardens and watching *Hockey Night in Canada*. When the sun rose on 1968 for the first time, it also looked like January would be typical weather-wise in London: bitterly cold. At the mercy of Great Lake effect snow and wind, temperatures during the first week of the year—still listed in imperial Fahrenheit in the local newspaper—plunged the city well into frostbite territory.

London wasn't the type of place to spend a winter, back in 1968, if one could avoid it. One could set ones watch to the certainty of watermain breaks and ensuing road closures as a merciless wind chill tore at the aged Forest City's crumbling infrastructure. A tortuous assemblage of snow squalls, freezing rain, and impenetrable, depressing, ash-grey skies greeted the city with each new morning, every day looking indistinguishable from the last—other than maybe, perhaps, just a little more drab. The coldest recorded intersection in Canada might very well have been Portage and Main in Winnipeg, but January in London was operatic in its dreariness.

On January 9th, only a few days after the school year was back in session following the Christmas and New Year break, with holiday lights still lingering on the façades of homes the city over, the local forecast once again called for snow—a forecast proven accurate with a dusting of a fresh few centimetres by mid-afternoon. London had certainly seen Januaries with greater accumulation, but on this particular date the weather itself would help trigger a series of circumstances that sent the city even farther down the rabbit hole into darkness. It would also set in motion a succession of events that would grip the city in the throes of a horrific murder mystery that endures to this day. It turns out that the weather might also remain one of the best enduring clues to helping solve it.

## VICTIM: JACQUELINE DUNLEAVY, AGE 16

In January of 1968, the Stanley Variety was a fixture in what remains an eclectic neighbourhood just west of London's downtown. Wedged into a tiny plaza at the corner of Stanley Street and Wharncliffe Road, the Stanley Variety was a definitive neighbourhood store that mimicked a bodega one might find in a denser city like New York. Appealing almost exclusively to the nearby foot traffic and neighbourhood passers-by, the store sold a curious assortment of just about everything, from consumable goods such as dairy, candy, and cigarettes to housewares and basic party supplies. It was a true smörgåsbord of miscellany, strewn on rickety shelves fabbed from Gypsum Board in a space no bigger than most living rooms of the day.

Years before coffee shops became Canadian institutions, the Stanley Variety also served both regular and decaf by the Styrofoam cup, with two self-serve glass pots always brewing on a hotplate, alongside an empty cakebell. For customers who had the weekly password, the money, and the right connections, that same cup of coffee could be sipped in the privacy of the store's basement, behind a locked metal door. The musty light-bulb-on-a-wire cellar is where the owner kept more than just the store's bargain inventory. Along with some cheesecake pin-ups and garden variety mail order smut, it's also where he kept his collection of home movies, bootlegged 8mm stag films, and fetish porn—all of it screened on a sheet for a small cabal of loyal "customers" on a pay-per-view basis.

The one-time owner of the Stanley Variety, Joe Clarke, in a January 1968 photograph that appeared in the *London Free Press* following Jacqueline Dunleavy's murder. Jacqueline had been working at the store for several months at the time of her death, one of numerous teenaged females employed by Clarke during his ownership. Courtesy: Western University Archives.

The owner, a shifty fiftysomething named Joe Clarke, had a talent for recruiting and hiring young girls, most of whom would find themselves being a captive audience to the motley assortment of customers who frequented the store for its fringe benefits. For some, these benefits included Clarke's collection of questionable amateur pornography; for others, these benefits were purely financial. From the cross-dressing hack chemist who gave Clarke knock-off, homemade cosmetics to sell illegally on consignment to the revolving door of teenaged boys pulling daytime B&Es and using the store to fence stolen merchandise, Clarke was more than accommodating. For some the benefits were even more sinister: access to the attractive and unsuspecting teen girls working there, usually alone. Regardless of the reason for why customers ended up darkening the door, the Stanley Variety was a magnet for some of the shadiest characters inhabiting the city's downtown, west end, and Old South neighbourhoods. All the while, the young girls working the counter and locking up after dark were at the mercy of who might show up next, who might be waiting outside—who might come up from the cellar.

Aside from the generally heterogeneous nature of the surrounding neighbourhood, the Stanley Variety was also the last stop on the way home for most of the city's suburbanites heading west from the downtown on weeknights. The small contingent of high school girls working at the store also lived in the recently annexed western suburbs themselves, with the London Transit Commission's daily bus service to what was previously the Village of Byron ending just after the store's closing time of 6:00 p.m. It was this same nightly bus that brought the Stanley Variety's most faithful and popular part-timer, 16-year-old Jacqueline Dunleavy, home from her after school job two to three nights a week. It was waiting for just such a bus on Beaconsfield Avenue, directly across the street from the store, just after closing on Tuesday, January 9th, that Jacqueline was last seen alive.

Just as Georgia Jackson had done on an equally blustery winter night three years earlier, Jacqueline Dunleavy hung the "closed" sign on the front door of her part-time workplace just after the last customer was rung through at 6:15 p.m. By 6:30 p.m., she had her coat on and headed out into an unlit, snow-dusted street. She walked as she had countless times before to a city bus stop, located just two blocks to the south. Witnesses would later confirm that she had been seen standing at the Beaconsfield stop in anticipation of catching the last bus back to her family's home on Griffith Street, near the London Ski

Club. What exactly happened next remains unclear, but at least one passer-by would later describe seeing Jacqueline getting into a white four-door sedan, described as likely being a Chrysler. The witness recognized Jacqueline, but didn't get a look at the driver.

On that Tuesday, Jacqueline had been working her usual 3:30-6:30 p.m. shift, and had had a number of visitors to the store, posing as genuine customers, in order to engage her in small talk. For most of her shift, Joe Clarke was also there. In only the few months that she had worked at his store, she had turned down the advances of countless of Clarke's associates, including one man who was a voracious viewer of his bootleg stag films. This same man was already married to a 16-year-old girl, and known to be violent when drinking—which was always. It would later turn out that he was only one of countless male customers who knew Jacqueline's routine and who would have had the access, motive, and opportunity to try to convince her to get into the car that night.

When 7:00 p.m. came and went, and Jacqueline had still not returned home, her parents started calling everyone but the police—the store, her friends, the neighbours, the London Transit Commission—all without luck. Jacqueline's father, a London police officer himself, as well as a police association representative, immediately went into cop mode, got into his car, and began driving the route Jacqueline would have normally taken home, either by bus or on foot. Before long he was driving in circles.

Jacqueline still hadn't been reported officially missing when, at around 8:00 p.m., three teenaged boys fishtailed a mufflerless winter beater into the parking lot of the Oakridge Plaza on Oxford Street West, about five miles from the bus stop where Jacqueline had been standing in the cold. The panicked trio pulled in and flagged down Constable David Clark, a London Uniformed Division officer and colleague of Constable John Dunleavy—Jacqueline's father—to alert him to what they saw while parking their car to go tobogganing at the nearby London Hunt and Country Club. Somewhat sceptical, Clark nonetheless called it in to dispatch and followed the boys back to the parking lot of what was then known, perhaps a sign of the times, as the Katherine Harley School for Retrainable Retarded Children—today, an upscale private school. When he arrived at the location and stepped out of his patrol car, Clark wasn't entirely sure what he was looking at but equally knew it would forever change him. At the same time, just a few miles away to the southeast, Dennis Alsop was getting out of his own car and walking into his house on Beachwood Avenue after pulling a seventeen-hour day at the London OPP detachment. He walked in the door and sat down to dinner, completely unaware that his predictions from two years prior were about to prove true. The other shoe just dropped.

## "PERVERTS DESTROY"

As Constable Clark squared-off his Sam Browne, radioed into 14 King for backup, and told the boys to stay put back at the road, the image before him and its implications slowly came into a focus: a young girl on her back in the snow, face bloodied, laying about fifty feet in from where Oxford Street dead-ended at the time. The girl's eyes were still open, her arms posed board-straight at her sides, palms down, and her legs carefully planked together as though positioned in a casket for burial. In a snowbank nearby was found her schoolbag with the contents spilling out. Just a few feet away, her shoes for work—leather slip-on flats—as well as snow boots, torn pantyhose, and underwear were found carelessly discarded around the body. Just beside the girl's carefully arranged corpse was her winter coat, covered in a mix of vomit and semen. The left side of her face had been severely beaten, and the scarf used to strangle her was still fastened like a garrote around her throat. Her skirt had been pulled up to her hips and her blouse had been torn open. Her exposed skin had been repeatedly scratched by the killer's fingernails, but there had been no actual sexual penetration. To the untrained eye it looked like amateur hour—the work of a frantic and sexually inept peer of the young girl following a botched rape. A closer look told the real story.

Before Constable Clark and the subsequent investigators even knew the body was that of Jacqueline Dunleavy, it soon became clear that the scene conveyed a host of contradictions. Deep ruts in the snow confirmed that the body was dragged over fifty feet from where the killer's car had been left idling on nearby Oxford Street. The assailant had then returned to the car to collect all of the girl's belongings—her boots, bag, and torn clothes—and walked them all the way back to the body, prolonging his time at the scene and leaving behind biological evidence on the coat—the technology of the time only being able to confirm that the killer was a secretor with relatively common type O blood. These same personal items belonging to the victim had been thrown into the snow without a care in the world, and yet the killer took the time to elaborately pose the body, placing it in a position that was equally contradictory. The arrangement of Jacqueline's body in a ceremonious, mortuary position would seem to suggest the presence of what forensic psychologists will often call "undoing," or an attempt to remorsefully restore order and dignity to either a victim's body or the crime scene. Yet, the efforts made to leave her sexually exposed to those who found her—to leave her in a position that removed rather than restored her dignity in death—suggests that the funereal posing was less about undoing as much as it was creating a visual that would sustain the killer for some time, perhaps through a mental snapshot, perhaps through an actual Polaroid photograph—perhaps both.

Had the Oxford Street tobogganers arrived just a few minutes earlier, they would have seen the killer and interrupted the whole iconographic process. The superintendent of the London Hunt and Country Club, an area resident named Morley Finlay, also looked after the Katherine Harley School parking lot, having ploughed it at 3:00 p.m., and was due to return again at 9:00 p.m. Had he arrived earlier or just driven by to check on his work, he also would have interrupted the killer, eyeballed the license plate, or even intervened. The chosen dump-site, in an upscale area that was still relatively active in the winter, in spite of numerous more isolated areas nearby, suggests that the killer wanted the body to be found relatively quickly and that he was not afraid of operating outdoors or being seen. He may have even banked on it.

The elaborate posing coupled with the lack of sexual penetration also suggests that the murder was of what is known as the power-control variety. Controlling every element of the crime and the subsequent crime scene, the killer was both excited and aroused by the visual he had crafted. It was a grotesque tableau that the killer would have rehearsed in his mind for a long time before, and later replayed on an endless loop-reel. Sadly, the most disturbing part of the inexplicable crime was yet to come, and would not be revealed until the body was sent for an autopsy at the city's St. Joseph's Hospital.

Inserted in the back of Jacqueline's mouth was a small travel pack of pink facial-tissue paper, the same type of cellophane wrapped Kleenex that someone might keep in a car's glove-box in wintertime. Apparently used as an improvised gag by the killer, the tissue didn't actually contribute to Jacqueline's death, a fact suggesting that it was inserted in the mouth either post-mortem or peri-mortem and done purely for expressive and paraphilic purposes. The necrophilic and necrosadistic actions of the killer in posing the body aside, Jacqueline was lured into a car, driven to her death, and defiled by someone who was clearly excited by the shock created by public exhibitions. He was in his element operating in a public parking lot at 8:00 p.m., leaving the body in a position that was both funereal and ceremonial on one hand, and sexually humiliating on the other. But the real signature—the killer's calling card and a window into his most aberrant fantasies—was the wad of tissues. For this very reason, no one other than the attending coroner, forensic pathologist, and handful of lead investigators within the inner circle of the case should have ever known about it. The exclusivity of this investigative inner circle is intended to function as something of a containment field, a way to keep what's known as "hold-back evidence" out of the public eye, and with good reason.

The value of having a hold-back evidence policy was first suggested in Edgar Allan Poe's 1842 short story *The Mystery of Marie Rogêt*, a fictional treatment of the actual 1841 murder of a young New York tobacconist named Mary Rogers, and arguably the first piece of true crime ever written. Hold-back evidence, as first recommended by Poe (although not using this precise terminology), is a list of facts about an open or unsolved case that is "held back" from the press and the public. The logic is that information or evidence relating to motive, profit, the MO, or the signature—not just in the case of murder, but for any crime—should never be revealed so as to prevent false confessions, and more importantly, deter copycats. The idea of crime scene copycatting, or the notion that one killer might change their MO and signature to match that of another offender in order to create artificial linkages, was not a term in use in London in 1968. It should have been.

Five years earlier, in 1963 Boston, a multi-agency task force known as the Strangler Bureau was assembled to catch the Boston Strangler—the man responsible for a reign of terror that included home invasion sexual assaults, murders, and similar necrophilic body posing in Boston's CMA. Questions remain to this day as to whether Albert DeSalvo, a hyper-sexual half-wit who had a history of ruse-style sexual assaults and who later admitted to being the Strangler, was actually the killer of all thirteen suspected victims. Questions also remain as to whether all of these victims were in fact killed by just a single offender. Some experts have suggested that there may have been as many as five Boston Stranglers—plural—and that the failure of the Boston Police to maintain a hold-back evidence policy, when the first linkages were made in

1962, actually opened the door for a wave of other paraphilic psychopaths to begin mimicking the Strangler's "successful" methods.

In the absence of an official hold-back evidence policy to help him follow the puck, London Police Superintendent Herb Jeffrey either didn't know about the Strangler Bureau or hadn't watched the news or read the newspaper to hear of the controversy surrounding DeSalvo's confession just four years earlier. He almost certainly hadn't read Poe. Otherwise he might have intervened, as the senior media contact for the Dunleavy case, to ensure that the details about the pink tissue were not printed in the *London Free Press* where the murder got a two-page play on the morning of January 10$^{th}$. Compounding the damage done by the most important detail with respect to the signature—a term still not having been coined and its importance to investigations not yet realized—having been leaked, was the manner in which Superintendent Jeffrey then went on to describe the cruelly sadistic crime. As both the de facto chief of detectives and the public face of the London Police for the purposes of the Dunleavy investigation, Jeffrey went on to curiously declare the murder as "the work of a healthy male." In later qualifying his remarks, he only made things worse. In claiming that, because "perverts destroy," the comparatively controlled and methodical scene suggested that the girl's murder was not the work of a "pervert" but that of someone more restrained, nuanced, and sophisticated. The term "pervert," even in 1968, of course had no consistent forensic definition. Even if such a definition had existed, Superintendent Jeffrey certainly had no credentials to warrant throwing around such a term to support his conclusions that were really apropos of nothing. None of it made any sense—not then, not now.

With one front page story and a reckless sound bite to accompany it, it was open season on London's most vulnerable victims among the sexual murderers-in-waiting who had simply needed validation, in their eyes at least, that their paraphilias were *not* perverse and were in fact normal, healthy, and merited indulging. Enough inside information on the mindset and sadistic fantasies of Jacqueline's killer had already been pro-actively disclosed to permit emulation and imitation of those same methods by others—either for their perceived effectiveness, or simply for the ability to pin future murders on Jacqueline's killer by having the police and media falsely connect them.

There are two types of crimes that will normally springboard the status quo of even the most idle police department into action with newly self-discovered rage, forcing its members into full throttle without as much as a second guess—cop killings and child killings. The bizarre necrophilic murder of 16-year-old student Jacqueline Dunleavy was an odd assortment of both. She wasn't quite a child but she was a cop's daughter, and while a cop hadn't necessarily been killed, Jacqueline's father and the London Police lost something forever with her murder. In light of this, a betting man might say that London Chief Finlay Carroll would have moved hell and high water to catch the so-called "healthy male" who murdered and desecrated the daughter of one of his own officers. For a month or two, that betting man would have been right, but soon the great flood would pour over the city, as Dennis Alsop had once predicted, and the Dunleavy case and others would be underwater seemingly forever. From February 1968 onwards, the back burner was to become a London murder cop's closest friend, second only perhaps to Detective Sergeant Alsop, who inherited most of the city's castoffs.

By the time young Jacqueline was laid to rest, there were in actuality a number of solid leads that suggested her killer would soon be in cuffs, with a formal city PD briefing and investigative brainstorming session having kicked loose a few key names. Unlike the most recent few murders in London's CMA, it looked as though the noose was tightening around some key suspects—at least a dozen. In the weeks after Jacqueline's death, and following an interview with the *London Free Press*, skeletons also started to walk out of Joe Clarke's closet; the Stanley Variety was then put up for sale. Before the ink was dry on a low-ball offer, Clarke had made a midnight move and had blown town for good. With his swift departure, information started to roll in as to who his regular customers were—customers who knew and *liked* Jacqueline. The list was a local who's who of sadistic deviants and paraphiliacs, all of whom it seemed shopped for cigarettes and penny candy at the Stanley Variety—but only when Jacqueline was working.

Beyond the middle-aged regular with the 16-year-old wife at home, there was the scatologist from the nearby town of Strathroy—a man who drove 45 minutes into London to shop at the Stanley Variety on Tuesday and Thursday afternoons when he knew Jacqueline would be there. The same man also had a history of exhibitionism and convictions for indecently exposing himself. Then there was a morgue attendant at a nearby London hospital, who hadn't coincidently been accused just months earlier of trying to force a teenaged girl into his car at the same bus stop where Jacqueline was picked up. Beyond these two discreditable types, there was another nighttime regular who lived in the neighbourhood. He had access to a car, and as a youth in 1962, had spent four years in reform school for hanging a defenceless 7-year-old girl and masturbating while he watched her die. A psychiatric report from before the youth's 18th birthday described him as a dangerous sadist with uncontrollable violent fantasies and recommended that he remain in secure custody indefinitely. The report was, of course, authored by a well-intentioned probation worker in vain, since upon the boy turning 18, everything he had done until that point was water under the bridge. He was cast loose upon society with a clean slate—allowed to move to the Forest City entirely unsupervised to be amongst like-minded compeers.

The reality was that Jacqueline, and the other girls working at Stanley Variety, had absolutely no clue who they were really dealing with at the store. In his interview with the local paper the day after Jacqueline's murder, Joe Clarke described his employee as "an extremely pleasant girl … happy as can be." His abrupt departure a short time after her death suggested, however, that he may have known more than he was letting on. This included the fact that the part-time job, which Jacqueline didn't need but genuinely liked at Clarke's hole-in-the-wall store, is what led, whether directly or indirectly, to her murder. Clarke, by virtue of his sketchy affiliations, had brought the wolves to the door of the Stanley Variety, and while he might not have killed Jacqueline Dunleavy, his store and some of the types it attracted no doubt helped seal her fate. Following his abrupt departure in the summer of '68, neither the city cops nor the OPP ever pursued the Clarke angle further. But beyond the laundry list of sexual psychopaths frequenting the store, the best lead actually remained on Oxford Street, embossed in the snow on the night of January 9th.

## JALOPY

The three teenaged boys who happened upon Jacqueline's posed body had quite incredibly managed not to run over the tire-tread impressions left by the killer's car in the virgin snow outside the Katherine Harley School. The nearby London Hunt and Country Club—still open for business in January to accommodate trap shooting and winter galas—had a methodical and diligent superintendent who ploughed and shovelled that same lot after so much as a single dusting of snow. Had he not ploughed both the parking lot and the adjoining laneway off of Oxford Street that afternoon, the killer's tire tracks would have been only one of an unrecognizable two-dozen or so left by other cars earlier in the day. But by ploughing the entire property between 4:00 p.m. and when Jacqueline's killer showed up four hours later, groundskeeper Finlay had inadvertently sprung the trap that might still prove key in helping catch one of the most mysterious killers in Canadian history—one who unquestionably later went serial.

With Jacqueline's body still at the scene, the London PD watch commander had the presence of mind to bring in professional stage lighting to enhance exposure and assist with the forensic photography. It was a move that allowed photos to be snapped of what were quickly confirmed to be the killer's tire tracks—caught on film just before the next wave of flurries moved in and buried them forever. The footwear impressions left by the three boys who found the body, coupled with Constable Clark's department-issue boots had destroyed whatever remained of the killer's shoeprints, but the tire tracks would actually provide just as clear a statement about for whom the local cops should be looking.

With the Ontario Centre of Forensic Sciences only two years old and still refining its protocols and case submission processes, private sector experts were brought in as the most timely resources to consult about the tire tread evidence. The crime scene photos, as well as plaster casts made from the impressions in the snow, were later turned over to the non-forensic experts—mostly dealership service techs and mechanical garage workers—whose independent assessments were unanimous in their findings: the car that drove Jacqueline to her death was a mechanical disaster. Most importantly, it had four completely different tires in terms of make, model, and tread depth, in addition to one of the worst alignment problems they had ever seen in a vehicle still operational and on the road in wintertime.

Crime scene tape delineates a horror story told in the snow. At first light on January 10th, the London PD day watch resumes control of the Dunleavy murder scene on Oxford Street, obtaining casts of tire impressions while scouring for other clues. Courtesy: Western University Archives.

It was yet another contradiction. Jacqueline was picked up in a densely populated neighbourhood and then driven, unclear if initially alive or dead, to a secluded property at the west end of the city. The destination was a property that, at the time, would only be frequented by parents with children attending the school for "retarded children" and who could easily be tracked. The surrounding area, the families of which used the dead end of Oxford for tobogganing, was buttressed by a newer and upscale suburb, as well as the London Hunt and Country Club—a private-members-only institution that was a home away from home for the city's blue bloods. Yet, the car driven there by the killer that night was a decrepit heap—a consummate clunker inviting unwanted attention. Four different tires haphazardly thrown on, and an alignment problem that, especially prior to the advent of power steering, would have made it nearly impossible to keep the car in its lane after a snowfall. Factor in the fact that, in an age of rear-wheel-drive vehicles, none of the four mismatched tires were designed for winter and the car would have been all over the road. Although it couldn't have been more out of place and would have stood out like a sore thumb, the killer remained unfazed—as if perhaps he had been there before and had an explanation at the ready if ever questioned. He knew the route well enough to find his way there under pressure and with a captive on board. Assuming Jacqueline had been alive when they got there, she would have known things were about to go bad and would have no doubt been resisting. The injuries to the left side of her face suggest a series of punches thrown from the driver's seat in response, while she was looking straight ahead, perhaps while staring through the frosted windshield in disbelief at where the detour had taken her. Whoever was behind the wheel of the jalopy that night knew the area and the Hunt Club's location well enough, yet was driving a mobile crime scene worthy of the scrap heap. There would seem to be little doubt that that's precisely where the car ended up within a matter of days.

Over the next few weeks, teams of officers fanned out from the crime scene in all directions, going house to house and business to business, checking the tires of every car in every garage, carport, driveway, and parking lot as they went. Every car under a tarp or in the shop was checked; every winter beater skidding down the road was pulled over and given the once-over, the screws being put to bewildered drivers by eager patrolmen who knew the girl's bereaved father. Everything on wheels, parked or stowed on Jacqueline's street was checked, as was every house and tenement on Stanley Street and surrounding area in search of the elusive white Chrysler with mismatched tires wobbling at different angles. They struck out. The student and teacher parking lots at Jacqueline's high school, Westminster Secondary, were also checked. Maybe the car was that of a cash-strapped young teacher, maybe a hand-me-down recently acquired by one of Jacqueline's schoolmates. No dice. Anyone living near the girl's home or school who was a known "rape-o" or who had sex-related convictions on their "jacket" was given extra special attention, but alas, nothing panned out. All the while, the Canadian flag outside Westminster Secondary's main entrance flew at half-mast. Beyond that simple gesture, mind you, the school wanted nothing to do with the whole ordeal. What happened to their beloved Grade 10 student was simply too terrifying and too graphic to repeat in mixed company, let alone on the school's watch. Bringing attention to it would just invite awkward questions from curious teenagers and panicked parents. The policy was to bury it, not mention a word of it. High school confidential.

## MURDER CITY

The Westminster yearbooks for both 1968 and 1969, printed in the months following Jacqueline's murder and then following the one-year anniversary in 1969, also make no mention of what happened. There is no memorial page, no reflections or poems offered, no photograph or tribute or any mention of the young girl of any kind, let alone of her having been taken. A single page in the 1969 yearbook and filed under the header "As the Months Go By…" lists the "wearing of black armbands" under the event calendar in January, but with no accompanying name, date, or context. Immediately below is the notification "radio installed in cafeteria," and just above it an announcement about changes to the school newspaper. Just another day at Westminster Secondary. By 1970, no talk of armbands at all, no anything, only good news stories en masse. Just two years out and it was already "*Jacqueline who?*" The London Police, it seemed, had an even shorter memory. A dedicated and well-liked cop's daughter being violated and murdered just about anywhere else would have meant a blank check to bankroll the midnight oil for as long as it took, until the killer was behind bars. But as leads began to wane and operational demands stretched the Chief's paltry force even thinner, the unthinkable happened: the man the media was already calling the Tissue Slayer struck again.

## VICTIM: FRANKIE JENSEN, AGE 9

Exactly one month to the day after Jacqueline Dunleavy's murder, February 9th, London had grown even colder. On that Friday morning, the overnight temperature had plummeted to nearly 40 degrees below zero, rising to just under the freezing point by first light and bringing with it blustery snow squalls that enveloped the city's west end. But in 1968, snow days were rarities and what they now call "cold days" all but unheard of. So shortly after 8:00 a.m., nine-year-old Frankie Jensen set out from his home at 382 Hazel Avenue to trudge his way to school. Located just over a mile from where Jacqueline Dunleavy's lifeless body had been found posed, four weeks earlier, the Jensen home was a peaceful and tight-knit place that seemed worlds away from the horror of the previous month.

The son of a Danish immigrant and local furniture magnate, Frankie, one of five children still living in the home with both parents, was in Grade 4 at what was then Westdale Elementary. The school's principal, a Mr. Pickles as he was known to the students, later reported that Frankie was a good-natured, punctual boy who had no issues with other students. The former was true but not the latter. Frankie had in fact objected to going to school that same Friday morning, not because of the treacherous weather but because he was being bullied by older boys on the playground.

Frankie's parents and older sisters, one of whom would normally walk Frankie to school, had told him not to back down and to carry on with his usual routine; after all, bullies could not be catered to or cowered from. Frankie listened to his family's Scandinavian wisdom and set out on his own that morning—his sister who often accompanied him running late—while waving goodbye to his parents. They stood in the picture window watching as he set out towards Riverside Drive, the first major road north of their home. From there, Frankie, who was carrying only a lunch box prepared by his mother and 40 cents in his pocket, would take Hyde Park Road to Valetta Street. From Valetta, he would cross to the dead end of Plantation Road, the quaint little street where the small, newly-built school was located. Total distance to be travelled: a little over half a mile.

The distance on foot at the time was actually even shorter, as students making their way to the school could shave about three minutes off their time by cutting diagonally north-by-northeast through a wooded area that was awaiting development, and where a foot path had been carved into the natural landscape by countless little feet. But as quaint and sedate as the area appeared on the surface, and as innocuous as the brief detour through the woods would seem, the daily journey was not without its risks.

On at least two occasions in 1967, boys walking through that same brush were ambushed and chased by grown men hiding amongst the trees. In the most recent incident prior to that fateful February 9th, a man emerged with a club and swung it at a young boy who was chased nearly to the front doors of the school. The protocol at the time was apparently just to report these incidents to Mr. Pickles, who might then call the police at his discretion. There is no indication that he ever did. In reality, most of the "men in the woods" incidents were either dismissed by the administration as embellishments, dramatic excuses for truancy, or just the imagination of school children. In cases where witnesses backed up the claims, the attacks were brushed off as the annoying but otherwise harmless conduct of the "mongoloids," as they were then insensitively and incorrectly called, who had wandered over from the nearby Harley

School, the same place Jacqueline Dunleavy's body was dumped, or the nearby Children's Psychiatric Research Institute (CPRI). Both institutions were precariously close to Westdale and had lax security measures to say the least. The CPRI—originally the Queen Alexandra Sanatorium for tuberculosis patients and since renamed the Child and Family Resource Institute—also housed clients up to the age of 18 who displayed concerning sexual behaviours. In reality, the Hyde Park shortcut is better understood today as fitting within a model of criminology and victimology that developed about ten years later, in the late 1970s, and which is today known as *routine activities theory*.

We all follow routines, and the structure of modern society is such that we seldom deviate from them. Suburban family homes are targeted for daytime break-ins because thieves know that the weekday routines of people who own those homes is one that puts the occupants at work, at school, or out running errands. The result is a predictive target that can be identified based on the routine of the owners. The routine activities theory of crime suggests that this same model can be applied to nearly all types of offending. The nuts and bolts of the theory state that, where a motivated offender and a suitable victim meet at a particular time and place in the absence of a "suitable guardian" (police, eyewitnesses, video surveillance, etc.), crime is more likely than not to occur. Children known to be using a certain footpath both before and after school in turn qualify as suitable targets for sexual predators and pedophiles, who themselves qualify as motivated offenders. With the location of the path removing it from public view, and therefore eliminating the likelihood of guardians and witnesses, these ingredients added together made the Hyde Park shortcut an ideal hunting ground for the deviants who pervaded the Forest City at the time. A full decade before routine activities theory was made public, and people were encouraged to switch up their daily routines and vary their routes home to help protect themselves against stalkers and other targeted stranger attacks, that same wooded area would soon be the focus of an intense search for Frankie after he failed to show up for school that day.

On the morning of February 9th, Frankie never made it to Westdale. A little over 24 hours later, by 10:00 a.m. the following morning, London Police had to actually turn away volunteers from the Oakridge subdivision where Frankie lived, with over 200 citizens showing up to complement the 60 police officers walking shoulder-to-shoulder as they scoured the area, searchers literally tripping over each other as they feverishly combed every inch of ground in search for the 60-pound, blue-eyed boy. Frankie had been reported missing to police on the previous evening after he failed to return home. His initial absence from school was first thought to have been perhaps due to his reluctance to face the bullies after all. Within 24 hours, however, while police were still—rather incredibly—ruling out foul play rather than misadventure, they also conceded that there was little chance Frankie would still be alive if he had been exposed to the elements overnight. Even in the daylight, officers had to limit their combing of the Hyde Park woods to fifteen minute shifts after exposed skin was found to be reddening almost immediately as a result of the severe wind-chill.

A new shift of London police officers and citizen volunteers heads out into sub-thermal conditions from the rear doors of Westdale Elementary on the morning of February 10th, 1968, preparing for a shoulder-to-shoulder search for missing 4th grade student Frankie Jensen. Courtesy: Western University Archives.

As the ground search proved fruitless, efforts to locate the boy expanded to include canvasses of rail and bus stations and even hospitals, the thought being that perhaps he had been injured and driven unreported to the ER by a Good Samaritan. Some even proffered the idea that Frankie might have somehow tried to run away from home. Although these theories also failed to yield any solid leads, the usual bogus sightings inevitably also began to surface—everything from his being seen shopping with another family to hitchhiking on nearby rural roads—in turn stretching the already thin resources of the police who tried to follow up on each tip. Return visits by police K9 units and the Legion of Frontiersmen to the Hyde Park Road and Valetta Street corridors in the coming days and weeks, in search of what by that time most knew could only be the boy's remains, also proved futile.

The reality is that Frankie never made it to the shortcut in the woods. As the routine activities model has taught us, while motivated offenders often rely on being able to predict routines, sometimes the routines of select victims are already known. Every day Frankie took the same route to school—a routine that changed only slightly on February 9$^{th}$ when he took it alone. For someone to know this, they would have needed to have been watching him when he first left the house. Frankie's parents said that the timid, gentle boy would have been too afraid to get into a car with a stranger, even in a blizzard. Although they were right, what no one considered was what might happen if he were offered a ride by someone who knew Frankie—someone who knew everything *about* him.

As the initial public statement by police, ruling out foul play in Frankie's disappearance, was beginning to look less and less genuine and the chances of the boy being found alive were looking less and less likely, the city—at least in the comradely west-end enclave where the Jensens lived—was galvanized by the horror of the whole situation, including the other unrelated attacks on children that prefaced his disappearance. The London chapter of the National Council of Jewish Women thus soon began brainstorming ways to better protect the city's young from the apparent proliferation of sexual predators and psychopaths walking and driving the Forest City streets. In doing so, they later hatched a revolutionary idea. The group, through their colleagues in the U.S., caught wind of a volunteer organization being used sparsely but successfully south of the border in towns about the size of London. It was known as the Block Parent Program.

London's—and Canada's—first Block Parents meeting the provincial Lieutenant Governor, Pauline McGibbon, at an unveiling ceremony in Hamilton in June 1979 to commemorate the start of operations in that city. The program began in London following attacks on children and teens in 1968 and within the decade had spread to cities and communities across the country. Courtesy: London Block Parent Program.

Designed to offer children a place of sanctuary if they felt they were being followed or were in danger during their travels to and from school, any home displaying the Block Parent placard in the front window was a safe haven that children could run to if danger approached or if a stranger was lurking. Catering largely to carefully screened stay-at-home mothers or retirees likely to be around on weekdays, thorough background checks—to the best of the police department's ability by 1968 standards—were conducted on all applicants. By the summer of that year, a pilot project was in place to help protect London's most vulnerable. Soon after, other Canadian cities followed suit, and by the turn of the millennium, there were over 1200 Block Parent cities and towns across Canada. While some good it seems did come from this period in terms of London's being—and having to be—ground zero for what later became a monumental national safety initiative, sadly it would take many years before violence against children in the Forest City receded.

By Valentine's Day, although Frankie still hadn't been found, his case was now being investigated as a suspected homicide—the police could no longer dismiss the disappearance as a case of playing hooky gone awry. A canvass of the surrounding neighbourhood—one much more sombre than the one conducted during those panicked first 48 hours following his disappearance—ensued as a small contingent of city detectives quickly found themselves juggling both the Jacqueline Dunleavy murder and the Frankie Jensen disappearance. This work overload was not simply a matter of staffing. The fact that the incidents occurred so closely together made daily trips out to the Oakridge subdivision to chase down leads a daily ritual for a small corps of detectives. Soon, the two cases would turn out to have more in common than just their unlikely geography.

By the third week of the month, a witness turned up who had seen something odd on the morning of February 8th. The witness told of a man sitting in an idling car on Valetta Street, at the very spot where Frankie and other Westdale students would customarily leave the road to take the hidden path the rest of the way to school. If the witness was right, the car would have essentially been blocking the path, as though anticipating that Frankie was going to be using it. The time was around 8:30 a.m., and the witness hadn't thought much of it until later asked—one of those predictable "actually…now that you mention it" moments that usually offers too little too late. The next time the witness drove past the spot that same morning, both the car and the man were gone. When asked to describe the driver, the witness predictably flunked. When asked to describe the car, the answer sounded eerily familiar: a white sedan.

## VICTIM: SCOTT LEISHMAN, AGE 16

In the dead of winter, little Frankie Jensen had literally vanished. The dread faced by his family was unspeakable, and the pressure on local police nothing short of remarkable. But as temperatures climbed and the snow began to thaw to reveal what lay beneath, the case of the missing boy would take on horrific new connotations.

Spring break in 1968—known back then as the Easter Break—fell between March 18th and March 22nd. Frankie Jensen had been missing for over a month but bad news travelled slowly. There is nothing to suggest it even travelled outside of the city at all, and certainly not beyond the local newspaper's circulation area. So, home from school for the break and headed to the local fishing hole following the first real spring-like day of the week, 16-year-old Scott Leishman left his house without a care in the world on the afternoon of March 21st. Scott, who lived in a rural home located just fifteen minutes east of London, in the township of West Nissouri, was heading to nearby Thorndale in the township of Thames Centre, all part of London's CMA and all located just a few minutes east of the city proper. Scott's preferred method of travel, along the county roads that encircled the Forest City, was the same as it was for so many others both then and now: thumbing a ride.

At just after 4:00 p.m. that afternoon, Scott was seen, with his fishing rod slung over the shoulder and tackle box in hand, getting into a car driven by an unidenfied male. The description provided by the lone witness driving by was, yet again, that of a white sedan. As had been the case with Frankie Jensen, Scott Leishman's family did their best to get answers before calling the police. Never mind the nonsensical "24-hour" missing-person policy that prevailed at the time, his parents thought. It simply made no sense that young Scott, a well-liked, outdoors-loving kid, would just up and vanish like that. Also, as in Frankie's case, the hours soon turned to anguishing days, the days to weeks, and the weeks to months. Like so many others, Scott Leishman's last confirmed whereabouts while still alive were while either walking or hitchhiking along London and region roads. It was becoming a familiar tale.

Just as with so many of the others—little boys, teen girls, and young women—it would be some time before Scott was found. His killer had intended it that way. Unlike in the case of Jacqueline Dunleavy, where the posed and very public disposal of the body satisfied the killer's dual needs for both a specific visual image and the shock and horror of those who found her, Scott's killer needed to put time and distance between him and what happened. But there was also one other fundamental difference between the Dunleavy slaying and the Leishman murder. Scott had vanished from rural rather than urban London, and so it was an OPP file from the start—and it was Dennis Alsop's turn to oversee new cases.

Within two days of the original missing-person report, the Leishman file landed on Dennis's cluttered desk which was already covered with the Jackson and Tedball files, not to mention his old crime scene photos of the Lynne Harper murder, which still nagged at him. With the Leishman file—at that point still a suspicious missing person case—being added to the pile, it would soon be joined by another, and then another, and then another. In time, Dennis would come to bear the brunt of London's record-setting tidal wave of murder and depravity, even snatching up and working cases that were not officially his, only because no one else was. Like the story of Sisyphus in Greek mythology, condemned for eternity to roll a jagged, crushing boulder uphill against all odds, only to have it roll back down before he had to start over, from March of 1968 onwards, Dennis would spend the rest of his life on an impossible mission. From frustration to obsession, the soon-to-be Detective Inspector Alsop would forever be haunted and tormented by the onslaught that followed.

## WATER'S EDGE

On the afternoon of April 12$^{th}$, 1968—Good Friday, and exactly nine weeks to the day after Frankie Jensen was reporting missing to London Police—fishermen located his body in the Thames River just east of London where it enters West Nissouri, Scott Leishman's hometown. Face down in the water near the shore, the recent thaw had revealed what the wrath of that winter had concealed: the nine-year-old boy dead in the water, and wearing only a button-down shirt and undershirt. A search of the surrounding waters turned up the boy's winter coat, the lunch box packed by his mother, and part of his thermos. All of these items were found between the body and a bridge located about two miles away. Had the boy's body not become unpredictably snagged on a downed branch sometime after the thaw, the swift spring current would have carried him out to Lake St. Clair, some two hours west, where the river's mouth is located and where he would have likely never been found at all.

In recovering his body from the river, Frankie's pants were then found submerged beneath the same branch on which the body was found hung up. The pants being found beside the body, especially with all of the boy's other belongings being scattered at random, suggested to investigators at the scene that he had gone into the water fully clothed, with no explanation as to how or why his pants came off. In a matter of hours, one of the officers at the scene was Dennis Alsop, already en route at the time to West Nissouri to look into the Leishman disappearance. Upon arrival in his department-issue '66 AMC Ambassador—mint green, zero trim—he very quickly deduced two things. Firstly, it seemed that the tragic end to the search for Frankie Jensen was likely an omen for how Scott Leishman would later be found. Secondly, he knew that based on the standing agreement between London PD and the OPP, the Jensen file, now officially a homicide, was also now his.

While Dennis was resigning himself to the certainty of what might come next, the autopsy conducted on Frankie's body was less than certain. A precise cause of death could not be confirmed, given the time elapsed and the interference of the water and ice. What was clear, even before the autopsy, was that the little boy had definitely suffered a massive blow—fatal or not—to the head, which would have rendered him unconscious and at the mercy of his killer. There was, however, no obvious indication of sexual assault, not unlike the earlier case of the Jacqueline Dunleavy, who had been found just blocks away from where Frankie was last seen, and whose sexual assault—within the type 4 range—was as unconventional as it was aberrant. But that's not where the similarities between the Dunleavy and Jensen cases ended.

Removed from the back of Frankie's throat by the forensic pathologist was a wad of pink facial tissue. It was not in a cellophane pack, like the wad found inserted in Jacqueline Dunleavy's mouth, but in everything else it was a match. The victimologies and MOs varied considerably: one was a teenaged girl disposed of on land, and the other a small boy disposed of in water. One was strangled to death, and the other beaten, if not to death then near death, before being thrown in the river, unconscious, from a nearby bridge. One was snatched at night near her work, and the other in the morning near his home. But even before the term "signature" was coined, the London Police at the very least (still running the Dunleavy investigation on its own) was sure that it was the work of the same killer. This conclusion appears to have been based on the lack of invasive rape, the scattering of clothing at the dump-site, and—the most obvious calling card—the pink tissue lodged in the airway, apparently after death.

But Dennis was sceptical. While not directly involved in the Jacqueline Dunleavy murder—at least not in the early days—he knew that excessive details about the property scattering and pink tissue paper in the mouth had been leaked to the press. He knew that a great deal of hay had been made by local news and in local taverns about it, and that the Tissue Slayer had fast become a household name in the city. On the other hand, the fact that the very next victim lived just around the corner from where Jacqueline Dunleavy was dumped seemed a little *too* convenient, especially with the story still in the news and the heat still on. To Dennis, it reeked of an impostor baiting the police—it bore the impression of being little more than subterfuge. But he was in the minority. It was soon Tissue Slayer this and Tissue Slayer that, as the beginning of a great public panic took hold.

With the Jensen murder, London yet again proved to be at the forefront of procedural and inter-agency issues in homicide investigations that in coming years would shock the world. Dennis was to some extent the Canadian progenitor to Detective Charlie Geunther, a Los Angeles County Sherriff's Department homicide cop whose name, like Dennis's, never made the history books, but is the man who actually—and almost single-handedly—solved the infamous Tate-LaBianca murders and brought down the Charles Manson "Family." After nabbing the two killers of a California man named Gary Hinman in July 1969 and noting that they wrote "Political Piggy" in blood on the walls at the crime scene, Geunther wisely teletyped his peers at the newly-minted Homicide Special Section with the LAPD and suggested they check out the known associates of the killers who were squatting at the Spahn Ranch in Death Valley, a deserted silent movie set with a senile caretaker. The LAPD quickly dismissed the tip that the Hinman blood scrawls might be connected, preferring instead to take the earlier "Pig" writings at the Tate-LaBianca murder scenes at face value and as the work of biker gangs, black radicals, or some anarchist group. The truth is that were it not for the LAPD getting a lucky bounce a few months later and solving the whole thing, Manson and his cult of homicidal hippies would have gone on to murder many more. The cases *were* in fact connected, and in the end the Manson Family was collared largely by luck. It was only the 1974 book *Helter Skelter*, authored by famed prosecutor Vince Bugliosi, that rewrote history to give the LAPD the win in the case. Like Charlie Guenther, Dennis's hunches—hunches that in this case suggested the copycatted pink tissue was intentionally bogus and the murders *not* connected—were ignored outright. Unlike Geunther, however, there were no lucky bounces to be had. The Tissue Slayer myth thus grew exponentially as the Dunleavy and Jensen cases grew colder by the day. As Londoners soon began looking over their shoulder before buying a box of Kleenex, lest they be accused of being the killer, a modern-day witch hunt in the tradition of Salem seemed to be in the offing. That was until just over a month later, on the afternoon of May 21$^{st}$, when it appeared as though every cop but Dennis had missed spotting the *real* signature in the Jensen murder.

Scott Leishman was taken from a county road near his home in West Nissouri, just on the outskirts of London. Frankie Jensen was taken from a city street near his home in London and his lifeless or near-lifeless body was thrown into the water from a bridge near the Leishman home in West Nissouri. The overlap was jarring when Dennis looked at it from a bird's eye view on a map. Then, on the afternoon of May 21st, Scott's body was found near the banks of the inner harbour in Port Burwell, located some distance away in Elgin County and roughly an hour's drive from where he was last seen getting into the mysterious white car. Suddenly the pattern was not as clear—at least not at first glance. It seemed that the 16-year-old boy was still definitely alive before going in the water. He was thrown from a bridge into the Big Otter Creek, and—just as it had been with Frankie—the intention was that he be swept out into a larger body of water, this time Lake Erie. Once again, nature intervened and the body later washed ashore after getting trapped in the inner harbour. An examination of the condition of the boy's body by Dennis and the other investigators at the scene quickly shed new light on the Frankie Jensen murder. In time, the boys' names would be forever linked in Dennis's mind.

Like Frankie Jensen, Scott Leishman was determined to have a number of items missing—though in this case, a dragging of the waters in both the harbour and the nearby Big Otter Creek failed to turn up any belongings. Scott's watch and at least one of his shoes—like both of Frankie's boots—were never found. Maybe they were washed farther out into the lake, or maybe they were taken as souvenirs. Unlike Frankie, however, Scott had no trauma to the head or face. If it was the same killer as Dennis was beginning to suspect, his MO was evolving, becoming more calculated and more sadistic. Also, unlike in Frankie's case, there was no pink tissue lodged in the victim's mouth this time. To Dennis, this all-but-confirmed that the Kleenex faux-signature in Frankie's case was an intentional attempt to throw the police off, to lead them down a garden path towards artificially connecting the murder to that of Jacqueline Dunleavy a month earlier. The tissue in the Dunleavy murder was an improvised instrument used to accompany the other acts of debasement after death, and it was information that should have never been released. The term "copycatting" in a criminal context hadn't yet been coined, but on the heels of the Boston Strangler case, Dennis had just seen the first documented case of its occurrence in Canada. Had he himself not headed the case, others might have fallen for it. There was no Tissue Slayer, or at least not just one of them. With the discovery of Scott Leishman's body, it was clear that they were dealing with someone else entirely—someone who, with Jacqueline Dunleavy's killer as his muse, was still out there and poised to strike again.

The comparatively quick discovery of Scott's body, relatively well preserved in the cold waters of the harbour, also allowed Dennis to gain better insight into why Frankie was found the way he was. Both boys, similar in appearance though seven years apart in age, were either lured or forced into a vehicle and driven a considerable distance before being thrown off bridges into bodies of water that fed larger lakes. While these similarities are compelling, occurring a month apart, they reflect only the MO—one that seemed to be relatively unstable and had changed considerably between the first and second victim. In Scott's case, the autopsy was more conclusive. The boy had been either strangled or suffocated to the point of unconsciousness and was then thrown in the water where his blacked-out state—coupled with the impact of the water landing—caused him to drown. It was a relatively prescribed process, and a method of murder that reflected total control and patience. It was the work of a sadistic and methodical killer who had been at this for a while. As with Frankie, there was no obvious sign of sexual assault, although the actions taken by the killer before sending the teen into the frigid waters and to his death seemed to reveal the real (rather than the faux) signature—the killer's true paraphilic calling card which had initially been missed in Frankie's case.

Whatever happened in that white car between the time Scott got in to catch a ride to Thorndale and when he ended up drowning in the Big Otter Creek some fifty miles away, his killer made sure that he had entered the water in a certain way. He made sure that he completed certain tasks that, in rewinding them and playing them over his head, would keep him cruising on the memory of the murder for a while, and keep his paraphilic and predatory drives at bay. As Dennis surveyed the boy's waterlogged corpse as it lay on the shore he noted that while certain items were missing, the boy was completely dressed aside from one anomaly: he had actually been *redressed*, and in a very specific manner.

It was never clear how or why Frankie's pants had come off and why they were found so close to the body, especially when all of his other garments and belongings were widely scattered. It seemed to Dennis that there was now an answer. The Leishman boy—who looked much younger than his actual age and more like an older grade-schooler—was found with pants still on but only barely, his belt refastened backwards and the zipper on his pants left fully undone. The boy's belt was in effect used as a cinch to keep the pants against the body until it hit the water, the apparent intent being that the impact, current, or—as in Frankie's case—a nearby branch or other debris would ensure they came off. While the posing in Jacqueline Dunleavy's case spoke to very specific necrophilic spectrum fantasies, as well as a need to defile and humiliate, the signature in the Scott Leishman case was much more obscure, its origins and symbolism much more complex.

There is no evidence that, in 1968, Dennis knew anything about the paraphilias of sexual psychopaths or how to distinguish a signature from an MO; no one did, at least not in Canadian policing. But as both the police and the media used empty and unqualified terms like "perverts" and "degenerates" to describe these people, and saw these murders as random, Dennis knew that there was a back story to all of it that was much more detailed and disturbing. He also refused to believe in coincidences, at least not in London. He also knew that there was a common dominator at work in both the Jensen and Leishman slayings. Someone with deep-seated, pedophilic proclivities, a reliable car, knowledge of the area, and the freedom to roam on weekdays had picked these two boys for a reason. The elaborate signature with the pants suggested that he had been rehearsing that routine either in fantasy or in practise for some time. But the brief span—a single month—between the kidnappings and murders of the two boys was also a short enough interval to suggest that chasing the fantasy was getting boring and that the intervals between the killings would start to diminish as the killer became more and more confident. It had already been a month since Scott was taken and killed. Dennis would need to act fast to save the next potential victim.

# THE NEIGHBOUR

On the day Frankie Jensen was buried, April 15th, 1968, his funeral brought out friends, neighbours, classmates, teachers, and everyday citizens—not to mention the London Police detective bureau. Although the original city investigators who were working what had been the Jensen missing person case had since relinquished the file to Dennis Alsop, now heading the dual investigation into both of the river murders, those original investigators had grown close to the

Jensen family over the intervening months. The case weighed heavily on them, especially now that it was evident just how terrifying the innocent boy's final hours and minutes alive would have been. Before leaving the chapel at Millard George Funeral Home on Ridout Street where Frankie's wake was held, one of the London detectives, keenly aware through the grapevine of the headway that Dennis had already made in linking Frankie and Scott's cases, offered a parting—and what he hoped would be a reassuring—statement to Frankie's bereaved mother. Before officially stepping off the case for good, London Detective Bob Young whispered *this* in her ear: "You can see the killer. You can see his house from your window. He can see you." Nothing else was said, and Detective Young, who would later become Dennis's wingman in future London murder investigations, then discreetly slipped out a side door before making his way back to 14 King. Within days, the local media seemed to echo these same reassurances, that closure was in the offing. Public statements made by both London and OPP boldly proclaimed that "an arrest [was] imminent," and that the public need not panic—that the killer was under constant observation and would soon be in custody. The bravado turned out to be premature, but the reality was that, for the first time, the killer was on police radar. As long as he lived in London, Dennis would shadow him everywhere he went and sweat him every chance he got. If he couldn't actually arrest him—the Truscott hangover having engineered a reliance on endless "wait-and-see" policies by police brass—he would at least ensure that he never hurt anyone else. In the meantime, there were also many inventive ways to try to crack him.

In 1968, Frankie's killer's house could indeed be seen from not one but many of the windows of the Jensen home. In the winter, from his elevated position just two streets over, around the corner from the Jensen house, the killer could see through the leafless tree line that separated the two properties and into the Jensen's single-storey Oakridge subdivision bungalow. Originally from the area surrounding the historic town of Simcoe, about 90 minutes from London, the Neighbour moved to London sometime in the mid-1960s and took a job as a travelling salesman. With a previous arrest for exposing himself to children, he managed—like so many sexual predators at the time—to elude conviction by virtue of his chalking the whole thing up to a big misunderstanding. Dennis knew better.

His road to shortlisting the Neighbour had been a winding and circuitous one. He had stumbled across his sexually depraved background largely by chance when running records checks on all males living in the vicinity of Frankie's home—a massive task four years before a national criminal database was even conceived. At the same time, Dennis employed a number of unconventional methods that, in retrospect, were hugely innovative, and which reflected his appreciation of the unbiased, third-party insights offered by civilian subject matter experts. One of these experts was Dr. John Morden, a theologian and professor of comparative religion at Huron University College, one of the affiliated colleges at Western University in London—one of Canada's "Old Four" institutions of higher learning. As an expert in demonology and occultism, the erudite professor was consulted by Dennis to try to gain insight into whether the river murders and the bizarre signature with the trousers perhaps had some historical significance in either scripture or pagan rituals. If nothing else, it would help Dennis put to rest rumours swirling around London that the Tissue Slayer was somehow affiliated to a satanic cult sacrificing children—one comprised of high-ranking officials who had protection. As the spate of 1968 homicides coincided with the release of *Rosemary's Baby* and the general religious crisis of the counter-culture 1960s, Dennis was well acquainted with the social context of the violence deluging the London area. In short order, he needed to rule out the rumours as little more than myth before the public panic worsened. Indeed, Dr. Morden confirmed, as best he could through discussions and the viewing of gruesome photographs, that the killings in no way reflected any known occult practice, and that like the existence of the so-called Tissue Slayer, the speculative satanic theme was little more than pure fiction.

Dennis was a man renewed. He punched out a one-page search warrant on an old-school IBM Selectric Model 72 typewriter—the document peppered with whiteout and correctable film marks—and executed it at the home of the Neighbour. The search effectively allowed, if nothing else, the Neighbour's life to be dumped upside down to see what might fall out. A few things did—big things, in fact. It turned out that the Neighbour was an exhibitionist, a pedophile, and a forger, but had until that time convincingly concealed himself in an upper middle-class subdivision and feigned conformity and normality. London at the time was the perfect concealing agent for high-risk repeat offenders and sexual deviants like him—nomadic predators who had endured high-altitude training elsewhere and could now wear a cloak of invisibility in a city like London, where people preferred not to know what happened behind closed doors. When Dennis and his skeleton crew of uniformed assistants, both city police and OPP, arrived at the Neighbour's home, they first confirmed that the attached garage concealed a car nearly identical to the one seen by witnesses picking up Scott Leishman. The car's interior was believed to have been the crime scene for both murders—a car which Dennis found to have been recently cleaned save for one item recovered from beneath the floor mat—a fine blond hair consistent in length and colour with Frankie Jensen's.

With no DNA testing available at the time, there was no way of conclusively linking the hair to the boy. The use of medulla patterning in the comparison of hair follicles as a common pre-DNA technique also didn't help given the state of Frankie's body once found, it having been submerged in the river for months. The Neighbour had successfully placed enough time and distance between himself and the body that, by summer of '68, the lone hair and the common make and colour of the car in the garage were little more than circumstantial pieces of evidence loosely joined. Alsop dug deeper. Inside the wood-shuttered, centre-hall home was a box of pink tissue paper consistent with the wad found inserted in Frankie's mouth. Yellowed copies of *The London Free Press* strewn around the main floor also confirmed the Neighbour read the local news—including the grisly details of the Dunleavy slaying and the leaked information regarding the use of the Kleenex pack. The house also revealed important evidence of the Neighbour's alibi on the date Frankie was abducted and murdered: it was fake. In seizing the Neighbour's work records and daily activity logs provided by his employer—the now long since extinct Acme Steel Company—as a result of the search warrant, it was discovered that he had falsified entries related to his sales accounts and customer visits on the morning and afternoon of February 9th. Dennis's notes from that day, April 19th, report:

*Re: Jensen murder case. Seized vehicle and company records. Checked on records, found many false entries.*

Based on these and other notations, the shopkeepers and hardware wholesalers alleged to have been met with and the addresses the Neighbour claimed to have visited based on the entries were all checked out by Dennis and all confirmed to be bogus. The persons named by the Neighbour in his ledger, once interviewed, had no recollection of ever seeing him that day. Demo versions of the various items being hawked and pedalled by the Neighbour during the course of his travels through the city and its outlying townships—including hand tools like hammers and wrenches—were all kept in his car as a matter of convenience but were all found cleaned when seized. With nothing directly linking him to either murder or either dump-site, Dennis had the Neighbour for misleading his employer and falsifying work records but not for murder. Before long, he had him for nothing, with the Neighbour seemingly also having read about Sandor Fulep and the murder of Victoria Mayo. As Dennis's notes report:

*On further investigation, suspect voluntarily committed himself to Ontario Hospital, London.*

With the Neighbour proclaiming himself insane and sowing the seeds of a future NCR defence, the forensic investigation into the car's interior and the entries in his work log carried on unabated. Curiously, no other entries in the Neighbour's ledger for 1968 had been doctored. Entries for the day of Scott Leishman's disappearance were not apparently falsified, but on the other hand, the distance from where he was last seen alive and where his body turned up was, unlike in Frankie's case, a mere matter of minutes and wouldn't have required a day-long alibi. With respect to Frankie's case in particular, the question asked by Dennis in his notes, and which endures to this day is why, on a blustery February Friday when treacherous county and highway road conditions would have prevented the Neighbour from running his usual sales route to begin with, he would feel the need to say he was somewhere he was not by falsifying his employer's date book. Once the Neighbour, like Fulep before him, was deemed "cured" and released from the hospital, Dennis asked him that very question on August 9th after tracking him to his hometown of Simcoe where he was in hiding. He asked him again after later following him to the Toronto suburb of Scarborough, where the Neighbour later checked himself into the then newly-opened Clarke Institute of Psychiatry. The answer was the same on both occasions—no answer.

Over the remainder of 1968 and into 1969, every approach made by Dennis towards the Neighbour was met with avoidance, disappearance, or self-committal to a psychiatric facility. Rather than "lawyer up," in each confrontation the Neighbour, living well beyond his means while in London, took the more affordable route of having himself locked in asylums. Psychiatrist after psychiatrist would in turn either tell the relentless Detective Sergeant that interviewing the Neighbour might push him over the brink to suicide, or that he was simply too catatonic or psychotic to speak with authorities in the first place. It was a masterful ruse that had everyone but Dennis convinced. Like in his body disposal methods and his work ledger forgeries, the Neighbour was a master manipulator and a consummate psychopath who was adept at buying himself time. Dennis pleaded with his OPP colleagues in the Toronto area to keep tabs on the Neighbour when he was not in the hospital, but it seems that few if any others were as invested in keeping him on the radar. They hadn't worked the cases, seen the boys' bodies, or met or consoled their families as Dennis had, and there were more than enough Toronto and area suspects in other murders to keep tabs on as it was.

One such murder occurred during the early morning of May 14th, 1975, just before 9:00 a.m., when 5-year-old Tracey Bruney was dropped off outside her school in Etobicoke, near where the Neighbour had re-settled at the time. She never made it inside the building. Her body was later found in Etobicoke Creek, apparently thrown from a nearby bridge—cause of death, drowning. The girl hadn't been obviously sexually assaulted, although her clothing was said to have been "disarranged." Her lunch box and bag were also found discarded some distance away. Dennis would never know of it. By late 1973, he had received an imperious call from an interceding, animatronic yes man named Superintendent Loree, directing him to cease and desist—that all surveillance of the Neighbour was to stop and that Dennis was to let it go. It soon seemed as though the Neighbour knew that Dennis had been ordered off his tail by way of an edict delivered from the OPP mothership because, only a year later, Simon Wilson, who was walking to school just like Frankie Jensen did back in 1968, vanished without a trace—his body has never been found. The Neighbour was living nearby at the time. In 1981, Erik Larsfolk—a blond Scandinavian boy almost identical in appearance to Frankie Jensen—also vanished and has never been found. At the time, the boy also happened to be in the company of his best friend John McCormack, who has also never been found. The Neighbour was coaching a minor league sports team nearby at the time.

The Neighbour died over forty years after leaving London and was no doubt surprised that he had never been caught for the Jensen and Leishman murders or for any other crime he had committed. By that time, the OPP had also "mislaid" the fine blond hair recovered from the floor of his car, back in April of 1968. As OPP brass later sent a retired Dennis Alsop letters, belatedly soliciting his insights into these cases years after the fact, he could only sit in anguish and anger as technologies like serology and DNA identification—methods that had only been a glimmer in the eye of police detectives back in 1968—had finally come to fruition, yet to no avail for these cases. With the only piece of physical evidence long since having disappeared, and with the Neighbour now dead and buried, an aging Dennis Alsop resigned himself to the fact that the London river murders of the young boys might never be solved, at least not by the police. From that point forward, he began to build his literary legacy—his notes relating the Jensen-Leishman killings packaged-up and stowed for future generations. Of course, by then there were countless others to be added to the list.

## VICTIM: HELGA BEER, AGE 31

In August of 1968, Helga Beer was newly single and working as a hairdresser in the Elizabeth Arden Beauty Salon, located within the walls of the iconic Simpsons Department Store at Dundas and Richmond Streets—at one time the city's premiere window-shopping destination. Helga lived due north, up Richmond Street beside the university, in a modest apartment with her brother and mother after splitting with her husband. Having arrived from her native Germany roughly seven years earlier, it's not clear why Helga chose to settle in London of all places, other than perhaps the considerable German community that had developed throughout the city following the Second World War. Her family later followed her there, including her mother who had been in Canada and living with Helga for only a few months at the time of her daughter's death. Newly available, attractive, and working in the public eye at what was perhaps the city's marquee department store at the time, Helga soon forged her own identity independent of her fellow ex-pats. There was also no shortage of London men who knew exactly who Helga was or where to find her.

On the evening of August 5th, something drew Helga back to her old apartment building at 186 King Street. The Jack Tar Building, as it was known at the time, housed many of Helga's friends of one type or another. It was reported that she was there to visit a female friend—reportedly also an occasional lover of hers—that same night after work. The female occupant of the building was later seen leaving from the back stairs with a suitcase in hand and apparently making the proverbial midnight move, never to be heard from again. Helga was then seen leaving shortly before 1:00 a.m., while being squired around by a man described as "well-built" and with a distinctly "wide nose." That's the last time Helga was seen alive—the last time the unknown man, like the woman with the suitcase, was seen at all.

The following morning, August 6th, at just past 6:30 a.m., Helga's '63 Volkswagen Beetle was found reversed into a vaguely marked parking space on the dirt lot of a service station, on what was then the west extension of Carling Street overlooking the Thames River, and just a block north of police headquarters at 14 King. From her last known sighting with the unknown male, her car had only been driven a distance of roughly 500 metres. The employee of the service centre, in preparing to open up shop, knew the VW wasn't one of the vehicles in for service. A closer look at the interior revealed what was initially thought to be a mannequin lying on the floor of the backseat. To confirm what he was looking at, the attendant opened the unlocked driver side door to find the lifeless body of Helga stuffed between the front and rear seats. She had been left wearing only a blouse and her brassiere, the rest of her clothes scattered throughout the car.

London crime scene identification officers photograph and process the 1963 Volkswagen where Helga Beer's partially nude and battered body was found at dawn on August 6th, 1968—the city's fourth, and still unsolved, sex slaying of the year, but sadly not its last. Courtesy: Western University Archives.

As Dennis Alsop continued to work the Jackson, Jensen, and Leishman murders, Helga Beer's murder would remain a strictly city PD case, although Dennis would catch wind of it and later do some digging of his own—all of it off the record. He seemed to know the sad truth that in the city, with the murders of Jacqueline Dunleavy, Victoria Mayo, Margaret Sheeler, and others still open and going nowhere fast, the murder of a swinging divorcée in socially conservative London would rank relatively low on the department's list of official priorities. A small quick-rigged delegation of detectives was sent out on a canvass run of the area bars where it was confirmed that, earlier in the evening of the 5th, Helga had indeed been out with two people—possibly a man and woman, and possibly the man with whom she was seen leaving the Jack Tar apartments. A composite sketch was then developed that looked as if it could be just about anyone Helga had ever dated or even talked to—or, for that matter, anyone who might be found shopping at Simpsons or wandering into any of the bars in the area. By the day's end, it was clear that the case would never progress beyond square one.

# QUARANTINE

While barkeepers, hoteliers, and Simpsons employees were being questioned in a roundabout way about Helga's usual haunts and hook-ups, at Victoria Hospital an autopsy was being conducted, one which would confirm that the young woman was beaten by a large fist and then strangled to death before being placed in the position she was found in the car. In all likelihood, she was killed elsewhere and driven to the location that appears to have been picked at random, the killer reversing rather than driving the car in forwards into the parking space—something Helga never did. She had engaged in sexual intercourse sometime prior to her murder, but it was unclear if it had been rape or consensual sex. What was clear is that she had either redressed herself or been redressed by the killer after the sexual activity, but before her murder. Either before or after parking the car, the killer took the extra step of removing the loafer-style shoes, green shorts, and semen-stained panties worn by Helga and then tossing them into the front seat so that the corpse would be found exposed—an indignity that recalled the Dunleavy murder from back in the winter. All the while, the London public and Helga's co-workers at the salon had no idea what was going on, with the story not being reported until later that afternoon in the *London Evening Free Press*. The front-page story also managed to feature a victim photograph depicting a woman who was definitely *not* Helga Beer. Someone in the newspaper's art department, it seems, had their wires crossed and mixed up the photographs for two different stories. A correction was published in the morning edition on the 7$^{th}$, and after running a couple of more paltry follow-ups, the murder was pushed to the back pages before disappearing from view entirely. For the police, Helga's case wasn't much of a story either.

In spite of the presence of semen on the underwear found tossed in the front seat, as well as inside the victim, for reasons that remain unclear, no efforts appear to have been made to obtain a blood grouping of the donor, a stark contrast with the forward-thinking efforts to preserve physical evidence in the cases of Jacqueline Dunleavy and even Susan Cadieux a full twelve years earlier. It is especially odd given that, at the time, some were drawing connections between the Dunleavy and Beer murders based on, if nothing else, the clothing scattering and post-mortem, necrosadistic humiliation. Even if such a biological sample were found to match the sample left on Jacqueline Dunleavy's coat, which could only be identified as type O using the technologies of the time, it would be far from a conclusive link. With type O positive and type O negative accounting for a combined total of nearly 50 percent of the male population's blood type in Canada, the last thing the London PD needed was to try casting an even wider net over the never-ending and ever-growing list of viable suspects.

Not only was a blood grouping never completed in the case of the Beer murder, but the underwear and any swabs or semen slides that were taken from the body were not stored in such a way that a donor profile could be developed when DNA technology came along thirty years later. It still remains unknown what the police actually did, of forensic significance, with respect to the Helga Beer murder, since few if any records or independent memories remain. What is clear is that, of the various men in Helga's life at the time, few of them showed up to mourn her. Even fewer could be found in later months. One even booked himself a one-way trip to Denmark as detectives were trying to arrange an interview. No doubt to his surprise, there was no one at the airport waiting to intercept him before he boarded the plane, and no flagging of his passport when he landed in Copenhagen a few hours later.

It might have occurred to him later on that no one stopped him because they were just as happy to see him go. Guilty or not, self-exile to Denmark was as fitting an end as anything the Canadian justice system might have meted out, and at no expense to the taxpayers. The woman with the suitcase and the mysterious "well-built" man were both quarantined safely away from the city until further notice. "Don't ask, can't tell" seemed to be the unofficial policy in place whenever people would ask whatever happened to the Helga Beer case. Few if any ever did.

By the time October rolled around, the Beer file was officially on ice, the list of persons of interest and suspects who could be located having long since been exhausted. Londoners were instead talking about the forthcoming one-year anniversary of the Tedball disappearance, wondering if it was somehow connected to what many still thought to be the ritual or occult killings of the city's young throughout 1968. Maybe it was because she was not one of their "young" and kept questionable company by the standards of 1968's disapproving London that Helga Beer's case never really became much of a topic of discussion. Maybe the killer, having left town for good, was the closest thing to a check in the win column that London could hope for based on its own recent track record. Either way, it seems that the voluntary quarantining of one and maybe even two of the people involved in Helga's murder amounted to some form of temporary closure for the city and its police. At least, for the first time in a while, it was something of an ending. And so the lid went on the box labelled Helga Beer—file number 110-4-68—and stayed there.

MICHAEL ARNTFIELD

# VICTIM: LYNDA WHITE, AGE 19

After Helga Beer was buried, the London Police Persons Squad—today rebranded as the Major Crimes Section—having been underwater for so long, finally seemed as though it could come up for air. In reality, the city and region's unprecedented and endlessly mounting number of unsolved sex slayings was just beginning. With a certain inertia having already built up, still more paraphiliacs and psychopaths were lying in wait. Some already called the city home while some, like Neighbour, would soon make their way there to follow their calling, migrating to London under various artifices while taking whatever chump change jobs allowed them the freedom to roam—the opportunity to hunt.

For those living outside the city and beyond the reach of its media and gossip networks, London was still the sedate Forest City where people left their doors unlocked and not much of anything ever happened. Roughly a hundred miles away in the city of Burlington, 19-year-old Lynda White was one such person. In the wake of the virtually unknown Helga Beer murder, Lynda was preparing to start her first year at Western University's Huron College—the same institution where Dennis Alsop had conferred with Dr. Morden just months prior about the water burials of the Jensen and Leishman boys. Unable to secure a room in the college's dormitory, Lynda was by late summer of '68 still scrambling to find a place to live off campus. An extraordinary and ambidextrous athlete, Lynda was excited to begin her undergraduate career at Western and was in no way deterred by the prospect of having to live away from its iconic campus. Just ahead of the start of Frosh Week festivities, Lynda had managed to secure a room in a rented house shared by high school friends from her native Burlington. Located on Argyle Street, over a half hour walk from Huron College, the redeeming quality of the little white house was that it was just a few blocks from her typing tutor, whom she would see at least a couple of nights a week. Factoring in that she already knew her roommates, the place seemed like the perfect fit, and in the nick of time.

With Lynda's move to London, she took her foray into university life as an opportunity to explore new ideas and new people. She dyed her black hair blond, and while maintaining close ties with a group of high school peers and other native Burlingtonians, she also branched out and made new friends. Two of these new friends were a pair of boys who were roommates and who shared a car. Given the long distance walked by Lynda to and from the campus, as the weather turned cooler she often accepted rides from them, normally not getting dropped off at her home on Argyle Street but about two blocks away, where Western Road turned into Wharncliffe Road North. Whether this was a safety measure used by Lynda to keep her exact address under wraps or whether she got dropped off there because it was just steps to her typing tutor, no one ever knew. What is for certain is that on November 13th, 1968, after writing an early evening French mid-term exam on campus, these same two boys dropped Lynda off at that same location. It was the last time she was seen alive, or at all, for nearly five years.

After the exam, Lynda had asked her classmates to go out for a drink at the nearby CPR Tavern, or the "Ceeps" as Western students had been calling it for generations. Finding no takers, she opted for the ride to her usual drop point. Lynda's two roommates, knowing she would likely head out—perhaps to the campus pub, perhaps downtown to the Ceeps as most students did at least one night of the week—were not overly concerned when she failed to turn up right away. When they found her bed empty the next morning, however, and discovered that she had never come home at all, they knew something was wrong. They called Lynda's watchful older brother John, in Burlington, who immediately drove to London with other members of the family. Lynda's tiny bedroom at the back of the rented house was searched for some clue as to where she might have gone, or as to whether she had snuck into the house to change in the middle of the night. It was hoped that she might have left *something* behind to let everyone know she was all right. The search of the bedroom, and the house itself, turned up nothing. Questions posed to her friends and classmates by her brother John also provided no indication as to where she might have gone after the exam. Strangely, the boys who dropped her off would deny doing so for over forty years, lying to both John White and later the police about their being the last ones to see Lynda. This suspicious omission on the part of the young men with the car served to unnecessarily rewind the time-line of events by nearly half an hour for four decades, wrongly putting Lynda's last confirmed whereabouts at the northwest door of the college, where she was seen exiting shortly after 7:00 p.m. following the exam. In reality, she was last seen walking south from the intersection of Wharncliffe and Western, nearly thirty minutes later and nearly three miles farther on.

People lie about what they see as insignificant details in police investigations all the time, normally to cover another lie or to distance themselves from matters they really want nothing to do with. The reality is that what are often dismissed as negligible white lies can end up having a profound impact on the speed, direction, and flow of an investigation, especially during the critical first 48 hours. The motive for the boys leaving out the details about their dropping Lynda off at the Western-Wharncliffe junction, during the first few critical days of the investigation, is still a mystery, as is why they stuck to the same story for well over four decades. Stranger still is why they came clean over forty years later, mentioning it off the cuff in an online forum and again during personal interviews. A reasonable assumption would suggest that the reason for the initial lie was perhaps considered to no longer pose any sense of jeopardy for them. The boys didn't kidnap Lynda or murder her, but their lies might have very well impeded the police catching the person who did. What was clear, after the sun set on the evening of November 14$^{th}$, when there was still no sign of—or word from—an otherwise conscientious Lynda, was that there was now good reason to worry.

John White had organized a search party at Western, where students and even faculty and staff came out en masse, as London citizens had in the Frankie Jensen case months earlier, to search on their own time for Lynda. Before the police got involved, and while the search teams were combing the area around Huron College and the university's main campus, John White drove to the London train station on York Street on a whim and showed Lynda's picture to the staff at the ticket window. "She just got on the train leaving the platform now, heading to Toronto" one of the counter attendants told him. Without missing a beat, John sprinted out the doors to the platform and jumped onto the train through the lone remaining open door, just as the engines were starting up and the "all aboard" was being sounded. Shoving his way past the conductor, John slalomed idle legs and bags the length of the train—car to car—while frantically scanning for his sister's face amongst the sea of anonymous passengers. Just as with the countless other alleged sightings of Lynda that were to come in following years, this one also turned out to be wrong—well intentioned, but wrong nonetheless. As the train began pulling out of the station and picking up speed, John leapt off the ledge of the rear car and barely landed in one piece back on the concrete platform, skid-stopping just short of the terminal doors. Undeterred, he headed back to the house on Argyle Street.

By the late afternoon, the remainder of the White family, including Lynda's parents, had arrived in London to help look and to find answers. In the freezing rain, Lynda's father paced back and forth along the banks of the nearby Thames River while using a long branch to probe the shallow depths of the murky water near the shore in his search for something—anything—that would lead him to his daughter. The image of their father standing in the rain and looking out to the river, apparently resigning himself to the worst-case scenario, would remain with the White siblings forever. Then, back at the house and in Lynda's room, the family made an unsettling discovery. A second search of her bedding by John White revealed a pile of clothes—the same clothes Lynda had worn to the exam—crumpled into a pile and stuffed under the bedspread. The clothing, Lynda's roommates assured her brothers, hadn't been there on the morning when her roommates had found the bed empty and realized that Lynda hadn't made it home. Neither John nor the other members of the family had noticed the clothing the first time the room was searched either, but in the span of the day the items seem to have spontaneously materialized. The clothing itself showed no sign of anything out of the ordinary—no stains or tears—and at face value it looked as though Lynda might have come home after the exam and changed before going out again. Either way, it opened up a realm of possibilities and moved the time-line forward well into the evening hours of the 13th, while also raising countless new questions—not the least of which was why the clothes were left hidden from view, and where Lynda was going and why she needed to change. Things were beginning to look more sinister.

When, later that night, a despondent John White walked out of the November rain and into the lobby of 14 King to report his little sister missing to the city police, Glenda Tedball still hadn't been found since vanishing in the woods on the previous Halloween. The murders of five London and area women over the previous few years—Sheeler, Mayo, Jackson, Dunleavy, and Beer—all remained unsolved and their killers still at large. The accumulating sex slayings of local girls in the last few months alone, in addition to the abduction murders and river dumps of the Jensen and Leishman boys—both also unsolved—confirmed that a city of then just over 190,000 people was at the mercy of at least three and as many as seven predators who, in increasingly brazen fashion, were snatching young women and children off the streets with impunity. Nonetheless, the officer manning the lobby that night didn't seem to bat an eye or find anything suspicious in Lynda's having uncharacteristically vanished. She "probably just ran away" the disinterested desk sergeant muttered, his eyes averted away to some other distracting paperwork, "…to become a hippie, or something."

## -CHAPTER 5-
# CRITICAL MASS: 1969

"In 1969 London, you did *not* walk the streets at night."
-Anne English, sister of Jackie English – murdered October 4th, 1969

# MARCH OF TIME

In many ways, 1969 represented not only the end of a pivotal decade in human history but also a punctuation mark on a socially tumultuous era when the world—especially in London—was in desperate need of some good news. If 1968 had started with Londoners longing for a return to being a simple city in the forest and for the madness sweeping the region to finally stop, the dawn of 1969 was met with genuine fear and loathing. But in spite of its spawning a sort of collective madness across the world, 1969 nonetheless emerged as one of the more nostalgic and iconic years of the 20$^{th}$ century.

The word "nostalgia" actually comes from the Greek *nostos*, loosely translating to homesickness—and until the late 19$^{th}$ century was actually considered a mental disorder across Europe and the Americas. Characterized by a melancholic longing for a place and time—in effect what we come to think of as "home"—it captures a sense of loss of something that we think we had, but probably never did. The year 1969, through the afflictions of nostalgia, is still held up as the mantle of a "simpler" or "happier" or "safer" time by those who choose to cling to some very idyllic, but in most cases fictional, memories of that extraordinary twelve-month period. In reality, as with most cases of nostalgia, these are people reminiscing about a past that never existed—an illusory time and place remembered only as they retroactively choose to remember it, not as it really was. The truth is that there was never a time when anyone was ever safe.

Beyond the self-perpetuating mythology of 1969 and its increasing historical revisionism in popular culture lies uglier truths about that same year and what was really going on. In London, the violence had reached critical mass, to the point that the body count showed no signs of waning. The murder of Jacqueline Dunleavy haunted every detective who ever looked at the file, and by 1969 had become a certified local boogeyman story. It was not a matter of *if* another London teen or child would be lured or dragged into a car and driven to his or her death but, sadly, a matter of when. Perhaps the killer would come right into your home instead, like what happened to Victoria Mayo, to attack you in your sleep—a nightmare you would never wake up from. These were the thoughts that began to creep into the minds of many everyday Londoners, many of whom had begun to wonder what the hell had happened to their city, and where it all went wrong.

## VICTIM: JANE WOOLEY, AGE 62

By the time the calendar flipped over to 1969, the Neighbour had a conniving system down pat for dodging Dennis Alsop's enquiries and invoking the protective services of the precarious Canadian mental health system. He had also left town for good, taking the scenic route to the Toronto area over the next few years following a long-term stopover in his hometown of Simcoe, near Lake Erie. Between keeping the Neighbour under loose surveillance—usually on his own watch—and spending sometimes days at a time going from farmhouse to farmhouse out in various counties, looking for either witnesses or the Jensen and Leishman boys' missing items, Dennis was consumed with solving the river murders while the Neighbour still remained within tenuous reach.

But if the Neighbour was a serial killer—albeit long before the terms "serial killer" or "preferred victim" began appearing in the literature—with a preferred male child victim, London had by 1969 produced another serial murderer with one of the more specific MOs and preferred victim types ever documented in Canada. On the afternoon of January 29th, 1969, Jane Wooley—a 62-year-old part-time hotel chambermaid—was seen leaving the London House on Dundas Street where she earned a mere $40 a week. A hole-in-the-wall weekly lodging house for drifters and other down-and-outers, the main floor tavern was reminiscent of London's frontier-like origins and was a throwback to the golden age of fist-fighting. It was a dump steeped in history, but few if any history books detail that afternoon of Wednesday, January 29th—payday for London House employees, including one Jane Wooley. Where exactly she went after collecting her money from the owner, no one ever knew. Given her solitary nature, and the fact that no one was expecting her anywhere, it is nearly impossible to conduct what is today known as a psychological autopsy to piece together her final movements or decisions before her death. But even with several hours missing from the time-line, the crime scene itself, located just a couple of blocks away and in her own rented room, certainly helped clear up the final few moments of her life. It confirmed that those moments were nothing short of horrific.

When Jane failed to show up for work on the morning of the 30th, not too much thought was given to her whereabouts. The turnover rate at the London House, especially for part-timers, was extraordinary and it was assumed that she had just quit without notice. Within the day, her position was filled by one of the hotel bar's regular loadies and neither her boss nor her co-workers gave Jane Wooley a second thought. It wasn't until February 3rd that the landlord of her own York Street lodging house, not having seen her for several days and waiting for an overdue rent payment, entered her unit just after 1:30 p.m., and found Jane dead on the floor. She had been severely beaten, with the cause of death being a combination of blood loss and a severely fractured face, which had sent her into shock. Found naked, except for a pair of stockings still on the body, she was lying on her back, and her severely beaten head and face were covered with three pillows and a sweater—perhaps remorsefully by the killer to conceal the gore of his heinous crime. Beyond this act of concealment, the scene presented as the work of a disorganized impulsive killer who appeared to have lost control during some sort of sexual rejection.

The scene additionally suggested that the murder was the work of an angry male who likely thought he was smarter than he actually was. There were additional questions that needed answering: how he was able to earn the trust of a reclusive senior and be invited to her apartment? Where (and how) had their initial meeting occurred? The ashtray on Jane's coffee table was full of cigarette butts, some with her shade of lipstick on the filters and many with no lipstick. Although it would be another thirty years before the National DNA Data Bank came into existence, the cigarette remnants in the ashtray provided the best clue the police had; they just didn't know it yet. No one could make heads or tails of the rest of the apartment. The telephone had been pulled off the receiver, but was still plugged into the wall. The victim's clothes were scattered widely throughout the unit; her purse was found upside down on the floor, the contents strewn about, and with no sign of the cash she had on her person when she was last seen alive. Strangest of all was Jane's pet budgie, found dead in its cage. With plenty of food and water still on hand to sustain it for days, it is more likely to have died, as birds sometimes do, from the stress of losing its owner—perhaps watching her murder.

Like the highly paraphilic sex slaying of Jacqueline Dunleavy the previous January, the year 1969 in London began with another "whodunit"—yet another horrific crime for immediate filing in the growing unsolved column. Aside from a canvassing run of the York Street tenement turning up a downstairs neighbour who reported hearing Jane's voice through the vents saying words to the effect of "no, stop it" followed by a dull thud, there was—in fairness—almost nothing for investigators to go on. The earwitness had only verified what the evidence at the scene had already told them—that Jane took the wrong man back to her apartment that night, and paid for it with her life. What local cops couldn't have known at the time was that Jane Wooley was merely his first murder. Using the Wooley slaying as his exemplar, he thought he had found himself the ultimate easy victim: older, indigent, and employed in the local low-rent hotel industry. He saw these women as naïve, lonely, and unduly trusting—women who nobody would be looking too hard to find. One of Canada's most peculiar serial killers, the London Chambermaid Slayer, had officially been spawned and spit out by the Forest City.

## VICTIM: PATRICIA BOVIN, AGE 22

The first of the chambermaid murders was likely one of London's lesser-known crimes of the late 1960s. But less than two months later, and just a few blocks east of the Wooley slaying, another indoor murder would preview what was soon to be a disturbing trend in London's CMA: a spate of apparently random home-invasion killings. Between senior-aged chambermaids and single mothers on welfare, the going solve rate, in 1969, for victims such as Jane Wooley and 22-year-old Patricia Bovin—the next victim of the city's crime wave—would not be good. About two days of media coverage—one day above the fold, one day below—and two weeks or so of earnest investigative work seemed to be the average elapsed time before things fizzled. It was two weeks on average until, like Helga Beer's murder, it was back-burner town.

The sad reality is that Patricia Bovin, a recently separated mother of two young boys on social assistance and living in a second storey tenement on King Street, although desperately looking to rebuild her life, had few advocates.

Patricia Bovin quickly became a second-class victim during a bewildering time when it seems victims either warranted an all out effort or didn't—period. Forthcoming chapters confirm that, even with solved crimes in following years, the courts also tended to regard young female victims as stakeholders in their own attacks, especially when without a voice from the grave. Patricia Bovin certainly seems to have been shunted into such a category. She had no cards to play, in life or in death, that gave her much of a fighting chance. Still, even by the investigative standards of the day, it was evident that at least three or four serial killers, plus an additional five one-off sexual murderers, all of them likely to strike again somewhere, were roaming the streets at once. By 1969, Dennis Alsop knew it—as he toiled away in his office, car, and under the Tiffany lamp in his kitchen at home—even if his city counterparts didn't. Within the year, things would get personal for him, with his cases taking him to a place where few cops before him had gone, at least in Canada.

In the meantime, much like Helga Beer's strangulation murder and VW body dump just two blocks from London PD headquarters the previous August, the investigation into Patricia's death was largely a post-mortem inquisition into her lifestyle and habits. Like Helga Beer, Patricia—young and newly single—had returned to dating a variety of men; however, unlike the newly unattached Helga, her number one priority had been being a mother and looking after her two young children, ages one and three. Together, the unsolved murders of these two London women, less than a year apart and both last seen alive on the same street in the city's core, seems to speak to the arbitrariness of how crimes got investigated, for how long, and by whom.

On the evening of April 22nd, 1969, Patricia was home with her two young boys, Clifford and Kevin, in her one bedroom upper duplex apartment in the 700 block of King Street, near the city's Western Fairgrounds, home of the Western Fair founded in 1868 and still one of the oldest existing fairgrounds in Canada. But in April of 1969, the fall fair was long since over and the grounds were empty; the area where Patricia lived would have had little reason to attract passers through. For all intents and purposes, the location was a "hard target," accessible only through a common ground-floor front door, in plain sight of dozens of other houses and accessed immediately off the one-way street. But as London's murders had already shown, "hard targets" do not always deter predators; for instance, no one would have likely guessed that Victoria Mayo's lower level apartment on the upscale Sydenham Street would have been a target either. In fact, as London detectives briefly mulled over a possible connection between the Helga Beer and Patricia Bovin murders in terms of demographic and lifestyle factors, they should have instead been looking at Victoria Mayo's case. But by the spring of '69, two years earlier in London must have seemed like ancient history given what the last twelve months alone had brought. The city police department's myopic merry-go-round transfer practises in its criminal investigation division had also helped with that. Many of the detectives who had worked the Mayo case had long since been re-routed into new postings driving radio cars, directing traffic, interviewing new recruits, or screening crossing guard applications.

It is now apparent that the overnight home invasion murders of Mayo and Bovin are in fact chillingly similar in terms of MO and victimology. This linkage is not just based on what was done to each victim, but also because of what was *not* done. Patricia Bovin was found dead inside her apartment mid-afternoon on April 23rd, discovered by a male friend who, having received no answer on the telephone, decided to go to the address to check on her. Finding the door unlocked, he entered and discovered her two children crying, soiled, and starving, but otherwise unharmed. Clifford and Kevin sat on the floor beside their mother, as if holding wake over her bloodied body. Lying on her back on the apartment's parquet floor, Patricia—like Victoria Mayo—had been stabbed, in some kind of frenzy, well over a dozen times. The graphic scene should have later looked familiar to the police, but with the revolving door policy across all detective units at the time in London—a system still in place today—lead investigators Detective Sergeant Lloyd Bryson and Detective George Burton hadn't been at Victoria Mayo's murder scene on Sydenham Street two years prior, and no doubt knew little about it. The Coroner system in Ontario at the time, and still in place today despite reforms elsewhere in Canada (many provinces moving to a concierge-style medical examiner system, where the same expert assumes carriage of the case from crime scene to autopsy), ensured that the Coroner receiving the call that night was a moonlighting general practitioner assigned on contract. Coroners attended scenes on a catch-as-catch-can basis and at their sole discretion, assuming whoever was on call even answered the telephone. Whoever got the call that night therefore also likely knew little of the Sydenham Street murder in 1963.

Like Victoria Mayo, the wounds to Patricia's body were numerous and erratic but avoided the face and throat—a notably unusual omission in the case of erotophonophilic murderers and one that, by virtue of its rarity, immediately suggests a behavioural link that we can today better understand. There was also no sign of defensive wounds, suggesting that Patricia—again, like Victoria—was fast asleep at the time she was attacked. Positioned beside the couch in the main room, which she used as a de facto bedroom, it appears as though she was sleeping on her back when ambushed by someone who had, yet again, made a stealthy entry undetected by the occupants or their neighbours. While the front door accessing the staircase leading to Patricia's second storey apartment was found unlocked, the original investigation never confirmed whether this was the method of ingress or egress used by the killer—or both. The finding of a bloodied pillowcase by a neighbour outside in the front garden several hours before the discovery of the body suggests that the main door was in fact used to leave. Also mirroring the Mayo case, a large sliding window was found unlocked in the apartment's living room, the same room in which Patricia slept so that her boys could share the one designated bedroom. She was found dressed in her nightgown, with blankets and a pillow matted with gore on the floor beside her. Patricia, like in the Sydenham Street murder, was also neither sexually assaulted nor moved from where she was killed. There was also nothing stolen and no harm was done to the sleeping children who hadn't been awoken by either the intrusion or the attack. The intruder came and went under the cover of night, without being seen or heard.

Police at the scene initially focused on the apparent disarray of the apartment, thinking that the murder must have followed a struggle or some kind of domestic dispute. Yet, a check with the neighbours confirmed that no noise was heard overnight between the paper thin walls and uninsulated floors in the converted duplex. The only exception was a toilet heard flushing sometime around midnight, a noise in itself loud enough to wake the female tenant one floor down who was an admitted light sleeper. With the only telephone in the apartment, as was common at the time, being a hardwired rotary dial unit mounted on the wall at the top of the stairs, out of the reach of children, the two boys—confined to the upper apartment by a baby gate across the stairs, and which had been skilfully vaulted by the killer in the dark—opted to use chairs and other stackable items to try to reach the food in the cupboards rather than try to reach and answer the ringing telephone while their mother lay dead. The disarray was not evidence of a struggle before the murder; it was the survival instincts of two now-motherless young boys.

Victoria Mayo and Patricia Bovin were both recently separated single mothers living alone with their children in core area apartments, what would in most other Canadian cities be considered low risk scenarios. Both were stabbed furiously and randomly in the torso while asleep and while clothed. There were neither defensive wounds nor a sexual assault in either case. The children in the apartments at the time of the murders were left unharmed and neither saw nor heard anything. Both crimes yielded no witnesses or obvious sign of forced entry, and both quickly became cold cases. In Patricia's murder, the police had two names with which to work—people they needed to clear. One was a friend whose alibi they would unsuccessfully try to dismantle. The other was a former boyfriend who would take his own life within hours of his being informed of Patricia's death. Perhaps he was despondent or heartbroken or perhaps he had a reason to avoid being questioned. Given the lack of any physical evidence recovered—the scene inadvertently trampled and contaminated by Patricia' a children and the friend who found her—it made little sense that a former lover, in the absence of any ties to the scene, would kill himself to avoid being implicated in her murder. Crimes of passion followed by the perpetrator's suicide are typically measured in seconds or minutes, not hours or days. Given that no commotion was heard by the neighbours below, and that her children were not awakened in their bedroom just feet away, suggests that if a heated argument or struggle had occurred, it was likely the shortest or quietest on record. The lack of defensive wounds or beating to the face or head also suggests that Patricia never saw the attack coming and didn't know her assailant. Although we will likely never know for sure, with Patricia's ex-boyfriend's suicide, there was likely deemed to be no imminent threat to the public which would have justified keeping the case open. Closing or solving the case would have been a luxury, but in the short term, the operational word of the day with respect to victims such as Patricia Bovin was *mañana*.

## VICTIM: ROBERT (BRUCE) STAPYLTON, AGE 11

Sunup on Saturday June 7$^{th}$, 1969 marked the unofficial start of summer in London. The weekend newspaper announced that Don Messer and his Jubilee Show would be performing at London Gardens the following week at $2.00 a seat, while Johnny Downs and his 12-piece orchestra would be at the Wonderland Ballroom that same night, performing for "ladies and escorts only." Guy Lombardo and his Royal Canadians would be taking the stage in the nearby town of West Lorne later that week to kick off a summer tour of the area, and a new episode of the locally-produced game show *Take Your Choice* would air on London's CFPL-DT local television station at 7:30 p.m. as usual, the city's various church organizations serving as the program's live studio audience. At dusk, the city's Twilight Drive-In would be screening the 1968 film *The Boston Strangler*, starring Tony Curtis as Albert DeSalvo.

On that same morning, Robert Stapylton, or "Bruce" as his friends and family knew him, began the day with his usual weekend routine of playing outside in his quiet Old North neighbourhood—the other side of the city's downtown from the Old South where some of the Stanley Variety customers had originated. Living in the sought-after 400 block of Piccadilly Street, Robert and his family were smack dab in the centre of what remains a stately neighbourhood. The murder of Victoria Mayo in that same neighbourhood in the summer of '67—the so-called "Summer of Love"—and the kidnapping and murder of Frankie Jensen in Oakridge just a year earlier, however, had proven that no area, however moneyed or apparently safe, was immune to the threat now invading the Forest City.

At 10:00 a.m. that same morning, Robert was seen by his parents on the front lawn of their home, in plain view of countless windows and passersby. Within an hour, he was gone. Some of the neighbourhood boys would later report that they had seen him as late as 4:30 p.m. at the nearby intersection of Pall Mall and Waterloo Streets near Carruthers Field—a soccer and rugby pitch used by local high schools and summer leagues. That was the last confirmed sighting of the small, imaginative boy who liked to play by himself and go exploring.

It was becoming a tragically familiar story in the Forest City. A child going about his or her normal, innocent routine in a neighbourhood where everyone is supposed to know everyone and the world is right side up. Then, suddenly, the child is gone and everything is upside down. Confusion turns to concern and then quickly to panic. Calls are made, habitual routes are driven, and usual hangouts are checked, but with no sign of the child. Families stay off the telephone, and in communities with primitive party lines they ask their neighbours to do the same—just in case the child rings home. But he or she never does. Then, out of desperation, the inevitable and defeated call to the police is placed. Some time later, a well-intentioned officer in uniform arrives, writes down some details, offers the usual reassuring platitudes and theories that run the gamut from the implausible to the impossible, and an all points bulletin is issued. In a rare handful of cases, such as Lynne Harper's murder back in 1959, officers will immediately chase down some initial leads and check a widened area. Unfortunately, more often than not, a perfunctory report gets filed and the tortuous waiting game begins. As the days and weeks pass, parents and siblings go through the five stages of loss, frequently more than once—denial, anger, bargaining with some higher power or even oneself, withdrawal, and then finally acceptance. When the child is found—if they are ever found—the process repeats itself. Few careers, marriages, or even entire families remain intact and survive it.

It would be September 23rd, 1969 when little Robert the "Bruce" was finally found. As with so many other London victims, his killer had taken him out of town and turned what should have been one case into two—a missing person file with the London city PD and a homicide case with the London OPP. Whether done as an investigative countermeasure to create friction and confusion—the killer dividing and conquering by ensuing duplication and redundancy—or once again the consequence of the city's odd frontier-style geography, it was clear that by autumn of '69 the city's child and sex killers were mimicking the strategies of their peers before them. Robert's body was found in a wooded area off of what was then Middlesex County Concession Road Six near Adelaide Street North. Now a densely populated exurb boasting a high school, strip plaza, and YMCA in the same block, it was at that time a scene right out of *Huckleberry Finn*—a rustic expanse of harsh forest dotted with small shacks and tree forts, housing everyone from country kids to aimless wanderers.

Amongst the tents, huts, and plywood shanties that made up this parcel of land, along what is now the eastern leg of Sunningdale Road, Robert's largely skeletonized remains were found, in a small clearing beyond some trees, by a group of boys who had eyeballed the location as a good spot to make camp. Robert's body, it was later estimated, had likely been at that same spot since the day of his disappearance. As a result of scavenging animals from the surrounding forest and Medway Creek, very little of the boy's body was still intact when he was found, but the remains did indicate that he was left there clothed. Just as with the other skeletons of London victims, which would be found in future years—albeit under different circumstances—no cause of death could be established in Robert's case.

With no obvious sign of murder, and the clothing still intact, the case quickly fell between the cracks and was classified as what is today known as an equivocal death, meaning undetermined in nature. Because it could not be conclusively established that a crime had occurred outside the city, there was no reason to try to hand the case off to the OPP this time, which would really have meant handing it over to Dennis Alsop. In fact, until Dennis took it upon himself to co-opt the file a year or two later as a matter of personal interest—or more likely obsession—no one else bothered to take a step back to re-examine the boy's death in the context of what else was going on in London at the time. Suffice it to say that, officially speaking, in the fall of '69, the OPP certainly wasn't interested in reclassifying the case as a homicide and adding yet another unsolved to the growing pile if it didn't have to. So the case remained a missing person file under the control of the London PD, albeit one that ended with that same missing person having been found dead. In the press releases that followed, London brass—including the same Inspector Herb Jeffrey who had publicly advertised Jacqueline Dunleavy's killer as a "healthy male" a year prior—were quick to rule out foul play in Robert's death. "Doubt foul play in death of boy" was the official headline in the *London Free Press* after word leaked out that Robert's remains had been discovered in a scattered state just north of the city. But in a September 24th morning edition, before the case became the talk of the town, Dennis had been more cautious, contrarily calling the death "most puzzling." The gauntlet had been thrown down and something of a rivalry established; Dennis was no longer towing the party line. The London rumour mill then began to fill in the cracks when the police would not, with wildfire scuttlebutt—similar to when Glenda Tedball had disappeared back on Halloween of 1963—soon becoming the order of the day. Faced with enormous pressure to avoid turning what theoretically could have been an accident into a murder, the initial investigation into what exactly happened to 11-year-old Robert Stapylton was soon deep-sixed by persons unknown.

MICHAEL ARNTFIELD

# THE LORDS OF HELLMUTH

Robert Stapylton's murder was an anomaly as compared to the surge of recent slayings in London and area, especially the pair of young boys. Unlike the Jensen and Leishman victims, young Robert was found on land and fully clothed, as best anyone could tell. After recovering the body, police at the scene located an abandoned shanty just a few dozen metres away, one known to be used as a "shack [by] undesirables" as the newspaper reported. It was also one that doubled as a fort and was used, when not occupied by hobos, by the assortment of local kids who went camping there in the summer months. Given the distance from Robert's Old North neighbourhood, where he was last seen, to where he was found—too far to walk, and his bicycle left at home that Saturday—all evidence suggested, as it does today, that Robert was taken by a vehicle and may have gone willingly to the site. What exactly happened after the driver arrived at the location remains a mystery, but something occurred there—perhaps in the fort nearby, perhaps in the woods themselves—that one way or another led to the boy's death. Robert was known to enjoy camping and was thought to have been one of a larger group of neighbourhood kids who had been there before—a straight shot up Adelaide Street for a distance of about three miles from Robert's family home on Piccadilly Street. This time, however, was different.

Although Robert may have previously cycled to the Sixth Concession Road site, he didn't get there on his own the day he vanished. So who would have brought him there and why? Perhaps it was the same person who introduced him to the location in the first place. Perhaps it was someone who had actually taken boys on camping trips at that very spot, or who was adept at scouting locations where he could be alone with them. Either way, on that afternoon, the killer was reasonably satisfied that he knew how to get in and out of the brush unseen and undetected, and, that by leaving the body out in the open, the elements and animals would together erase the cause and time of death. The killer no doubt knew that when the body was finally found, there would be enough doubt about what had happened to make it an equivocal death rather than a homicide. This indeterminateness would allow the killer to put time and distance between himself and his secret encounter with the boy—one that, for whatever reason, took a tragic turn that day. With the city police following the official tag-line, and later the pathologist's lead, by announcing that there was no evidence of foul play, for several months following the discovery they were relying on the absence of obvious trauma to the bones or skull to suggest there had been a beating or stabbing. After all, up until that time, those had been the preferred means used by London's growing faction of child killers. The advanced state of decomposition, the limits of forensic pathology in the late 1960s, and the damage caused by scavengers also made it impossible to determine if Robert had been strangled. Whatever the cause of death, the clothed body suggests that the killing may have been a heat of the moment and visceral reaction to something that Robert said or did—something that the killer no doubt felt might risk exposing him for who he really was—leading to the series of undetermined actions that claimed the boy's life. Sadly, Old North, like much of the city at the time, was wall-to-wall with pedophiles and sexual deviants masquerading under any number of community service positions, which in turn provided them with unbridled access to children. Even more regrettable is that people were prepared to keep the secret of being victims of these predators until long after Robert's case went cold. For years they lived in fear of the men who stole their childhoods and what else they might still be able to do.

Fast forward to 2010, over forty years after Robert's murder, when many of these same victims, now grown men, were finally prepared to lift the veil of secrecy on what was actually happening in Old North in the summer of '69. On one of those humid London city nights, a band of young neighbourhood boys with bicycles and big dreams assembled for the first time and christened themselves as the Lords of Hellmuth—a reference to Hellmuth Street as one of the more iconic streets in the city's Old North enclave. They considered themselves to be the guardians of their neighbourhood, with the assistance of a couple of adult role models and mentors. While the newly branded Lords considered that their mentors embodied their definition of cool, the children were in fact being groomed for years of abuse at the hands of two sexual predators—one a mechanic and one a school teacher.

The Lords of Hellmuth, all around the ages of ten and eleven, were routinely invited by one or both of these same men to convene in a red brick Victorian boarding house located at the corner of Colborne and St. James Streets, just two blocks north of Robert Stapylton's family home. The boarding house was owned by a man named Robert Hall, the mechanic of the pair, who had moved from Windsor to London in 1964, and who also strangely stretched himself thin to rent a second house during his time in the Forest City—a house located just one block from where Robert was last seen alive. Bringing the Lords of Hellmuth back and forth between the two rented addresses located just a street apart from each other, Hall was often accompanied by his sycophantic young sidekick: an elementary school teacher named Bill Yates, who was also a tenant in Hall's boarding house. At one point or another, nearly every one of Hall's tenants seemed to be present when the boys were over. It was as if Hall had selectively vetted rental applications to ensure that his tenants shared mutual interests in prepubescent males. With some certainty then, it can be said that at least two and as many as five known pedophiles were within two blocks of Robert's home at the time of his disappearance.

Between 1968 and 1974, a long list of young boys rotated through the ranks of the Lords of Hellmuth, a mythic name that bonded them together in childhood, and for a much different reason, in their adult lives. Going back to the beginning, it all started with Hall rewarding the boys with Popsicles and candy for doing laps around Old North's narrow tree-lined streets on their bicycles. The grooming eventually progressed to Hall hosting secret meetings for the Lords of Hellmuth, at either one of his two houses, and also taking several of the boys on camping trips. During each of these outings, Hall—sometimes with Yates enabling him or just watching—would expose himself to the boys, show them Polaroids of naked men engaged in sex acts with children, or would encourage them to inappropriately touch him. Hall also had an assortment of cars at the time that he would use to transport the boys between these various isolated camping locations when they were not at one of his houses. The vehicles included a vintage VW bus, a Jag, and even a James Bond-inspired amphibious car. All of these curiosities were used as icebreakers with the Lords to earn their trust. The same held true for Hall's elaborate workshop full of gadgets and tools—tools obtained, in some cases, from the neighbourhood hardware store owned and operated by Robert Stapylton's step-father. Whether Robert Stapylton was one of the many members of the Lords of Hellmuth over the years or whether he met Hall through his father's store or simply by virtue of living and playing in the same block of Old North where Hall was preying on other boys, is all still unclear. In fact, any one of Hall's tenants is just as likely a person of interest in the boy's death, which makes what later happened in 2010 all the more interesting.

As the advent of social media quickly served to make the world smaller, some of the Lords of Hellmuth, scattered across Canada and living in private pain for over four decades in some cases, gradually found each other and reconnected online sometime around 2008. The consensus amongst many of them was clear: it was time at last to expose Robert Hall for what he had done. The London Police criminal investigation division followed up diligently on the historical sexual allegations subsequently filed by members of the Lords, all now in their fifties, and, in so doing, set out to find the tenants in Hall's boarding house from the summer of '69. Most of the names were dead ends—aliases used by convicted molesters and drifters hailing from all over the place and possibly acquainted with Hall from his days working on the road as a trucker for Imperial Oil. But one name stuck out—Bill Yates. His career as a lauded London schoolteacher allowed his identity to be confirmed and his whereabouts verified. London detectives soon called him and explained that they needed to ask him a few questions about Hall and their time at the boarding house on Colborne Street so long ago. The award-winning teacher indicated that he would be pleased to help and confirmed an appointment for the following week, doing so with the usual courtesy one would expect from a retired educator. The interview would never happen. Soon after booking the appointment with police, Yates committed suicide by throwing himself into the freezing Thames River from the banks near his home. His body was fished from the water only a day before he was supposed to have been interviewed about his old friend Robert Hall.

Yates's suicide only delayed the inevitable. In November 2010, the Lords of Hellmuth would reunite one last time, now in a London courtroom. Following a week-long trial, heard by Superior Court Justice Kelly A. Gorman, the then 72-year-old Hall—described as a "rabid animal" by one of his victims—was convicted of various historical sex offences and later sentenced to three years in prison. It was also revealed that Hall continued to abuse boys after moving from London to the town of Aylmer in the 1970s, there being arrested and later receiving electroshock therapy by psychiatrists of the day in a flawed bid to correct his perversions. No one at Hall's trial ever uttered the name Robert Stapylton. In fact, to this day Hall has never been questioned about the real identities of his other tenants, any knowledge of Robert Stapylton, or any camping trips with boys at the Sixth Concession location where Robert's remains were found. Perhaps it would have been pointless since Hall claimed, at his 2010 sentencing, that the corrective electroshock therapy had completely erased his memories of the late 1960s, specifically that fateful summer of '69. It seems that Hall, like many others in the Forest City, had a ready-made excuse for forgetting what happened in London back then.

## VICTIM: JACKIE ENGLISH, AGE 15

Saturday, October 4th, 1969—a date forever imprinted on the collective hard drive of the city of London and its enigmatic criminal history. It's a date that would change countless lives forever, and which would destroy most of them. To trace the antecedents of what happened that night, it is first necessary to rewind the clock to more than a year earlier, back to the winter of '68.

Sometime just before Valentine's Day 1968, Anne English embarked on one of the last nighttime promenades she would ever take in London. Before long, she knew better. On that night, a ruthless freezing rain had blanketed the city, downing trees and power lines that heaved under the weight of the ice, leaving much of London eerily quiet, even pristine in its glass-like state. With the power to much of the Forest City knocked out by the downing of many of its signature trees, and only the moonlight to guide them, Anne and her friends roamed the vacant streets of London's Old South and talked about the recent murder of Jacqueline Dunleavy. They commiserated about what they had heard, what might have happened, and who might have done it. Everyone by that time had a theory. One of these theories was offered up by Anne's classmates, her name since lost to history, who was part of the group that night. Whoever killed Jacqueline Dunleavy, the girl suggested, would no doubt do it again. Even if he didn't, others would surely follow suit. Like Dennis Alsop, the group of high school sophomores had a prescience of what was to come—something few wanted to acknowledge—with London creeping ever farther towards a very dark place. A sense of dread overwhelmed the girls. "I wonder who will be next?" one of them asked somewhat sheepishly, even fearfully. It was a question that would remain with Anne English forever. The next year, her little sister Jackie would be one of the city's next victims, a murder case some would later describe as hexed—a murder with one of the most astonishing set of characters one might ever imagine. Amazingly, even with everything else going on, Dennis Alsop was also assigned this case, and it was one that would haunt him until the day he died. It was a murder without precedent, and one that would set into motion a series of disastrous events that no one could have ever predicted.

By October 1969, less than a year after her ominous winter walkabout, Anne English was accelerated into adulthood at lightspeed, and her younger sister Jackie even more so. With their mother in the hospital and finances tight, the family had splintered apart by necessity, moving from its long-term home on Elmwood Avenue in London to various locations throughout the city. Jackie ended up billeting with friends at a house on Kent Street while holding down two waitressing gigs. During the week she worked at the Latin Quarter Restaurant on what was then Maple Street in the city's downtown, along with her boyfriend, Dave. On weekends she took a seemingly endless bus ride to the city limits and then walked an extra mile or so to the Metropolitan Store restaurant, on the outskirts of London's southern boundary. As was then not uncommon, the "Met," as it was known, was one of the area's "five and dime" stores that had an eat-in diner for weary bargain shoppers. It was the type of smoky cafeteria that also proved particularly appealing to truckers and other motorists passing by London, especially given its proximity to Highway 401.

The Met itself was located in what was then known as the Treasure Island Plaza, now a multipurpose commercial building following London's annexation of the area in the 1970s. Working two jobs and staying in school with the family in disarray wasn't easy. Despite the challenge, those who knew Jackie all remember her as someone who always had a genuine smile on her face, and who never in a million years let on that anything was less than perfect or that her life was anything less than a charmed one.

Most or all of the money Jackie earned went to helping out her father and siblings, one of the many selfless acts she prided herself on during her brief life. As with so many of London's victims of this era, it was doing things for other people and living lives the way they were taught was proper—going to work, going to school, running errands, and being responsible—that led so many of the city's young into the clutches of their killers. While Jackie was certainly doing everything as she had been taught, her case today serves as something of a watershed in the study of victimology and victim-offender encounters in terms of forecasting risk. After aggregating decades' worth of data, it turns out that nursing, modelling, and waitressing are the riskiest job categories amongst females, all three being the most over-represented categories of victims holding "legal" occupations. Just as with so many other findings recently made with respect to criminals and their victims, London it turns out was the social laboratory where these results were first validated—the canary in the coal mine with respect to warning us about previously overlooked trends in criminal violence. Before such facts became the fodder for worldwide research in criminology and the subject of conferences and conventions stewarded from the safe confines of the ivory tower, the people of London lived this reality—they were actually *in* the coal mine.

On the evening of Saturday October 4th, 1969, Jackie didn't want to go to work at the Met. Despite her strong work ethic, after spending the day with her boyfriend, the idea of getting on a city bus to travel for nearly an hour to the Treasure Island Plaza and waiting tables for only a few dollars was getting her down. But in the end, her sense of responsibility took over, since she knew that people were counting on her. Also, her new grey overcoat, the only significant item to which she had treated herself since becoming a teen-aged workaholic, had set her back in her monthly budgeting. She needed, she thought, to keep up the pace. So on the bus she went, while dressed in her candy-striped blouse, chequered skirt, and diner-style smock—the restaurant staff uniform—her work gear covered with the fancy new overcoat she cherished so much. In her purse were the usual contents that a 15-year-old girl would carry, in addition to some schoolbooks and stationery supplies so that she could do her homework after she punched-out for her dinner break. As she began the trek southbound through the city to work her usual Saturday shift, it seemed to be business as usual. As it turns out, there was nothing usual about it, at least not according to the restaurant witnesses who later told police that Jackie appeared frightened that night.

After the store and restaurant closed at 10:00 p.m., Jackie set off into the night with a few dollars in tips in her pocket and was last seen walking northbound over the Wellington Road highway overpass, heading back into the city to catch the last bus home from nearby Exeter Road. She never made it to the other side of the overpass. Multiple eyewitnesses would later come out of the woodwork, all offering varying descriptions of a vehicle that she was seen entering, midway across the bridge. Some descriptions were of a blue car with square taillights bearing one occupant, some of a white car—the same description as in the Dunleavy and Jensen murders—bearing two occupants. Eyewitness descriptions, extremely useful when accurate, always have the potential, when conflicting, to be more harmful than helpful. True to form in this case, with one red herring after another, the cops were soon chasing their tails.

Twenty years later, in what would be one of the most infamous serial killer cases in Canadian history, the horrific crimes of Paul Bernardo and wife-turned-accomplice Karla Homolka, history would repeat itself. After months of looking for a Chevy Camaro in the case of the Niagara schoolgirl murders in the early 1990s, and after hauling in every owner of that particular make and model on record for an interview, it turned out that the real killer, Bernardo, actually drove a Nissan 240sx—not even close. Back in 1969, with only a handful of makes and models on the road, asking civilians with little eye for detail of this type to identify features of a car, let alone its license plate, was an exercise in futility given that, for many, nearly every car looked like some version of the same.

Back in London, in addition to issues surrounding correct identification of the suspect vehicle, there was also the fact that no one managed to get a good look at the driver who picked up Jackie. There was, however, one detail on which witnesses agreed—Jackie had climbed into the back seat of the car from the passenger side. It seemed puzzling that she would choose the back if the front seat was vacant. It still does. Perhaps there had, in fact, been two occupants on board as some asserted. Perhaps whoever picked up young Jackie knew that the rear was an easier place to confine her, the interior handle being out of reach from the back seat in a two-door model. Perhaps whoever picked her up had learned, from picking up his last nightwalker, that if the girl struggled in the front seat, she could grab the wheel causing the car to lose control. Maybe it was simply instinctual for Jackie to get in the backseat as a result of previous rides taken or taxis hailed while working downtown. Either way, it ended up not being as significant as some people had hoped.

Given Jackie's displaced living arrangements at the time, no one initially reported her missing when she failed to return home that night. Reporting her missing right away, as the police notifications of the missing boys or Lynda White the previous year confirmed, would have done little good in any event. But by the evening of the 5th, when still no one had heard from or seen Jackie, her father called the police and reported her missing, just as the Cadieux, Harper, Tedball, Stapylton, White, Leishman, Jensen, and other London and area families had done before. Then, four days later, just before 5:00 p.m. on Thursday October 9th, two duck hunters, having parked their pickup truck beside a newly constructed bridge on Cornell Road just outside the town of Tillsonburg, headed down an embankment towards the Big Otter Creek—the same creek where Scott Leishman's body had been submerged a year earlier. In the water, one of the men noticed what he would later describe to Dennis Alsop as "just a dummy … a mannequin" floating in the creek. The two men paused for a moment, returned to the truck, and looked a second time at the figure with the aid of a telescopic sight mounted on a rifle they had brought. The magnified image permitted them to see two identifying features that made it clear that the body in the water was in fact real. They were able to discern a vaccination scar on the left arm and a black Alaskan diamond ring on a left hand finger—the only item still on the body.

The two hunters were of course accustomed to seeing dead fowl, but not what they saw on this particular afternoon. In horror, they retreated to the truck, rushed to a nearby pay phone in town, and called the OPP. After meeting with a handful of officers at the local volunteer fire hall about twenty minutes later, the hunters led the police back to the same secluded spot where the body, soon confirmed to be that of Jackie English, was still floating naked and face up in the frigid water. By the time Dennis and his entourage of other plainclothesmen reached the scene, the sun had moved westward across the sky and was shining down directly on Jackie's watery grave. With the body in the spotlight, Dennis, looking down from the bridge, had one of those road to Damascus moments—a personal transformation and conversion from which there would be no return. Dennis had a son, Dennis Jr., but also a daughter of Jackie's age, named Liz, and who, in light of what he saw at dusk that autumn Thursday, he swore he would never let out of his sight again. Soon enough, the villains of the city would leave him no choice. In the meantime, he had returned to thinking in professional rather than personal terms. He could tell that the state of the body suggested Jackie hadn't been in the water and exposed to the elements for the full five days since she was last seen. The body had been there at most a day, and someplace else between the night of the 4th and the afternoon of the 9th when the hunters found it. The question was where.

Police scour the dirt road and adjoining bridge above the Big Otter Creek, where the body of 15-year-old Jackie English was discovered by duck hunters on the evening of October 9th, 1969. Courtesy: Western University Archives.

As Jackie's body was later pulled from the murky waters of Big Otter Creek, there was an even more unsettling discovery from the police recovery team—Jackie's drop earrings, apparently unclasped and removed after her death, were placed in the water alongside her. It was physically impossible for both earrings to have become simultaneously unclasped yet also have remained intact upon her impact with the water. The cheap teenaged costume jewellery would have had no monetary value to the killer, but he had nonetheless chosen to remove them for some intrinsic, expressive purpose. He had chosen at some point in the murderous time-line to remove the earrings and then, from atop the bridge, throw them into the water to land alongside Jackie's body. It was to be the first of many chilling finds that made it clear the killer was both browsing for souvenirs amongst Jackie's apparel and toying with authorities at the same time.

On the morning of the 10th, a post-mortem conducted at Tillsonburg District Memorial Hospital confirmed that there were no ante-mortem injuries to Jackie's body save one—a severe single blow to the base of the skull with some kind of edged instrument, likely a crowbar or tire-iron. Death would have been near instantaneous and the primary crime scene would have been copiously covered in blood. Although it was unclear if Jackie had been sexually assaulted, there were no obvious signs of penetration. Notwithstanding that semen consistent with a type O donor was found inside the body, it would later be revealed that this was the same blood type as Jackie's boyfriend, with whom she had been on the afternoon prior to her disappearance. With some internal post-mortem trauma consistent with her having been thrown into the water, from the same bridge on Cornell Road where the hunters had parked, Jackie's body was otherwise in a pristine state. All clothing and jewellery, other than the ring still on her left hand, had been removed without damaging the skin. Then, there was the state of the body itself.

While the pathologist suggested that the death occurred sometime overnight on the 4th, after she was picked up on the overpass, the body *looked* as though it had been dead less than a day, and certainly not partially submerged in the water and exposed to animals, insects, and the elements for nearly a week. While no efforts were made at the time to x-ray the body for signs of preservation or freezing in the bones as would ideally be the case today, it increasingly appeared that Dennis's hunch at the scene might have been spot-on. Somewhere between where Jackie was picked up along that London overpass and the creek 45 miles away where she was found five days later, there had clearly been a secondary crime scene where it all happened. It was too complex, too fastidious to have all happened in the car that picked her up. It was likely at that scene where Jackie was killed, and then kept until she was moved to the creek overnight on the 8th in order to be found on the 9th. As talk in squad rooms in both the Oxford and Middlesex County OPP detachments turned to shaking down the usual perverts, current and ex-boyfriends, and even jilted admirers, Dennis knew that he was dealing with a new kind of killer entirely: one who was already running the show. Jackie's killer was not only a sexual psychopath but also some kind of twisted theatre impresario. In a matter of days, it would become painfully obvious.

On the evening of October 12th, a week to the day that Jackie was first reported missing to police, her Metropolitan store smock and her chequered skirt—torn in two—together with her underwear, a torn set of pantyhose, and her brassiere—also torn in half—were all located at the side of County Road 46 in Bayham Township, roughly 18 miles south of where Jackie's body was found. After the clothing was positively identified as hers, an analysis of the underwear turned up a second semen sample, different from the one previously found inside her body. Although the sample was too degraded, based on the technologies of the time, to obtain a blood grouping, it was at least clear that Jackie—or perhaps just her clothing—had been subjected to sexual activity with an unidentified male sometime after the afternoon of the 4th of October.

Then, eight days later, on the afternoon of October 20th, a pair of brown penny loafers that were confirmed to have been worn to work by Jackie on the evening of the 4th, turned up in a most unusual location. The shoes were found by a farmer in Malahide Township, some distance back from the road beside a pond. It appeared that someone had pulled off the concession road and tried to propel the shoes into the water, had failed to hit the target on account of the distance, and had then elected to simply drive away. The pond itself was located off the same unmarked rural lane joined by a county road switchback where Georgia Jackson's body was found in March of 1966. With the distance between the location of Jackie's shoes and the location of Georgia's body, over three years earlier, being only a dozen metres, they were in effect in the *same* spot. Unlike in the case of the so-called Tissue Slayer back in London proper, information as to the precise location of Georgia's body had, by that time, never been formally published and widely discussed. It was a detail that only Dennis and an inner circle of lead investigators, a handful of volunteer searchers, and of course, the killer himself would have ever known. Still, no definitive link between the two murders—both waitresses, both brunettes, both walking home after work—was made at the time, not even by Dennis who, in fairness, was now carrying over twenty cases of his own. These active and competing files included his chasing down petty thieves, extortionists, and rubes stamping parking meter slugs or fencing stolen farm equipment, all on top of pursuing the region's more elusive serial murderers. In addition, there were the idle London city cases for which he speculated there might be interconnections. These included the growing list of open/unsolved cases like Dunleavy—file number 110-1-68—that he had slowly started to work off the books and on his own time, one of several cases vouchsafed by city PD colleagues secretly eager for outside help and Dennis's insights. At that time in his career, Dennis was also still willing to believe that no one would be so brazen as to take on the police the way Jackie English's killer seemed to be doing. It was almost an article of faith that no one would be that cunning in trying to outsmart the authorities by using their own jurisdictional policies against them. That type of behaviour was thought to be limited to one-in-a-million psychopaths like the Zodiac Killer—still recent headline news at the time—who sent clues and taunting letters to the press and police, and who muddied the waters by choosing different counties and cities as hunting grounds for his victims. That was Big City, USA behaviour—or so it was thought. Dennis was not proven wrong too often, but he was about to be.

The most disturbing discovery that made it clear the police were dealing with a type of Zodiac Killer knock-off in the Jackie English investigation came nearly a week later and just before Halloween—just ahead of the two-year anniversary of the disappearance of Glenda Tedball. On the evening of October 26th, a man out walking with his young son along Wortley Road in the city's Old South neighbourhood stumbled across what seemed to be a small shrine on the sidewalk at the corner of Wortley Road and Elmwood Avenue. On the ground, the man found a bottle of perfume, a cosmetic bag, and a pencil case containing stationery supplies. Naturally curious to determine if someone might have dropped the items, the man unzipped the pencil case and rummaged through it in search of any identifying information as to its owner. In doing so, he retrieved a red Laurentian-brand pencil crayon from the case and looked at a white field on the side of the pencil intended for inscription with the owner's name. The owner was in fact identified in the white field. In red font was the inscription: "J-A-C-Q-U-E-L-I-N-E E-N-G-L-I-S-H."

The man couldn't believe what he was seeing. He recognized the name not just from the local papers following the discovery of Jackie's body outside of town, but also as a former resident of Elmwood Avenue in the immediate neighbourhood. Crouching down on the sidewalk, beside the assembly of items, he looked up to see what was, until only a month earlier, Jackie's family home address on Elmwood Avenue in a direct sight-line from where her belongings were left—belongings which had all been in her purse the night she disappeared. Although the English family had moved from this address just a few weeks earlier, the London telephone book still listed Elmwood Avenue as Jackie's address in October 1969. Her killer had, two weeks after the murder, driven back into the city and carefully arranged these items in front of what he thought was still her family home.

Long after she had been murdered, Jackie's killer was still playing out his sadistic fantasies and obtaining paraphilic mileage out of the active criminal investigation, at the expense of the grieving English family, the city police and OPP, and perhaps the entire city of London. As with all sadists, whoever was doing this needed to incite a response or an image of destruction and pain to capture in his mind before he could feel truly fulfilled. This compulsion included his need to leave clues scattered widely across the region during his travels—evidence leading through the Forest City and beyond. Like breadcrumbs left throughout the dark forest in a Grimm fairytale, it was a series of acts that seemed to revisit the mystery phone call to Georgia Jackson's parents in 1966, and the surreptitious return of Lynda White's clothing to her rented London home in 1968. Perhaps not surprisingly, given that an apparent paraphilic souvenir collection was at work, some items such as Jackie's new beloved overcoat, as well as her tan purse, identification, and other jewellery items were never found at all, much like in the earlier murders of London and area girls.

Dennis's boss, Inspector James McBride, was a man of true grit. When it came to expressing his opinions he was about as subtle as a heart attack and then some. He had always thought that his protégé Dennis was on to something in terms of the connection between the recent London murders, but this latest development was a definitive game changer. The day after the chilling Elmwood Avenue discovery, McBride called Dennis into his office for something of a fireside chat *sans* fire—the standard OPP-issue plastic fern in the corner would have to do as the atmospheric background. The files for the boys—Jensen, Leishman, Stapylton—as well as the cases of Tedball, Jackson, and the ongoing assistance that was being given to city detectives on the murders of Dunleavy, Bovin, and Mayo would all need to go on hiatus. The killer of Jackie English had made it clear that, before the police could find him, he had found them—it was *he* and not the police now controlling the investigation. Dennis needed to go at the English case full bore, and McBride would stand behind any findings and wherever they led him. Neither man could have possibly foreseen where exactly that would be.

## "BURIED WITH ME"

Things started to go sideways within the month, quickly going from bad to worse. On the evening of November 21st, 1969, Constable Ron Harris of the London Police responded to a call from the night watchman at the Simpsons Department Store downtown—the same store where Helga Beer had worked until her death—about an unresponsive 16-year-old girl found on the ground near the rear freight loading bay. When Constable Harris arrived, he found the girl propped up in a chair in the building's security office still in a stupefied and semi-conscious state. The girl's name, Marilyn Hird, didn't initially mean anything to the patrolman. On the surface, it seemed as though it was just another attempted overdose, the girl having seemingly taken a random assortment of sleeping pills and over-the-counter painkillers just this side of fatal. But, as was starting to become clear to just about everyone, nothing in London was ever as it appeared on the surface.

In preparing to take the girl to the hospital to be checked over, Constable Harris looked through her coat for the pill bottle or anything else that might help determine what exactly had occurred. In doing so, he found something in the pocket that suddenly made him reassess the whole situation—a crumpled photograph of Jackie English, just like the one plastered all over the newspaper. Stranger still was what was written on the back of the photograph. In elegant-looking ballpoint pen script, Marilyn had written what seemed to amount to something of a suicide letter: "Let her killer remain a secret to be buried with me." With Marilyn soon sedated in hospital and the photograph tagged as evidence, a call went out to Dennis Alsop from the city cops. As it turns out, Dennis and Marilyn were already well acquainted.

Beginning in the days following the discovery of Jackie's body, Marilyn had been interviewed upwards of five times by Dennis about what happened the night of the English murder. Marilyn had worked with Jackie at the Metropolitan and would, in the wake of her death, claim to have been Jackie's best friend and confidante. Although few people outside the circle of girls working at the restaurant knew that Jackie and Marilyn were acquainted at all, let alone "best" friends, Marilyn told police that she first knew Jackie was in danger the night she disappeared, her guilt over this supposed inaction having prompted her to later take the overdose. In the days leading up to the overdose, Marilyn kept coming forward with new information—always new details only ever recently recalled—that she thought was useful. The one consistent element of each new interview is that the latest version differed significantly from the last, Marilyn always saving the new ending for the next interview.

Marilyn's meandering versions of events ranged from the assertion that she and Jackie, in the days before the murder, had been getting picked up from work and taken cruising by a group of American men to a theory she had that two London PD plainclothesmen were responsible for the murder and had sought to silence Jackie about something she had seen at the Met one night she was working—that she knew *too much*. With the cryptic note written on the back of Jackie's picture on the night of November 21st, Dennis began to wonder if there were perhaps some grand design to all of Marilyn's monkeyshines—a common denominator to all of these misleading fabrications and embellishments. After the overdose, and after police found the inscribed photograph of Jackie in her pocket, it appeared Marilyn was officially done talking. At the behest of the attending psychiatrist in the secure ward where Marilyn was taken, Dennis backed off of further questioning about the "secret" that she was apparently willing to die protecting. Just as his pursuit of the Neighbour had ended in the man committing himself to an asylum, cowering out of the reach of the law behind a cordon of white coats, Dennis had once again been shut out—stonewalled by a system that at the time seemed to equate deception and cruelty with clinical insanity. The one item that her doctor did let slip, however, was that he considered Marilyn to have more knowledge about the case than she had ever shared with police. In reality, the best suspect tip didn't end up coming from Marilyn but from another London woman who herself was now in danger.

MICHAEL ARNTFIELD

# THE TELEPHONE MAN

On the evening of October 4th, London resident Elizabeth Harrison, along with her husband and teenaged son, had been inside the restaurant at the Metropolitan Store and seated at the lunch counter near the kitchen's short order window. On October 19th, the 43-year-old Elizabeth belatedly came forward and confirmed with police that she and her family had been served by Jackie English that same night and had been witness to something unnerving. During the hour or so they were at the restaurant, near closing, the Harrisons watched as Jackie was approached by two separate men on two separate occasions. The description of each man was similar, with both males roughly ten years older than Jackie and both with short dark hair and medium builds. The first of the two to approach her was described as wearing a "work overcoat," as though he were perhaps employed in some outdoor capacity. The second man, who approached sometime later, looked almost identical other than that he was dressed in casual clothes. Neither Elizabeth nor her family could say for certain whether the two men were in the restaurant at the same time or whether they might have actually observed the same man dressed differently on the second occasion. The Harrison family, however, was unanimous in saying that, after the second encounter in particular, Jackie looked frightened.

Although these encounters might have meant nothing, it was the most consistent piece of information Dennis had to go on, especially given the wildly varying descriptions of the car that Jackie entered that night. Dennis considered it the most valuable lead and arranged for the Harrisons to meet with a police sketch artist using a new technology that had recently made its way to Canada: the Identi-Kit.

Developed by firearm manufacturer Smith & Wesson—a preferred supplier of revolvers among Canadian and U.S. police departments of the day—the Identi-Kit was a spiral-bound set of transparencies featuring standardized sets of stencilled facial features that, it was hoped, might allow for an equally standardized system of suspect composite sketching. The Identi-Kit first gained notoriety in 1954 when it was used to create the composite of the unidentified "bushy haired man" described by Dr. Sam Sheppard as being the intruder to his Ohio lake house and murderer of his wife. Sheppard was himself later tried and convicted for the crime and his case became the inspiration for the acclaimed television series *The Fugitive*, where the Identi-Kit's "bushy haired man" composite was replaced with the elusive "one armed man" and Sheppard was fictionalized as Dr. Richard Kimble. Then, in 1966, after the Identi-Kit proved its worth by successfully helping to identify Richard Speck for the massacre of eight nursing students in a Chicago hospital dormitory, it eventually found its way north. By early November 1969, it had made its way to London and was used to create a composite of the man seen by the Harrisons speaking to Jackie English just before her disappearance and murder. A Photostat of the composite was later circulated throughout London and the surrounding region with a plea for tips as to the person's identity. London PD and OPP patrols also rode with the composite portrait on board, its being appended directly to the dashboard of their squad cars in some cases. Tipsters who caught a glimpse of the portrait also began phoning in all sorts of red herrings—most unintentional, some intentional. But while London citizens took the time to call police with their tips, someone else who saw the composite decided to call witness Elizabeth Harrison.

Dennis Alsop's commanding officer and staunch supporter, Inspector James McBride, holding a composite portrait of a person of interest in the murder of Jackie English, a portrait created used the Identi-Kit system and with the assistance of eyewitness Elizabeth Harrison and her family in November 1969. Courtesy: Western University Archives.

Incredibly, by today's privacy standards at least, the media publicly released Elizabeth Harrison's name as one of the people who had assisted with the creation of the composite, and who could possibly identify the only person of interest at the time in the investigation. Worse yet, to rule out any other Elizabeth Harrison who might have lived in London, the media also revealed her home address—just to be sure.

The first predictable retaliation occurred on November 14th, when the telephone rang at the Harrison home, on Elgin Street in East London, shortly after 7:00 p.m. Elizabeth picked up the receiver to hear heavy breathing, followed by someone making guttural noises and telling her in a demonic sounding voice what he was going to do to her sexually—what would today be recognized as a textbook case of telephone scatologia. Elizabeth hung up and called the London Police. A marked cruiser was later sent by the house, but two and two were never put together. Missed was the possibility that the obscene call might be related to the composite, and that the call might have been made by the killer himself—the Identi-Kit creep. That omission must, however, be viewed in the context of the era. The Jackie English file was in a box at the OPP Middlesex detachment, sitting on Dennis Alsop's desk. Other information relating to the case, and some contents from the file, were with him at home as he studied them on his own time into the wee hours of the morning. The attending patrolman at the Harrison home that night, aside from having no access to any of this information, also had no knowledge of Jackie English or who else was involved in the case. With no computer, database, names, or go betweens on which to rely, he also lacked essential knowledge or the training available today. This includes the now-known connection between telephone scatologia—a preparatory paraphilia that has since been linked to everything from exhibitionism and pedophilia to necrophilia—and violent stalker-like behaviour, a knowledge base that might have suggested the Harrison caller was likely very dangerous. This was also a time when the section of the *Criminal Code* now prohibiting indecent telephone calls was not yet the law of the land. Callers spouting obscene or harassing content were during this historical period treated as the adult equivalents of adolescent crank callers—dismissed under the law as nuisances who would simply iron themselves out. It wasn't until the theatrical release of the Canadian psychological thriller film *Black Christmas* in 1974 that the clinically established link between obscene calling and sexual homicide was first unveiled for a mass audience, after which time both law enforcement and law makers finally began to pay attention to the related paraphilic research following increased public attention.

Today's advances in investigative analysis and paraphilic scholarship were, of course, not the reality in London and area in the late 1960s, with scatologists and other paraphiliacs roaming the city like the proverbial kids in a candy store. The local police lacked the technology to share information on cases, the ability to immediately access the criminal records of offenders, and the training to identify high-risk preparatory behaviours when they saw them. At the same time, governments, courts, and medical institutions of the time were wilfully oblivious to the fact that sexual psychopathy and sadism were not necessarily tantamount to insanity. They refused to accept the fact that these people could not be corrected with counselling, let alone LSD or electroshock therapy—two preferred experimental procedures of the time that, not surprisingly, failed to work.

After the London PD took a quick report from Elizabeth Harrison about the obscene caller, a report that should have set off alarm bells but didn't, things quickly escalated. The next day, November 15th, at 6:30 a.m., within minutes of Elizabeth's husband and son leaving the house for the day, the telephone rang again. Elizabeth picked up the receiver to hear the same voice as the night before, this time making more specific threats: "I saw you had the police over last night ... I am going to cut you up real good and we will see what that will do to your husband and kid. I am really going to enjoy this." Elizabeth gasped, slammed down the receiver and immediately called back to the London Police. This time, the day watch was now back on shift, including the criminal investigation division detectives who had investigated Jackie's initial missing person report and who had also been recently talking with Dennis Alsop. This time, word of the calls to the Harrison residence made it to the higher-ups, who then briefed OPP Inspector McBride. So, without hesitation, McBride took the information to Dennis, who knew that, as far fetched as it seemed, they needed to treat the two incidents as connected. The caller *could* be Jackie's killer. It could also be the man depicted in the Identi-Kit portrait who, even if not the actual murderer, might not be too happy about seeing his face circulated in every media outlet and police station throughout the area. Then again, it could just be some other London paraphiliac aroused by all the carnage befalling the city and region. At Dennis's insistence, and with McBride's backing, both the London Police and OPP, beginning that same night, started rotating officers in and out of the area of the Harrison's home as part of a dedicated "surveillance patrol" that would, it was hoped, smoke out the deviant caller and determine whether he was in fact watching the house as he claimed. On some occasions, when Elizabeth would get spooked by a hang up call or a noise heard in the backyard, this meant actually posting a uniformed officer to the front door overnight. The strategy seems to have worked as the telephone calls stopped—at least for a while.

By the first week of December 1969, the surveillance detail was pulled, with the thought generally being that whoever the caller was, he had since moved on to bother someone else. Conventional thinking—at least in the London ranks—now seemed to be that the caller and the killer were separate individuals. Then, in the early morning hours of December 7th, at just after 4:30 a.m., a loud thud was heard at the Harrison's front door. Elizabeth's husband, Verdun, and his son ran to the door together, only to see a car speeding away, headed east towards the Highway 401 interchange. Elizabeth's husband would later describe the car as likely a Ford—either a Falcon, Fairlane, or a Meteor.

Things were then quiet until the afternoon of December 11th, four days later, when Elizabeth went out to get the mail. Among the usual bills, flyers, and Christmas cards in the mailbox that day there was another type of card entirely: a sympathy card. No name or stamp was on the envelope, since it had been hand-delivered to the home's mailbox by the sender. The card was the type that one would send following a sudden or unexpected death, with the front covered in sketches of doves and flowers in soft pastels and muted colours. Inside the card was a simple, ominous inscription in red ink, using wooden stencil letters: "WATCHING YOU." For whatever reason—perhaps denial, perhaps defeat—Elizabeth didn't immediately report receipt of the card or its threat to the police. She perhaps had had enough of being tormented and would no longer let the calls, nighttime knocks, and now ominous letters disrupt her life. Instead, she continued on with her day. This included taking her dog to the off-leash park down in Westminster Township off Wellington Road, just a few minutes from the Metropolitan Store. It would be the first time she had returned to that area near the Met since the fateful night of October 4th.

Just after 5:30 p.m., Elizabeth stopped at the local Sayvette, a now defunct discount department store located on the site of what is today White Oaks Mall on Wellington Road, just north of the Metropolitan Store in the Treasure

Island Plaza. During the nearly thirty minutes she spent in the store, her dog, a black mutt named Cindy, was secure in her Volkswagen Beetle in the parking lot. Elizabeth later loaded a hodgepodge of housewares into the trunk of the car and then headed to the dog park to the south, just outside the city on what was then the deserted 4$^{th}$ Concession. With the winter solstice just over a week away, it was long since dark and the off-leash greenspace was predictably deserted. Using the high beams of her car as ambient lighting, Elizabeth played with the dog in the snow, against the shadows of the trees, for roughly fifteen minutes before getting back in her car. By that time she was no longer alone.

As Elizabeth placed Cindy in the back seat and sat down behind the wheel to head home, she flicked off the high beams only to witness a dark figure, having seemingly materialized out of nowhere, standing beside her passenger side window. Before she could throw the manual transmission into gear, the shadowy figure was in the seat beside her, holding a knife to her throat. Although it was an unbelievably swift and feverish sequence of events, the attacker remained calm, as if stoic. He had ambushed and attacked before. It was old hat for him.

With her dog barking and growling relentlessly in the back, the shadow told her to turn the interior light on so that he could see her face more clearly before he cut it apart. "I like to watch," he said, with a sinister confidence. Elizabeth was too paralysed with fear to summon the fine motor skills to locate and adjust the car's dome light as she had been ordered. The attacker took this as defiance and immediately sliced open her cheek as he held her by the throat. As blood trickled down her face, it would have no doubt felt warm against her skin, still numb from the wind outside. The figure, still concealed by darkness, then leaned in, licked the blood, and kissed Elizabeth on the same cheek. He whispered in her ear that he liked the sight of blood and also preferred women who were dead so he could do what he wanted with them. But it was soon clear that he didn't want Elizabeth dead and that this fantasy wasn't about that. It was about something else entirely. While fondling Elizabeth over the top of her clothing, he broke a button off her blouse and seemed to be trying to excite himself by terrorizing her and eliciting a response—textbook sadism—but it wasn't working. So he started cutting.

A puncture wound to Elizabeth's right shoulder caused her to shriek, a response her attacker seemed to enjoy, and which additionally seemed to provide him with short-lived arousal. Over the next few minutes, a time-frame

Elizabeth would later say felt like hours, he slashed her face upwards of twenty-seven times. He also stabbed her in the thighs and back, and ended up mutilating her hands as Elizabeth tried to shield herself against each thrust of the knife. Elizabeth's loyal dog Cindy, prepared to defend its owner to the death, latched onto the attacker's arm while biting and snarling, doing its pint-sized best to fend off the maniac. Whether it was the dog, the fact that he simply could not incite the terror necessary to perform sexually, or the fact that the slashing and facial mutilation (amokoscisia) was an end in itself, following one final slash to the face, he abruptly stepped out of the idling car and fled into the rural darkness beyond.

The passenger door still swung open, Elizabeth put her bloodied hands around the shifter, popped the car into first and floored it. She spun out onto Wellington and barrelled north to Southdale Road. Back inside the city limits, she pulled off at the first sign of street lights and potential witnesses, threw the VW into neutral, and dove head first into a snow bank as a form of improvised first-aid for her facial injuries. Placing snow and ice on her wounds to numb the pain and slow the bleeding, no one was around to help her—all the stores in the area were closed, pay phones apparently non-existent. She packed a snowball to hold to her face to prevent the blood from running into her eyes and then drove due north on Wellington for a distance of just over three miles to the front doors of the city's historic Victoria Hospital where she ran screaming into the emergency room, her dog Cindy in tow, before collapsing.

From that night onwards, while Elizabeth languished in serious but stable condition, a uniformed officer was posted to the door of her room at all times, with another patrolman at the outer entrance to the ward. Whoever had done this had bided his time and waited until he had Elizabeth alone—until the police sentry was no longer guarding her Elgin Street residence. There could be no more slip-ups. Dennis Alsop, knowing what Elizabeth Harrison didn't about the state of Jackie English's body when found, visited her in hospital. In hearing the attacker's confession to Elizabeth about his preferring the company of dead women, Dennis knew that whoever did this and whoever killed Jackie English had disturbingly similar preferences. One problem for the investigation was that the attack in Elizabeth's car had been under the cover of darkness and had occurred so frenetically that she was unable to say if it was the same man she saw at the Met and the one depicted in the Identi-Kit portrait. Although she had only heard his voice, she was, however, able to confirm it was the same voice as the mystery caller who had been tormenting her. Had she turned on the car's interior light, as he had demanded, she might have been able to recognize him. The fact that she didn't turn on the light and was unable to put a face to the attacker might also have saved her life. Whoever it was, a new chapter in the Jackie English murder was unfolding and a new saga beginning for Dennis and the city as a whole. From the day the composite had first hit the newspapers, it appeared all bets were off in the new sadistic game being played by Jackie's killer.

# HINTERLAND

It soon dawned on Dennis that he was dealing with a new breed of enemy, one that not even his time in combat could prepare him to fight. After all, even in war there is some semblance of rules. But this was a different type of conflict entirely. Dennis was without a doubt at a significant tactical disadvantage. After inheriting so many murders of London residents whose bodies were found in OPP territory, and now having to deal with the bizarre Elizabeth Harrison attack, he realized that he was woefully outnumbered. As a reluctant middle manager at a skeleton crew detachment, which had found itself underwater in next to no time, he soon sent word to the OPP General Headquarters in Toronto pleading for competent reinforcements, a task force—anything. He had spent days at a time as a lone wolf canvassing farmsteads in the counties in relation to the Jensen and Leishman murders and inventively consulting with a divinity and demonology expert at the university about occult killings. He relished being the dogged investigator, but now he simply needed more boots on the ground. It was a simple question of supply and demand—a matter of basic arithmetic. With limited resources and no apparent end in sight to the torrent of violence in London and region, he was getting desperate.

After the Harrison dog park attack upped the ante, a reward of $20,000 dollars—roughly $130,000 by today's standards—was offered for information relating to the murder of Jackie English. Dennis later helped author the first of several reports to be sent to the senior brass at the OPP and their retinue of bean counters who quickly wanted to know if they were getting their money's worth for the resources devoted to the lives taken in London and region. A communication sent to General Headquarters, authored by Dennis and McBride and signed off by McBride's boss—a Detective Chief Inspector Pelz—laid it all out in black and white:

"*I cannot close this report without bringing to your attention to [sic] several other unsolved murders or deaths in the area [...] Having examined the files available to me, and talking to the officers concerned in these investigations, I find that there are several common factors to one or more of them [...] If one can believe any of these deaths are related to the English murder, coupled with the manner of the attack on Mrs. Harrison, e.g. the stabbing, the kissing of her bloodstained cheek, the remarks 'I like to f\*\*\* (sexual intercourse) a woman after she is dead', one can only conclude that in all probability, we are searching for some form of (sexual) psychopath(s).*"

The term "psychopath" showing up in an interim report of this vintage, let alone an accompanying parenthetical reference to a sexual psychopath—both terms barely out of the ivory tower and having only been household terms since the release of Hitchcock's 1960 film *Psycho*—should have raised the alarm among those reading this same report. These are certainly not descriptors that would have been used among lay persons, or that most cops of the era would have even known existed, much less have been willing to cite in official correspondence. The reality is that Dennis was right and had clearly picked up on the vernacular used by the experts—like Dr. Morden and others—with whom he was consulting. Sadly, it seems to have never registered with the OPP brass. Forty years later, there is no record of anyone ever having heard of the report or having spoken to anyone who may have read it. Dennis's report also makes it clear that he knew, along with a small cadre of bosses, that multiple sexual murderers were on the loose in the city and region. While the term serial killer hadn't yet been coined, Dennis instinctively knew that each of these killers was responsible for more than one murder and that they would continue to claim new victims until they were stopped. The "several other unsolved murders" that Dennis refers to in this official communication are also spelled out in the same document, but to no avail. These cases range from the Mayo and Sheeler murders back in 1963 to Georgia Jackson in 1966, the city murders through 1968 and 1969, plus the three boys—Jensen, Leishman, and even Stapylton. The murder of Jackie English and the attack on Elizabeth Harrison were the final punctuation mark on the list. It all fell on deaf ears.

By 1969, Dennis Alsop was essentially on his own to work the London and area murders—no partner, no support from Toronto, and investigations running on fumes. Things would only get worse the following year, when his own children became apparent targets of the city's predators. Courtesy: Dennis Alsop Jr.

As the 1960s drew to a close, Dennis would remain a lone voice in the wilderness, a lone warrior in the hinterland surrounding the Forest City. By 1969, he was inheriting murder cases from London where the victims were killed or dumped out of town, plus homicides from London's CMA which straddled three surrounding counties. Larger cities with only a fraction of the murders going on during this same period had detectives working on rotation, and with at least a week or so of breathing room between absorbing new files. As 1969 became 1970, Dennis on the contrary was largely still a one man show. He *was* the rotation—no relief cycles and no days off for good behaviour. At the same time, the overflowing caseload included his chasing down other run-of-the-mill hoodlums engaged in various assortments of rural and agricultural crime. A pair of country-fried knuckleheads using a stolen Buick to knock off the local Canadian Legion for till cash and bottles of Crown here, a series of overnight safe jobs using Metabo power grinders at mom-and-pop stores out in the boondocks there. Most of them weren't criminal masterminds, no

Professor Moriarty-like foes to be tracked down to a grand finale. But between the sheer volume of cases and the accompanying machinations of the court process, like London itself, Detective-Sergeant Alsop had reached a boiling point. Moreover, London had reached what is known in criminology as critical mass.

Not unlike how critical mass in physics describes the similar "boiling" point required to create nuclear fission, critical mass as a social concept describes a similarly self-sustaining chain reaction. It describes the wide adoption of a new idea or way of doing things that soon becomes so pervasive and widespread that it sustains itself without any outside intervention—an endlessly repeating pattern. More commonly today, people refer to it as the "network effect" or the process of trends going "viral" in the context of popular culture. London, by the close of 1969, had reached such a viral point, but it would by no means be a short-lived trend. The city had created or otherwise unwittingly invited in a sufficient number of psychopaths and paraphiliacs to ensure that London's descent into violence and depravity had reached a sort of terminal velocity—a point of no return for the foreseeable future. Like a twisted game of whack-a-mole, if and when one killer or other predator was to be caught, another would immediately pop up elsewhere as if part of some sympathetic response. The problem was that the worst ones weren't being caught at all.

Today, we see subtle indicators of how the Forest City, as a case study in critical mass, has either directly or indirectly influenced police publicity and media relations practises across the whole of Canada and beyond. When viewers see "perp walks" on the evening news as the police parade arrested suspects in front of the camera going to and from court, or when readers see photos of "dope on the table" in their local newspapers—seized guns, drugs, and confiscated cash fanned out in front of a media scrum—the police are deferring to a propagandist crime control strategy known as *general deterrence*.

To put it simply, general deterrence describes the logic that aspiring offenders with half-baked ideas about experimenting with certain types of crime will be deterred from committing those crimes if they see other like-minded people getting caught. This process creates its own type of critical mass where, on one hand, a domino effect can restore order and confidence in the police and reinforce the rule of law. On the other hand, when no one is getting caught, when there are no perp walks and no "good news" stories to tout in the press, but only new murders to report and add to the old ones, the opposite effect can occur. In terms of high profile sexual homicides, when similarly like-minded offenders who may just be in the preparatory phases of their paraphilias see that there is no certainty of being caught, the chain reaction moves in the opposite direction—towards a culture of disinhibition and criminal fission that becomes self-sustaining. By December 1969, Dennis was tired of putting out fires on his own, and tired of following the manual. With his own people, other than perhaps his mentor and loyal boss Inspector McBride, leaving him twisting in the wind, the citizens of London and area sat in the cross-hairs of a new type of killer for a new decade yet to come. As bad as 1969 might have been, the irreversibility of London's plague would soon make sure things got worse—not to mention a whole lot weirder.

# -CHAPTER 6-
# LOST AND FOUND: 1970-75

"The world is full of obvious things that nobody by any chance ever observes."
–Sherlock Holmes, *The Hound of the Baskervilles*

# THE PORN MAN

As Dennis Alsop was pleading in vain for reinforcements and additional resources, which would of course never arrive, all the while churning out reports and requests in assembly line fashion on an old typewriter, he knew—as no one else seemed to—that there was no end in sight to the sex murders that had the city under proverbial lock-down. Well ahead of his peers, he also knew, even if he didn't have the precise terminology at hand, how to identify serial indicators, evidence of process-focused killers, and even sexual psychopaths. These were specific behaviours he had seen first hand, and which were already haunting his dreams. There was nothing in his training or stale-dated field manuals that taught him how to approach these cases. It was simply a matter of confronting it head on and hoping for the best, but preparing for the worst.

Even without any official training in paraphilia or criminal-signature identification, Dennis knew that a person does not just arbitrarily decide to start attacking strangers at random and in high-risk places without earlier warning signs, especially when those strangers are teens and children—comparatively risky targets even for experienced predators. Nor, he thought, does a person wake up one day and instinctively start sneaking into occupied apartments with surgical precision to slaughter sleeping young mothers without waking her children or neighbours. He knew there would have to be some earlier sign of escalation, likely some antecedent that would have predicted or in some sense approximated the now more serious homicidal offending that was taking the city and region by storm. Without his knowing it, Dennis was likely one of the first documented law enforcement professionals to begin looking at cases in the context of preparatory paraphilias as a type of distant early warning system. No one else was listening.

One of the other problems at the time was of course the absence of both a sex offender registry to track these earlier behaviours and a central police database to permit timely searches for criminal records, parole conditions, or even pending charges for persons of interest. With the Canadian Police Information Centre (CPIC) not going online until 1972, a repeat criminal or sex offender who was a little too well-known by police in one city could simply move to the next town or province on the map and start over again—resume offending with impunity. The paper files containing his criminal background and other useful information would remain black-boxed and self-contained back where he came from, in some room of some station house in the previous jurisdiction. By the late 1960s, a number of deviants employing this very tactic came to London to start over and launch a new career of offending amongst like-minded and empathetic paraphiliacs. Some were also homegrown. One name that stood out in the early days of the Jackie English investigation was not so much a name as it was an unsettling sobriquet, or an alias with an accompanying legend. It was one that London and area parents had learned to fear: the Porn Man.

Talk of the so-called Porn Man had surfaced as early as the Jensen and Dunleavy murders in the winter of '68. Both victims had lived in the general vicinity of largely unacknowledged complaints about a grown man approaching children to show them graphic sexual photographs. Unlike Robert Hall's photographs, later shown to children in the summer of '69, these were not images of grown men engaged in sex acts with each other, but were images of men engaged in sex with animals—bestiality pornography—a fetish within the spectrum of zoophilia and a predictor of both pedophilia and necrophilia. Although these stories of the Porn Man and his catalogue of grotesque images had been treated for months as urban legends, by 1970, with several West London cases and countless others in the city and area still cold, someone was finally taking reports of these incidents seriously: Dennis Alsop. With the murder of Jackie English on the other side of the city, Dennis determined that the composite drawing enabled by Elizabeth Harrison not only matched earlier descriptions of the Porn Man, but also of the man now tutoring Marilyn Hird, Jackie's former co-worker at the Met. More importantly, this man was found to be living equidistant between the Jensen and Dunleavy homes. Perhaps even more significantly, he worked as both a teacher and senior administrator at the CPRI, which bordered the property where Jacqueline Dunleavy's body was found. He was also one of the regulars at the Stanley Variety and knew Dunleavy's boss, Joe Clarke. For Dennis, things were beginning to add up.

This was years before necrophilia and necrophilic spectrum homicides were even remotely understood by law enforcement, let alone publicly discussed. Nonetheless, the spontaneous statements made by the obscene caller during the attack on Elizabeth Harrison about his preference for "dead girls," coupled with both the Dunleavy and English murders, strongly suggested a necrophilic element. It seemed as though the Porn Man with his interest in zoophilic fetish pornography might well be the common denominator to all of these crimes. By January 1970, Dennis concluded it was time to get to the bottom of the legend and ferret out the Porn Man.

Investigation into the attack against Elizabeth Harrison unearthed some other interesting facts. The man tutoring Marilyn Hird and widely believed by some to be the infamous Porn Man had turned up late for work at the CPRI the day after the attack at the dog park, and also had an injury to his right hand without a logical or consistent explanation. Investigation also determined that a plumber had been called to his Headley Drive home a month or so earlier—around the time of the English murder—for a clogged pipe. After pulling the couplings apart, it was discovered that spools of 8mm film had been flushed down the toilet in an attempt to destroy them. While not exactly a smoking gun, it was still one more piece of the puzzle. A suspect seemed to be coming into focus.

This time, the London police saw fit to act on Dennis's insights. Cobbling together these loosely connected pieces of information, they were able to obtain a search warrant and raid the suspected Porn Man's Oakridge area home. Once inside, they found no 8mm film, as hoped. What was reportedly found, however, were numerous photographs of young boys—origins unknown. As with so many other delinquencies and paraphilias that were rampant in London at the time, possessing these images was also—and somewhat remarkably—treated with discretion and often as little more than a nuisance crime, warranting a stern finger wagging and nothing more. After all, child pornography was quite incredibly not even identified as meriting Parliamentary discussion until 1978, the current laws in that regard being on the books only since 1993. Although the photographs were seized as potential evidence of something else, there was no arrest made for simply possessing them. The continuing search of the home then resulted in an even more bizarre discovery.

Inside a locked steamer trunk in the basement, near where the cache of photographs had been found, investigators were later said to have discovered a collection of sealed mason jars—lots of them—filled with human feces. While it was not illegal then or now to be what is known as a fecophiliac, if so inclined, and to keep a collection of excrement on hand for ones own pleasure and curiosity, the homeowner would find himself in police custody within the next few weeks for something that *was* a crime. On April 26th, 1970, the alleged Porn Man was officially arrested and charged by Dennis—who was now also heading the investigation into the attack at the dog park—for the forcible confinement and mutilation of Elizabeth Harrison. Shortly after the execution of the search warrant and recovery of the troubling items at his home, his image was also selected by Elizabeth Harrison from a packet of head-shots as being her attacker—what is today known as a photographic line-up. At last, newspapers could assign a name and a face to the so-called Porn Man: 37-year-old Glen Fryer, the school principal at the CPRI.

The case against Fryer in the Harrison slashing was largely circumstantial. In addition to the photographic line-up selection, there was his mysterious hand wound the day after the attack, the lack of an alibi for the night of the attack, and a voice identification made by Harrison herself after she called Fryer's listed home number posing as a prospective home buyer. She would later state that the man who identified himself as Glen Fryer on the telephone had the same voice as the man who, while attacking her in the car and cutting her face, also made her listen to his twisted and horrific necrophilic fantasies. The report of the photographs of young boys and the collection of feces—not directly relevant to the facts of the Elizabeth Harrison attack and not widely known until a *Toronto Star* exposé in the 1990s citing unnamed sources—ensured that Fryer was convicted in the eyes of most police officers before the official trial had begun. The prevailing theory was that the attack on Elizabeth Harrison amounted to a deliberate attempt to silence her with respect to the Jackie English murder, with by the summer of '70 the London court of public opinion having reached its verdict against Fryer. Police and citizens alike were now hoping, based on the available evidence, the real court would follow suit and lock him away for good.

The trial of Glen Fryer would go on to be what was probably the biggest legal spectacle in London since the prosecution of those considered responsible for the nationally infamous massacre of the "Black Donnellys" in 1880. Fryer's trial was also reported on in the local news with the same fervour as were the trials of OJ Simpson and Oscar Pistorius in the age of 24-hour news cycle decades later. Londoners knew that a conviction of Fryer for the attack on Elizabeth Harrison was to also convict him—albeit indirectly—for the murder of Jackie English. This was because the prosecution's theory was that the motive for the attack against Harrison was her ability to provide some linkage that would end up identifying him as a suspect in the English slaying. There was, however, one lingering question: if Fryer had in fact already killed at least one young girl, why then resort to the theatrics of stalking, attacking, and carving up the witness's face, only to leave her alive so she could identify him for this further crime?

Glen Fryer poses smugly for newspaper cameras at a pre-trial appearance for the mutilation of Elizabeth Harrison, a potential key witness in the murder of Jackie English in October 1969. Courtesy: Western University Archives.

Fryer's criminal trial saw a cast of characters paraded before the court that seemed to pry back the cover on London's fungal undergrowth, doing so against the subtext of Jackie English's still unsolved murder. In the end, Fryer would receive what would be the equivalent, if it existed in Canada, of a Scottish judgement—a verdict of not *yet* proven. Although Fryer was officially found not guilty and acquitted, the closing remarks of Judge W.E. Colter, whose voice wavered and eyes watered towards the end of his ruling, clearly suggested that he thought there was more to the story. In looking at Fryer, the judge concluded his ruling with the following: "Y*ou* are the only one who truly knows whether you are innocent or guilty." As though he were perhaps speaking on behalf of the entire city and region and channelling the raw emotion, frustration, and fear of all Londoners, Judge Colter for a moment seemed to have lost the judicial and gentlemanly detachment for which he was known and widely respected. His words in acquitting Fryer suggested that he too seemed to know what Dennis Alsop had all along—that there was no apparent end in sight to the storm, and no going back to the way things were thought to be in London.

Judge Colter knew that Fryer's trial would not bring closure to anyone or likely serve to dam the city's cresting homicide problem, and that it all—the charges, the trial, the circus of witnesses and media—seemed to have been for nothing. The rule of law had prevailed, but there were still myriad unanswered questions. Judge Colter did urge Fryer to seek help, in "the name of God" no less. It was essentially a warning to leave town—and that's exactly what he did. Over two decades later, however, Fryer issued a bizarre invitation to Jackie English's sister Anne to attend his wedding anniversary gala, being held in the Toronto region where he had since relocated. Anne English accepted the rather odd invitation, hoping it might be the prelude to some kind of latter-day confession in the twilight of Fryer's life. Instead, after attending some nondescript rental hall in a random and lonely-looking plaza near Toronto, Anne as a reluctant guest would witness an eccentric and vaguely threatening monologue in which Fryer vowed that "everyone gets their just desserts" before he faded into the geriatric crowd, never to be seen or heard from by Anne again. Fryer might also have had the audacity and vindictive instinct to invite his accuser Elizabeth Harrison to the same tacky venue, but history as it turns out had other plans.

London Police cordon off the charred remains of the Harrison home on the morning of January 8th, 1973 while awaiting Fire Marshal's investigators from Toronto. Elizabeth, her entire family, and her dog Cindy all perished in the overnight fire that was eventually ruled accidental. Courtesy: Western University Archives.

Overnight on January 8th, 1973, Elizabeth, her husband, son, and even her beloved dog, Cindy, who had fought off her concession-road attacker back in December 1969, all perished in an overnight fire at their home on Elgin Street. The cause of the blaze was eventually ruled accidental, the result of some faulty illegal wiring installed the previous summer. This conclusion was reached following a joint investigation between the London Police, OPP, and Office of the Ontario Fire Marshal. It was a multi-death inquiry that, given the possibility that the witness was targeted for reprisal a second time, was also scrutinized by London and Middlesex Crown Attorney Michael Martin who personally attended the scene. Martin was the same prosecutor who had run the trial against Glen Fryer, and he had a heightened interest in finding out what had happened to his star witness and what the outcome of the police investigation into the fire would reveal. To this day there are those who believe, regardless of the fire being officially classified as accidental, that it was the same Telephone Man who attacked Elizabeth Harrison in her Volkswagen, and that he had returned years later to finish the job. Urban legends aside, the timing was certainly suspicious, especially in the context of another fatal fire that occurred just two months earlier.

On November 17th, 1972, the charred remains of a young mother and her three children were found inside the apartment house at 133 Elmwood Avenue in the city's Old South. When police at the scene strung up the crime scene tape around the tenement, some thought the address sounded familiar. It was. The scorched apartment house was the same building where Jackie English had lived until just before her murder, and the same address near where, three years earlier *to the day*, her killer had left her cosmetics and pencil case to taunt her family and authorities. As with the fire that later claimed the lives of the Harrisons, the Elmwood Avenue blaze was also ruled accidental, apparently the result of an overnight grease fire. The key witnesses to the Jackie English murder and the new family occupying Jackie's former home were all now dead in overnight fires in only a matter of months. Although experts ruled both fires as accidental, for some the urban legend only grew. Talk of a curse surrounding the English case soon surfaced. It was becoming the proverbial Hope Diamond of murder mysteries; anyone with a connection to the case, direct or indirect, would soon be met with some horrible fate.

Worse yet, even with Fryer's arrest, acquittal, and abrupt departure from the city, reported sightings of the Porn Man continued well into 1971 and beyond. For all the reported accounts of lewd photographs, 8mm films, and mason jars of excrement, and for all the trial testimony of his former colleagues and secretarial staff about his various proclivities, it turns out that Fryer was likely *not* the Porn Man after all. He was little more than a social pariah, albeit one who did little to avoid courting controversy and inviting the enmity of Londoners. While the case built against him by Dennis for the Harrison attack was rock solid, the urban legends and subsequent newspaper accounts of the crass items allegedly recovered from his home simply aren't corroborated by Dennis's original files or the trial transcripts. Once again, it would seem, a case of historical revisionism at its finest. To this day, whether it was a Porn Man or Porn Men—plural—stories and sightings still live on about a time when the Forest City was a breeding ground for villains—murderers, pedophiles, and others, all stranger than fiction and impossible to contain.

Unfortunately, the breeding ground was not to be contained to those tumultuous years of the 1960s. London was to face another wave of serial killers—some old and some new—during a new decade which made the prospect of nabbing the Porn Man as a local bit player a luxury that no one could afford. On a weeknight in August of 1970, less than a month after Fryer was acquitted for being Elizabeth Harrison's attacker—an acquittal tantamount to "acquitting" him—all at once—of being the Porn Man, the Telephone Man, and Jackie English's killer, the rotary telephone at Dennis Alsop's home rang shortly after 8:00 p.m. Twenty-five years before call display and mobile phones, his 15-year-old daughter Liz, who was the same age and had the same general appearance as Jackie English, picked up the receiver completely oblivious as to who might be calling. Her instinctive "Hello?", spoken into the plastic receiver, was met with dead air on the other end. A second "Hello?" was this time met with a sinister voice uttering, "You're next!" before the call ended with a click. Dead air again. The call bore a chilling resemblance to the calls received by Elizabeth Harrison a year earlier. Locally, at least, it was thought to be the first time that someone had called a cop's house, threatened a cop's daughter, and crossed a line that even the most brazen of criminals dared not. The London files were already personal for Dennis, but this was on a whole other level. It might have been a crank call, but it might also have been one of the innumerable killers he was chasing. It might have been the Neighbour, the Porn Man, or even Fryer himself. It didn't matter. The simple fact was that the man trying to solve a dozen murder mysteries and protect the city's young and innocent was now left trying to protect his own family from perhaps one of the killers he was pursuing. For the next several years, Dennis had an intermittent police wiretap placed on his own home telephone.

## VICTIM: SOROYA O'CONNELL, AGE 15

The year 1970 had begun in London with an eerie calm. Aside from the spectre of the Fryer "wounding trial" as it was commonly referred to in the media, as well as the natural calamity surrounding the Hotel London sniper incident later that same summer, there was little in the way of noteworthy crime. It had been the quietest twelve months in nearly a decade, murder-wise at least, the year ending with only two, both of which were solved in what seemed like record time. One was a wife-stabs-husband job, and the other a man-kills-girlfriend incident. Drunken bozos got collared at or near the scene in both cases and booked for non-capital. Things were looking up. As in the past, however, cautious optimism got the better of the city, with the first seven months of 1970 being little more than the calm before a new storm, or more accurately, a rolling barrage of storms.

Toward the end of that same summer of '70, and only a couple of weeks after the mystery call to the Alsop family home, Soroya O'Connell was just fifteen years old. Living with her parents on the Bridle Path—the same street as the Sheeler murder back in the winter of '63—her father worked for the Canadian Forces out of a centralized office in Toronto and was out of town on Friday, August 14th. Shortly after 7:00 p.m. that same night, Soroya was driven to a youth drop-in centre on Fanshawe Park Road, in a section of London Township not then annexed by the city of London. It was also the same area where Robert Stapylton's body had been found less than a year earlier.

On that night, Soroya, a diminutive brunette of mixed ethnicity, was relaxing with friends at the now long-since demolished youth centre located only a few miles northeast of her home, and her regular weekend haunt in the summertime. The spot was a social meeting place for both urban and rural teenaged kids, a safe place in which to play cards, darts, and other innocent games. When Soroya was dropped off by her mother to play euchre with friends that night, it had been agreed that she would return to pick her daughter up at closing, three hours later. When her mother returned, as promised, just after 10:00 p.m., the few remaining teens there explained that Soroya had left on her own about thirty minutes earlier. An older boy still hanging around, one with a driver's license and a car, said that he had initially agreed to drive Soroya home when she voiced her desire to leave earlier than planned. When the boy decided to stay a while longer, Soroya subsequently set out on her own. To this day, no one knows why she wanted to leave early and why she left just ahead of mother's arrival. The same older boy with the car later reported that he last saw Soroya walking alone, westbound along Fanshawe Park Road just before 10:00 p.m. That was the last time she was ever seen alive.

Somewhere between the span of a little over three miles between the drop-in centre and her home, and sometime within the 20 to 30 minutes between when she left the club and when her mother arrived, Soroya had vanished into the night. Given that her mother never saw her while driving the only direct route between the two locations, it seems likely that she may have entered a car somewhere along the first mile or so of her journey. Whether she was walking or hitchhiking, like so many other previous and future London victims, no one will ever know for sure. Either way, the timing of her disappearance along that three-mile stretch was puzzling. It was either an extraordinary coincidence or—more likely—a matter of someone having his eyes on the drop-in centre that night and waiting to strike if given the opportunity.

Soroya's mother drove home shortly after midnight, hoping to find her daughter there safe and sound, believing they had perhaps missed each other while separately coming and going. She instead found the house empty and telephoned Soroya's father at his Toronto office to alert him to the fact that something was seriously wrong; he made the drive home immediately to begin the fruitless search for his young girl. By sunup on August 15th, the O'Connells had, out of nowhere, joined the growing ranks of London parents whose happiness had been instantly wrung from their peaceable quiet lives in the Forest City. Overnight they joined the other London and area families—the Sheelers, the Tedballs, the Jensens, the Leishmans, the Stapyltons, the Englishes, the Whites, and others—who would wait with unbearable anguish for days, weeks, months, and even years for an answer. Unlike so many of the other city cases on which Dennis Alsop had been briefed, only after they had run a gauntlet of city officers and lost momentum, this time he was brought on board from the outset. Two years after the disappearance of Lynda White, no longer was anyone suggesting that missing girls were just runaways. Soroya's case was rightfully treated as probable foul play from the start, and when it came to missing and murdered London girls, no one had insight like Dennis. On the invitation of London brass, he made his way to 14 King to compare notes. His diary entry from August 27th of that year reports:

*At London PD with Insp. McBride re: missing person Soroya O'Connell - suspicious.*

Dennis, with McBride at his side, knew that Soroya's disappearance had to be connected to the other missing nightwalkers in London and region. He had already seen an obvious nexus between the existing cases and knew that this was now another one. He had, of course, also previously sent alerts to OPP HQ in Toronto about the likelihood of several London serial offenders all being at work at once—with a response of deafening silence. There seemed to be little discussion, if any, about the degeneracy consuming the city, with Dennis's take on the situation having been all but ignored by every higher-up except for McBride. London and its most vulnerable citizens, it seemed, would be left to the wolves for another decade as Dennis's coterie of bosses enjoyed the rarefied air of the upper ranks from their offices in Toronto and left him to his own devices. Beyond the pain of the O'Connells and their pleas in the newspaper, the frustrating and fruitless investigation into the disappearance of young Soroya did manage to turn up a significant and familiar detail. An eyewitness driving by that night later reported seeing Soroya enter the *back seat* of a dark-coloured sedan. Young girls being picked up and entering back seats of strange vehicles seemed to be a yet another emerging pattern, but a larger picture was not yet clear.

## VICTIM: EDITH AUTHIER, AGE 57

Although the first eight months of 1970 had been suspiciously quiet in London, it was as if, with the disappearance of Soroya O'Connell that August, someone had pulled his finger out of the dike and the flood had resumed with a vengeance. The truth was that the next five years would see more bloodshed than anyone had imagined after the crest of violence in the late 1960s.

Just a few weeks after what seemed to be just the latest snatching of a teenaged London girl from a city street, the small farming village of Merlin, Ontario, located about 80 miles southwest of London and well outside its CMA, would find itself unexpectedly linked forever to the Forest City as one of the last confirmed serial killers from this period—the London Chambermaid Slayer—had decided to broaden his horizons. After a one-year respite following the murder of Jane Wooley, he had changed his MO and target location just enough to make sure the police were unable to conjoin the murders—at least not for some time.

No one knows how or why the Chambermaid Slayer ended up at the William Pitt Hotel in the city of Chatham on Labour Day weekend of 1970, and no one knows for sure how or when he managed to earn the trust of 57-year-old widow Edith Authier, the housekeeping attendant on duty that weekend. Somehow, he ended up back at her white, wood-sided country home in nearby Merlin, on what seems to have been the evening of Friday, September 4th. The following morning, friends of Edith's who carpooled with her into Chatham attended her home to pick her up for work. Finding the door unlocked and assuming she had slept through her morning alarm, they entered to wake her up only to find her bed empty. In calling out her name and looking around the house, they eventually found her at the back of the kitchen, lying face-up on the floor beside the table. The wainscotting by the body was covered in blood spatter, it later being apparent that two butcher knives taken from her own kitchen drawer had been used to repeatedly stab and slash her in the chest and throat. A third knife, unused, was located nearby, as though the killer had abandoned his frenzy after the insertion of the second blade. A subsequent autopsy confirmed that Edith had also been bludgeoned, her face pulverized with a nearby clothes iron left out from laundry day earlier in the week. It was during this brutal beating that Edith was also sexually assaulted and knocked unconscious, her killer inflicting peri-mortem knife wounds to ensure that she never woke up.

The scene was similar in its brutality to the murder of Jane Wooley on York Street in London a year earlier, other than for the completion of the sexual assault in the latest case. The Authier murder also marked an evolution and escalation of the killer's MO. Compared to the earlier Wooley homicide, the murder of Edith Authier—although no one knew the terminology at the time—pointed to an increasingly process-focused and thrill-seeking killer. These similarities between the victims and disorganized behavioural indicators at both scenes all but confirmed that the Chambermaid Slayer was also a category 3 rapist who, like the Boston Strangler already mentioned, was targeting women of a certain age and income bracket—punishing them, it would seem, for something. In fact, in spite of the noted differences between the London and Merlin murders, the victimology couldn't have matched with greater precision. Both victims, of similar stature and appearance, were older females living alone; both were chambermaids in low-rent hotels; both were heavy drinkers and smokers willing to take a hotel guest back to their own home with them; both had their purses emptied and money stolen in an act of post-mortem petty theft that suggested this was all just a twisted lark for the killer. One big difference, however, was that Edith Authier worked in the territory of the Chatham Police and lived in OPP jurisdiction. While Dennis Alsop was stationed in Middlesex County and was catching murder cases from all over Southwestern Ontario—including neighbouring counties like Elgin, Oxford, and Norfolk—the town of Merlin was located in Kent County in the opposite westerly direction, just far enough away that very little of what happened there made its way east to London. While today it's no doubt difficult to imagine, by the informatic standards of 1970 no one who knew of the Jane Wooley case would know of the Edith Authier case. Not until three months later, when the sadist, revenge rapist, and thrill killer struck again.

## VICTIM: BELVA RUSSELL, AGE 57

Sometime just before midnight on January 22nd, 1971, the Chambermaid Slayer walked into the Merrill Hotel in Chatham in search of his next victim. The Merrill was an old-time inn where the bar was still divided into a men's side and a ladies' side. Seated on the ladies' side with a male acquaintance was 57-year-old hotel chambermaid Belva Russell, who was just beginning her weekend off. Within an hour, when Belva got up to head to the bathroom she was followed down the dark, dank hallway by another patron from the bar—the Slayer. What he and Belva may have discussed when he followed her to the ladies' room is, of course, unknown. It's also unknown if the two were previously acquainted or whether she was selected purely at random once he realized that she was the Merrill's chambermaid and fit his preferred victim profile. The Slayer returned to the main bar by himself a short time later and asked the bartender if he could move to the ladies' side so that he might be closer to the cigarette machine. While the Slayer was sitting there alone and plotting his next move, the Merill's waiter, a man named William Bezzo, pulled up a chair and introduced himself. The mysterious lone guest in the bar that night followed suit and shook hands. It was a chance meeting but one that would later prove momentous. For the first time, the police would soon have a name and face for the Chambermaid Slayer—Gerald Thomas Archer, from London.

After Bezzo's shift came to an end, he sat drinking with Archer, making small talk and learning some basic biographical facts that would ultimately be key in later taking down the Slayer. He revealed that he had recently made his way to Chatham to work as a forestry labourer—now known to be, strangely enough, the most common semi-skilled occupation amongst male serial killers. At the time he had also been working as a highway tree cutter along the same Highway 401 and 402 routes that allowed so many other predators a pathway back and forth between London and the surrounding towns and hamlets where their victims were dumped. He was married and had a daughter, lived on Adelaide Street in town, and, as it turned out, was the same age as his previous 57-year-old victim. What Archer said next took Bezzo by surprise: if "she didn't smarten up, [he] would have to kill her!" Asking who "she" might be, it was made obvious to Bezzo that Archer was talking about Belva Russell, now back from the toilet and seated just a few tables over, laughing and carrying on with her male suitor. Dismissing it as the typical drunk talk he heard from most of the louts who passed through the Merrill Hotel bar at one time or another, Bezzo brushed off the remark and called it a night. But for Archer, the night was still young, and it hadn't just been talk.

A few hours later, Belva's severely battered body was found in a pool of blood on the dining room floor of her Chatham home. At the time she was also living on Adelaide Street, only a few blocks from where Archer and his family had settled. Just as was the case with the Wooley and Authier murders, Belva had been furiously beaten about the face, head, and neck, suffering multiple fractures and significant trauma. Unlike the other murders, the scene seemed to suggest what's known as a personal cause rather than a sexual homicide. The killer hadn't spent long at the scene, especially in comparison to the Authier case, and all indications were that someone had followed Belva home from the bar that night with the intention of dispatching her quickly and for a specific non-sexual motive. That same bar is where Chatham detectives naturally began their investigation after later retracing the victim's final movements. Once they had a chance to talk with bartender William Bezzo, that's also pretty much where things ended.

## INTENTIONAL WALK

Four weeks later, Chatham Police picked up Archer while he was working as a contractor for the then Ontario Department of Highways along the 401 at Highgate Road. He was charged with the murder of Belva Russell as a result of overwhelming circumstantial evidence uncovered by investigators—evidence that was lacking in the cases of Edith Authier and Jane Wooley before her. Archer, in relying on what is sometimes called the jungle telegraph—an underground and informal system of oral communication used among fringe groups—certainly seems to have picked-up on the trends that his fellow London murderers had established years earlier with respect to exploiting the city's geography and awkward assemblage of police jurisdictions. In just under two years, he had killed three women in three different locales and involved three different police departments, seemingly walled off from what was happening outside of their own backyards. He had also managed to stay off of Dennis Alsop's radar and had been able to select victims whose deaths saw only limited media coverage. Much like what pioneering Yale victimologist Hans von Hentig, in his 1948 treatise, *The Criminal and His Victim,* called the "lonesome victim"—one of thirteen victim types in a detailed taxonomy he created—Archer had preyed on these women not simply because they worked in hotels. He knew from experience that the unsavoury hotels where he liked to go boozing often employed aged housekeepers who could be easily conned and who would often tolerate the risk of taking a creepy stranger home in exchange for a little company. It was a remarkably cruel and sadistic ruse that helped confirm that Archer killed for sport but only when he was able to rig the game.

Archer's crimes were little more than a new spin on the similarly specific and callous want-ad murders committed by Harvey Glatman, the so-called "Lonely-Hearts Killer," back in 1957-58. A sadistic TV repairman who targeted LA-area women by responding to lonely hearts club personals ads and other classifieds under various sinister pretexts, Glatman was caught red-handed by a California Highway Patrol officer while trying to kidnap what would have been his fourth victim on Halloween 1958. In a case that still epitomizes the unapologetically swift and decisive nature of American justice, Glatman was tried, convicted, and gassed in the green room at San Quentin State Prison—the infamous "Big Q"—within just eleven months of his arrest. Ruse attacks targeting von Hentig's "lonesome victim" in the tradition of Glatman are still, unfortunately, rather common, as seen in the accumulating number of "Craigslist Killers" today—killers whose victims are targeted by virtue of their unknowingly advertising their personal details and vulnerabilities online, including their routines and the fact that they live alone. In Archer's case, however, in spite of the obvious pattern in victimology, a lack of tangible evidence at the time meant that he was only ever charged with the murder of his final victim, Belva Russell. Once convicted and sentenced to life imprisonment, Archer still knew he had beaten the system and that a life sentence was not actually for life, at least not in Canada. Smug, defiant, and remorseless to the end, Archer was hauled out of the courtroom screaming, "That's only the first strike against me! The ball game isn't over yet!" His metaphorical bravado was more literal than most people realized. He had killed three women, but had only been caught for one. He was still in the game and had two more chances before striking out.

But in a matter of months, the London Chambermaid Slayer was yesterday's news. No one came looking for him or was able to secure the evidence to get the other two strikes against him. He was for all intents and purposes given an intentional walk—allowed to go on his merry way provided he never came back to the Forest City where his murderous rampage and visceral hatred of spinsters and widows working in hotels first began. Archer was paroled in 1985 for the murder of Belva Russell and subsequently walked out of prison a free man with no restrictions. He spent the next ten years as a nomad, drifting from town to town throughout Ontario and staying in many of the low-rent dives where he used to go trolling for his victims. During those ten years, from his early seventies to his eighties, Archer no longer had the rage or strength he had between 1969 and 1971—a criminological process known as "aging out"—and there is no evidence that he ever harmed another chambermaid, or anyone else for that matter. Archer, penniless and anonymous, would later die unmourned of heart failure in 1995. He was buried as an indigent in a small plot funded by taxpayers after his remains went unclaimed. But he wouldn't stay in the ground for long.

Shortly after his death, Archer's estranged wife and daughter went to police and explained that more than two decades earlier he had confessed to killing Edith Authier. The spontaneous admission—really more an act of boasting than confessing—had been made after a story about the murder had been published in the local newspaper and Archer had a few drinks in him. Like William Bezzo at the Merrill Hotel in Chatham, they had initially dismissed the confession as a drunken cry for attention from a pitiful man looking for notoriety. Once Archer began to look more and more like the Chambermaid Slayer and was convicted for the murder of Belva Russell, however, they soon started to think differently. In now coming forward, they also mentioned having heard about something called the *DNA Identification Act* and new techniques that could help cops solve cold cases—techniques which would have seemed like science fiction back when Archer first got a taste for murder. As it turns out, they were right. In 2000, a disinterment order was made, Archer's body exhumed, and tissue samples were taken for comparison to the crime scene samples from both the Wooley and Authier murders. While the Chambermaid Slayer had apparently confessed to killing 57-year-old Edith Authier in her Merlin home in September 1970, the way the crime scene was processed and the evidence mishandled precluded Archer's involvement from ever being verified. The murder of Jane Wooley was a different story. It turned out that DNA from one of the non-lipstick coated cigarettes plucked from the ashtray in Wooley's York Street apartment was conclusively shown to belong to Archer. It was finally strike two—by that time nearly thirty years later. The Edith Authier case could never be officially credited to Archer, but between the detailed anecdotal evidence about his confession and all of the other factors linking her murder to him, today the case is considered less unsolved than it is officially uncharged.

# THE SECTIONMAN

The Chambermaid Slayer wasn't the only killer being brought to justice in 1971. In the neighbouring town of Aylmer, 20-year-old Georgia Jackson had been raped and murdered five years earlier. Although Dennis Alsop had always kept the file open and active, from 1968 onward he had been deluged with a horrific spate of new slayings and was no longer able to commit the time or resources to it he wanted. He had been especially consumed by the murders of the boys—Jensen, Leishman, and Stapylton—while the English case had become something of a personal obsession. But back at the same Kingdom Hall where Georgia Jackson had been an admired and respected member prior to her murder, tremendous progress was being made off the record. There was a member of the local community of Witnesses who had recently become the subject of disturbing rumours. As a sectionman for the Canadian National Railway (CNR)—a nomadic job that required scouring sections of rail track for deficiencies or dangers, sometimes for the entire length of a line—he had already been investigated by the railway police for fencing stolen equipment, tools, and other goods purloined from rail cars to crooked store owners across the province. An internal CNR investigation in March of 1970 had concluded that this same man was "not too intelligent" and that he had likely been duped into trafficking in stolen property by another more venal employee, one who later became the patsy and was summarily fired.

Beyond the happenings at Canadian National, this same member of the Kingdom Hall had already begun a more serious criminal career. In the spring of '70, he had been arrested in the city of Kitchener for exposing himself in public, as well as breaking and entering. At the time, few people—including purported experts—understood how exhibitionism functioned as a gateway to a host of more serious attack paraphilias. He was thus declared a "pretty standard" exhibitionist by a court-appointed forensic psychiatrist, although we now know that there is really no such thing. Today, his being an exhibitionist and sex offender with an extraordinary degree of mobility, not to mention an aptitude for criminal versatility—petty theft actually being the second most common first adult crime among all serial killers—would merit his being flagged for surveillance or earmarked for continued monitoring. But by the fall of '71, it was only the overseers at the Kingdom Hall who were watching him. As the year was drawing to a close, and stories of his perversions began to escalate, these same overseers finally made their move.

It was the mother of all long shots. They put the sectionman in a room and told him that whoever killed Georgia Jackson would be punished by the Creator, that the killer would not be saved when the world ended in 1975 as they believed at the time and as was corroborated in *The Watchtower*. The only way for the killer to be saved was for him to confess and beg for the Creator's forgiveness. It was the ultimate inducement and one that no cop could ever get away with; but the overseers at the Kingdom Hall weren't cops. They were civilians with a hunch, and a good one at that. Within the hour they had a detailed confession about the kidnapping, rape, and murder of Georgia Jackson, complete with crocodile tears and the sectionman pleading for mercy. There would, however, be no absolution for him as promised—no saving by the Creator or anyone else for that matter. He was ex-communicated by the overseers on the spot and was soon meeting with a uniformed OPP officer following their notifying police of the confession. After attending the Kingdom Hall to effect the arrest, the officer then called Dennis Alsop at home. News of the arrest blindsided him. Out of nowhere the case had been brought in from the cold. The twisted and sadistic killer who had mutilated Georgia's body to take trophies, had scattered her clothing, and had even participated in the Kingdom Hall's volunteer search for the girl while at the same time toying with her family and authorities was finally in custody after five long years. In a matter of hours, Dennis would at last put a face and a name to Georgia Jackson's killer: 26-year-old David Bodemer, CNR sectionman.

In January of 1972, Bodemer underwent a series of psychiatric tests to determine his mental fitness to stand trial for the Jackson murder. In due course, fitness was established and the trial proceeded, commencing in June of 1972 with Bodemer being charged—like Gerard Thomas Archer before him—with non-capital murder. The trial ultimately revealed some disturbing facts about Bodemer's sexual preferences when his wife later took the stand. Although he had fathered four children with her, he was only ever aroused when she would play dead. If she did, he was hyper-sexual and never satisfied. When she refused, he would fly into fits of rage and then leave the house for sometimes days at a time. Upon his return, he was always calm and apologetic, as well as newly renewed in Kingdom Hall activities, even displaying what was described at trial as what we now classify as religious mania. From child killer and cannibal Albert Fish—electrocuted at Sing Sing in 1936 and one of the oldest men ever executed in America—to Gary Ridgway, the so-called "Green River Killer" who endures as the most prolific serial killer and necrophile in American history, displays of religious mania involving emotional outbursts during prayer or religious ceremonies—even among non-religious offenders—have proven to be a widely documented common denominator amongst some of the most sadistic of sexual murderers. No one has ever been able to explain why.

David Bodemer's wife, accompanied by her father and senior Kingdom Hall overseer Albert Crocker, arrive to testify at Bodemer's murder trial in July, 1972. Crocker—Bodemer's father-in-law at the time—along with fellow overseer Arthur Powley, were instrumental in obtaining the confession to Georgia Jackson's rape and murder that later resulted in Bodemer's conviction. Courtesy: Western University Archives.

Throughout Bodemer's trial, Dennis followed up on each new grisly development as they were distilled from various pieces of evidence or testimony entered on the record. Prior to the case going to court, he had also managed to track down the navy blue '57 Ford Meteor that Bodemer had owned in the 1960s, locating it in a Kitchener scrap yard and then asking himself, in fountain pen scratch, in one of his diary entries:

"Could D. Bodemer's car have had a faulty alignment in Jan. 1968?"

He was of course drawing potential connections between the car where Georgia Jackson was killed in the winter of '66 and London's unfinished business from the past, specifically the mechanical condition of the car that drove Jacqueline Dunleavy to her death on January 9th 1968. He was essentially spitballing and brainstorming, but it was more than anyone else was doing—not to mention that the Dunleavy file wasn't even his case.

Questions Dennis posed to himself, and conclusions he had already drawn, serve as an early example of the type of signature analysis and linkage methodologies used today. He was also seriously troubled by the thought of what Bodemer had been up to between the Jackson murder and his arrest in the fall of '71. Assisting locomotive engineers and inspecting tracks all over Southwestern Ontario had allowed Bodemer to develop an encyclopaedic knowledge of the region's geography—every hidden cubby and county road scouted along his travels had become committed to memory. His movement from train yard to train yard with the CNR, coupled with his itinerant lifestyle, moving from Aylmer to Stratford to Kitchener and other points in between, had equipped Bodemer to become something akin to an Aborigine in the Australian Outback—a master trekker and hunter with a cognitive map of an expansive area, one who knew how to exploit the natural landscape to his advantage. But while Dennis still hadn't necessarily figured out *what* Bodemer had been up to since the Jackson murder in 1966, he soon discovered *where* he had been secretly spending his time.

From the mid-1960s to sometime in 1971, just prior to the confession extracted by the overseers at Kingdom Hall, Bodemer had been secretly renting a small and isolated work shed at the back of a farm property near the town of Avon, a short drive from the CNR yard in Ingersoll where he was stationed at the time. Immediately after the murder of Georgia Jackson, Bodemer had driven to this same shed and had hidden the souvenirs taken from the dead girl's body there; he had confessed to as much. By the time the police had this information, first revealed by Bodemer during his interrogation by Dennis, follow-up investigation confirmed that the farm's owners had demolished the shed to allow for new construction on the secluded site. Dennis—a soon-to-be Inspector but forever someone who was never afraid to get his hands dirty—went so far as to manually search the dump-site in the nearby village of Springfield where the original shed's building materials and contents had been taken after the demolition. Sure enough, the search turned up one of Georgia Jackson's winter gloves which had been taken as a souvenir and later walled-up in a devious hidey-hole in that same shed, just as Bodemer had admitted. Given the time elapsed since the demolition and Dennis having limited resources available to conduct the landfill recovery at the time, no other items thought to be relevant were located. Of course, Dennis and his team were also only looking for property belonging to Georgia Jackson.

Whatever else had been hidden by Bodemer in his secret hideaway might also have been removed by the killer prior to its being torn down—Georgia's glove being the one item overlooked on move-out day. What Dennis was able to confirm, in later contacting the shed's original owners in the neighbouring village of Avon, was that the crude building had electrical service, and thus could have supported refrigeration devices.

With Bodemer's conviction for non-capital murder in July of 1972, he was sentenced to life in prison, but, like Archer before him, "life" was a misnomer, especially when convicted of only *one* murder. Because dead women can't talk and the system at the time seemed to have had very little regard for victims of sexual crimes in any event, Bodemer's version of events about getting carried away once his sexual advances were rejected by a chaste Georgia prevailed as the version of record—one that was ultimately deemed sympathetic to his cause by the parole board. After serving the ten-year minimum for non-capital murder, Bodemer was released in 1982 after being considered rehabilitated.

Of course, no one at the Parole Board of Canada ever bothered to ascertain, assuming as Bodemer claimed that the murder was a type of date rape turned fatal, what exactly he had done to Georgia's arm and her ear, and why he'd scattered her clothing, kept souvenirs, and participated in the community search for the girl to divert authorities. No attempt was made to determine if he also had any role in the subsequent cruel crank call placed to Georgia's mother. Because all of it was apparently deemed immaterial, in 1982 Bodemer was free to walk the streets without restrictions. One of the first things he did was go back to what he knew—an itinerant life in logistics—but on a much larger scale. Abandoned by the Witnesses and his family, and unable to return to his job as a sectionman with Canadian National, Bodemer later secured himself a tractor-trailer trucking license, enabling him to drive long-haul rigs all over the country completely unsupervised. Although, as a convicted murderer, he was declared an "undesirable" and banned from entering the U.S., he would—in theory—be able to travel anywhere he wanted within Canada. It was, however, the time that Bodemer had previously spent in prison that ultimately provided the most interesting revelations. Following the demolition of his devious lair in Avon, his arrest for Georgia's murder, and his subsequent incarceration all occurring in immediate succession, various items—and bodies—soon began surfacing all around London and region.

## VICTIM: PRISCILLA MERLE, AGE 21

March 4th, 1972 was a Saturday, and an unseasonably warm one at that—not to mention a full moon. Just after 2:00 a.m., 21-year-old Priscilla Merle returned to the home on London's historic Hill Street where she had been staying with her sister. Priscilla had been out with friends at the nearby Clarendon Hotel where, following a dust-up with some of the regulars, she stumbled back to her sister's home in a tipsy and agitated state. After unsuccessfully trying to then goad her sister to head to an all-night bush party in Exeter—a nearby town that figured prominently in the Truscott case of 1959—Priscilla left the apartment to use a nearby pay phone to call and ask her boyfriend to come and pick her up. A few minutes later, Priscilla stumbled back into the house and said that her boyfriend was still out but that—good news—his brother was en route to take her instead.

What happened next was no real mystery. Unlike the other victims of London's dark era, whose final hours remain forever in the grey in terms of what may or may not have happened, who they may have met, or where they might have been taken, the end to Priscilla Merle's life seemed to follow a predictable itinerary. At roughly 2:15 a.m., she was seen by her sister walking out of the house on Hill Street and into a station wagon, unknown make, model, or colour, but being driven by her boyfriend's brother and with no other passengers in the vehicle. Priscilla has never been seen alive since. Unlike the other cases of London women and children seen getting into unidentified vehicles being operated by lone mystery men, Priscilla's final trip could be linked to a specific car and person—one known to her and positively identified by one of the last people to see her alive. For this very reason, Priscilla was never reported missing. She was assumed to be with her boyfriend's brother, or perhaps back at her boyfriend's house, or perhaps still safely up in Exeter. Conventional thinking was that she would make her way back to town after the bender was over. She was 21 years old and seemingly didn't have a care in the world—no job to report to, no kids at home, and no one to worry if she failed to turn up after several days, a week, or even three weeks.

Then, on the morning of March 26th, a fisherman on the shore of the Kettle Creek near the local beach town of Port Stanley—a favoured summer destination amongst Londoners then and now—made a gruesome discovery. Carried to the beach by the morning tide was a human arm that was soon determined to be female. The OPP arrived on one of Dennis Alsop's rare days off and recovered the limb. When word of the find reached the countless London families who had children or siblings still unaccounted for, they all wondered if this is how it might have ended for their loved one. For Priscilla Merle's sister, despite Priscilla's prolonged absence, the thought of linking her with the recovered arm was both gruesome and largely unfathomable. Three weeks later, the unthinkable became the reality.

On April 13th, about four miles downstream from where the arm had been located in the same Kettle Creek, a fisherman in a rowboat came across the dismembered and mutilated upper torso of an adult female, floating supine in the water. Then, on May 11th, just over half a mile from where the upper torso was discovered, a recreational boater braving the choppy spring waters came upon the lower half of the same torso—the abdomen and pelvic area—floating amongst some flotsam and jetsam near the marina. It was the last of the body parts of the Jane Doe to be found. Police divers and search teams deployed in OPP boats failed to turn up the head, legs, or any other identifying features of the body. Following a methodical federal fingerprint check, the remains were eventually identified as those of Priscilla Merle, whose prints were on file as the result of a previous burglary conviction. No clothing or other items were ever found, and no one could recall having seen her arrive in Exeter on the night of March 4th or anytime after. Yet again, like clockwork, a London girl had been taken from the city, murdered, and placed in OPP territory. In similarly predictable fashion, it was also Dennis Alsop's turn to catch new cases, and Priscilla Merle was added to what seemed to be a never-ending pile of manila folders, each bearing a name and a life for which he was now the sole custodian. He must have thought it was all a bad dream, a surreal nightmare that might, like all nightmares, eventually end. It didn't.

MICHAEL ARNTFIELD

# THE TAXI DRIVER

An autopsy of Priscilla's dismembered and waterlogged remains was, not surprisingly, inconclusive. No cause of death could be confirmed without the head or the remainder of the body to submit to a post-mortem examination. Even with the torso recovered, given the time elapsed and its having been bisected, no histamine levels or other peri-mortem data could be obtained to help determine whether she was killed quickly, or whether she was still alive when the dismemberment began. The torso, showing no stab wounds as best as it could be reconstructed, suggested that whatever weapon had been used to sever the limbs and head had only been used after death, at least in terms of the visible damage done to the body. Then, a more detailed story emerged, when looking at the severances and the wounds to the flesh and bone of the recovered pieces.

It seemed as if the killer had attempted to at first make the cuts with a hand tool before moving on to a power tool to expedite the process, likely using either a circular saw or chainsaw. Priscilla's dismemberment it seems was less about erotophonophilia, lust murder, or some other paraphilic indulgence as much as it was an attempt to efficiently dispose of the body—the panicked work of an amateur. With both sections of the torso and the left arm having been found in close proximity to each other and apparently thrown from the same bridge outside of Port Stanley, it seemed as though Priscilla's killer—whether because of time constraints, a lack of gas money, mere laziness, or any number of reasons—wanted to minimize his trips out of town. He was not prepared, as Bodemer had been, to drive across expansive areas to maximize the greatest number of disposal sites and evidence recovery locations. What the only known dumpsite did clearly show, however, was that Priscilla's killer had a car, a private place to desecrate the body without having to worry about eyewitnesses, earwitnesses, or nosey neighbours, as well as immediate access to professional-grade power tools on a weekend night.

Dennis Alsop—cruising on caffeine and adrenaline for nearly six years now—began the Merle investigation with interviews of the last people to see Priscilla alive. These people included her sister and her boyfriend's brother, a 39-year-old man he confirmed was named David Pullin. A laborious manual background check of both names, the only way possible then, had revealed that both individuals checked out clean—no prior records. However, it certainly wasn't the first time that Pullin had been checked for priors. He had previously been successfully screened by the London Police when applying to be a taxi-cab driver, a calling he later gave up in May of 1972 after Priscilla's body parts were found. After the identification of the remains, Dennis, on first going to interview Pullin that same summer, had no reason to expect anything less than full cooperation from a man with no criminal record who had last been seen with Priscilla and who no doubt was the key to helping solve the case. But when Dennis Alsop and David Pullin finally met, the sleep-deprived detective was gob-smacked by the chilly response he actually received. Pullin prickled at Dennis's introduction, and refused to speak to him—refused to answer questions about what happened to his brother's girlfriend. It was, of course, the same girlfriend who was last seen alive in his company—in *his* car. In the blink of an eye, Dennis's best witness had morphed into his best suspect.

For the next several weeks, in a reprise of his thwarted attempts to apprehend the Neighbour, Dennis shadowed Pullin nearly everywhere he went, continuously changing up his pitches. From fastballs and sliders to change-ups and even knuckleballs, Dennis tried to find a combination that worked and that would prompt Pullin to take an irrevocable swing and commit to an answer. Putting all his cards on the table, he let Pullin know that he was confirmed to be the last person with whom Priscilla was seen alive and was now the prime suspect. All the while, Dennis had Pullin under technical surveillance—a now largely obsolete wiretap variation known as a pen register (dialed number recorder) on his phone—and had also seized his '61 Pontiac station wagon under the authority of a search warrant. With Detective Bob Young at his side and as impromptu backup—the same London city investigator who had initially caught the Frankie Jensen missing person case and who by that time was considered a master interrogator himself—Dennis ventured into East London to finally confront Pullin head-on. Dennis let his suspect know in no uncertain terms that a search of his car had turned up traces of human blood diluted with cleaning chemicals, and that a search of the garage at his rented Hale Street address had uncovered a blue toolbox containing a hack saw with the blade inexplicably removed. The noose seemed to be tightening, but Pullin knew that even on a good day all this evidence would not likely be enough for a guilty verdict in a Canadian court. Since the Truscott hangover was still in full force and effect, absent a confession or Priscilla's remaining body parts actually turning up in plain view inside Pullin's house, car, or taxi cab, Dennis himself knew deep down that he would never get the go ahead to make an arrest—not even from McBride. Pullin, sporting a mirror-perfected tough guy smirk, subsequently gave Dennis the same line he had during every previous shakedown. On March 28th, 1972, as Bob Young stood quietly and toed the gravel on the ground outside the garage at Pullin's dilapidated Hale Street address, letting Dennis do his thing without interjecting, the ad hoc interrogation served as an omen for what would be the suspect's recurring tag-line for years to come. Dennis's notes from that afternoon report Pullin's statements verbatim:

*"Well, what if a person had picked up a person?... it didn't mean he did anything else. He could have dropped her anywhere in town or in the country. So, I'm innocent!"*

Dennis didn't have to rely on his code-breaking skills to decipher that Pullin was spelling out that he had and would always have reasonable doubt on his side. There was no smoking gun to be found—none of the wish-list items that since the early 1960s had been the frequently unreachable benchmark for justifying murder prosecutions post-Truscott. So, before long, there would be few people besides Dennis who bothered to care about Priscilla Merle, or at least what remained of her. It was to be yet another case to add to the seemingly interminable unsolved pile. But with the march of time, and as Dennis climbed the OPP ladder, the aging detective still had a few more tricks up his sleeve. The problem was that London's scourge did as well.

By the summer of '72, the threatening mystery call to Dennis's daughter two years earlier seemed to be a mere blip on screen and had for the most part been forgotten. Liz Alsop, by then a sophomore in high school, was in the living room of the family home one weeknight while her father was at work and everyone else out and about. With the place to herself, she cranked the volume up on the 45-RPM record of Ashton Gardner & Dyke's "Resurrection Shuffle" as she danced across the room. She suddenly stopped in mid-step. Looking out the home's front picture window, she caught sight of a lone car parked on the street in the evening twilight, and what appeared to be a male driver watching her through the window with a set of binoculars. Her heart stopped and she drew the curtains after sweeping the needle off the vinyl and hunkering down behind the chesterfield. She sat paralysed with fear in that same spot until her father came home later that night. From that point forward, both David Pullin and Dennis's own daughter would have one thing in common. Before long they would be followed by unmarked surveillance details everywhere they went, many of the officers volunteering their time off the clock for fear that Dennis and his family were now squarely in the sights of the city's faction of psychopaths. Neither surveillance project offered any new leads, however, and by summer's end the tails were pulled off.

Then, on Tuesday, September 26th, 1972, as Dennis digressed into what by then seemed—at least for his daughter—to be a weekly dinner-table pep talk about the dangers of hitchhiking, the dangers of getting into a car in London, and—the most recent rule—always keeping the front curtains closed, the telephone on the kitchen wall suddenly rang. It was McBride. They had found Priscilla Merle's head.

Without so much as a pensive pause, Dennis rushed full bore to an abandoned and decrepit bungalow on Chesley Avenue in South London. Several local schoolchildren had reported to the principal of the Chesley Avenue Public School that they had seen a plastic bag in the garage of the home in question containing the head of a woman they had recognized from the newspaper as being Priscilla Merle. By the time Dennis arrived, the London PD who were already at the scene had determined that there was no such head, although the place was certainly creepy enough for the story to ring true. It later turned out that one of the boys who got the whole rumour started was an inveterate glue sniffer and exhibitionist, who within the year would end up in a secure reform school for high-risk delinquents. Soon after, the same boy's psychiatrist sent the OPP a letter reporting that he was still telling the same story and that it sounded cogent and genuine. Following the receipt of the letter, on July 5$^{th}$ of 1973, near the same Chesley Avenue garage searched the previous fall, a plastic bag containing clumps of human scalp hair was discovered in a culvert at the side of the road. The hair was slightly lighter than Priscilla's was thought to have been at the time of her death, but Dennis nonetheless contacted her sister and mother in a bid to try to find a sample for comparison. Once again, no luck. The head was never found, and to whom the scalp hair in the bag belonged was never determined. It is also unclear what, if anything, ever became of the discovery.

Every year on the anniversary of Priscilla's murder—right up until the time of his retirement—Dennis went back to see David Pullin to sweat him, relentlessly asking him the same questions time and again. The answers always remained suspiciously the same, with Pullin always speaking in the third person and speculating "he" could have dropped the girl off just about "anywhere" prior to her murder. Of course, Pullin never could expand on the story to describe—speculatively or otherwise—where exactly that might have been.

# HILLCREST

In April of 1973 in Bayham Township, the same speck on the map where Jackie English's torn bra and underwear were found in the fall of '69, a farmer was doing a spring perimeter check of his property when he discovered what was later revealed to be clothing belonging to Lynda White. The items were identified by one of Lynda's Argyle Street roommates, whom police were able to track down now five years after the fact. The clothing was found wrapped up with a broken piece of what looked like a land surveyor's range pole, all of it seemingly thrown as one pile of debris from the window of a moving car. Where exactly these items landed also happened to be 26 miles due west of another curious landmark.

At the corner of Charlotteville County Road and Vermeulen Road in a tiny Norfolk County village known as Forestville, there lies an old pioneer-era graveyard, most of the headstones covered with the patina of age and largely illegible. Some markers at the Hillcrest Cemetery date to when the area's earliest non-Native settlers first arrived and began farming the region nearly three centuries ago. Until 1962, the now-extinct South Norfolk Railway, a subsidiary of the famous Grand Trunk Railroad, ran right past it. Having been acquired by the Canadian National Railway that same year, sectionmen from all over the region were brought in, beginning in the summer of '67, to pull up the track of the abandoned line. Six years later, in May of 1973, just a month after Lynda's clothing was found, the little-known place was once again a hub of activity, and was crawling with OPP black and whites. Soon, the police caravan parked along Charlotteville Road was joined by Dennis Alsop's latest company sled, an unmarked '69 Dodge Polara—his first "executive" model as a newly-minted Detective Inspector.

Across from the cemetery's rustic wrought-iron gates, which still serve as the property's official entrance, was and remains an unmarked and unassumed old horse-carriage lane which leads from the county road into the brush to snake through a network of farm properties, mostly fields of tobacco and other cash crops. Just a few feet off the desolate main road and covered in deadfall from the canopy of trees above, yet another farmer stumbled across an unusual find, in this case a nearly complete human skeleton. Dennis's suspicion that the skeleton was that of Lynda White, in light of her clothing having been discovered just a month earlier and some miles away from this same scene, was later confirmed by dental records. At last, Lynda's family had some kind of an answer, but also a host of new questions. One of these questions was how and why Lynda's remains could be found nearly 70 miles from her last known whereabouts, and nearly 30 miles from where her clothing was located—with both of these finds occurring years after her disappearance.

Dennis, with a host of his own questions, had also been to this dance before. He immediately knew something was familiar about the state in which Lynda's body was found. The skeleton was on its back in a carefully arranged position, having been carried from the killer's car, which had been left on the old carriage path, to a concealed spot amongst the trees some distance away. Although concealed at first glance, the spot was also easily locatable should the killer ever venture back to review his work. The body had been posed with some degree of intricacy, and with some unsettling similarity to the famous da Vinci sketch known as the Vitruvian Man, had all of the limbs splayed in different directions. It was as though Lynda's killer were looking to replicate a long-standing image in his mind or perhaps fuel new fantasies. The fact that her body was placed on the surface and that no attempt was made to conceal it is in keeping with what is generally seen in cases of bodily posing—versus crime-scene staging—as well as surface burials and limited attempts at concealment. Such behaviour is historically not uncommon with necrophiles. Gary Ridgway—already mentioned in this same chapter—would frequently return to his body disposal sites surrounding the Green River in Washington State to compulsively review and admire his handiwork. What immediately stuck out for Dennis was the fact that the body had been completely stripped of all clothing and jewellery, right down to the earrings and other personal effects. These items included Lynda's MedicAlert bracelet, which was never recovered. No jewellery or personal identification was ever found with the discarded clothes that turned up a month earlier, either. But perhaps most familiar to Dennis was what had been done with Lynda's right arm.

The right arm of the skeleton, severed from the shoulder joint with relative precision, was missing in its entirety and was never recovered. The conclusion of the attending pathologist—in summarily backing up the unqualified opinions of a number of the officers at the scene—was that the arm was taken as a result of "apparent animal activity." No proper archaeological excavation of the site was conducted and no forensic anthropologist was consulted, as would ideally be the case today. The scavenging theory with respect to the missing arm thus remains doubtful at best—even by the standards of 1973. Animal scavenging in rural Canada has, especially in the last thirty years, become an extraordinarily well-studied phenomenon, leaving the "animal activity" thesis to make even less sense today than it did then. Simply put, there is no known scavenger or other animal who takes only one limb from a corpse in the wild. Smaller animals have neither the strength nor the teeth required to remove or carry away a full human arm. Larger animals such as coyotes inevitably pull a body apart and take the richest sources of food back to their dens. Even properly buried bodies in the same part of Canada have been disinterred years later to find that remains were attacked and scattered from within the grave by scavengers in such a fashion. Then, of course, there was also the state of Lynda's skeleton proper: bleached white by the sun's electromagnetic rays.

Had they chosen to either listen to Dennis's wisdom or consult an accredited anthropologist, the Norfolk County investigators at the scene might have also learned that it was not only improbable but actually impossible for such a whitening process to occur had Lynda's body been deposited at the location in November of 1968 when she vanished. The state of the bones would have instead confirmed to the trained eye that the body was placed at the Hillcrest location during the hotter and drier summer months when decomposition was accelerated. Bodies left outdoors during the late autumn through to the spring inevitably develop a waxy coating on the bones known as adipocere, the result of dampness and humidity affecting the decomposition process, especially in Southern Ontario's climate. Soil samples taken from this same location forty years nearly to the day after Lynda disappeared, as part of the research conducted for this book, and then later submitted to laboratory testing by a certified expert, confirm that the conditions and acidity levels of the soil at Lynda's recovery site were and remain optimal for the formation of adipocere during the month of November. All modern and reliable biological evidence and related testing therefore indicates that, between the fall of '68 and the spring or summer of '71 when decomposition began, Lynda's body was kept somewhere else, somehow preserved or frozen to delay decomposition. As in the case of Robert Stapylton, no cause of death could ever be established—a fact that on its own also seemed to negate the pathologist making any attempt to more thoroughly examine the precise nature of the arm's amputation, or recruit outside assistance in examining the molecular structure of the bones for evidence of freezing and thawing.

So, as the coroner's service removed Lynda's remains from the scene, Dennis drove back to London alone in his opinion that the recovery site and state of the skeleton simply didn't feel right. Although he had spent what seemed like a lifetime pursuing these unsolved cases, he also knew that his days left in the London area were numbered—that Lynda's case would no doubt be his last, at least officially speaking. With this latest promotional bump to Inspector, Dennis knew he was at the mercy of the bureaucratic machine that had been churning at full throttle since the Truscott disaster. Just as with so many good cops before and after him, he soon found himself promoted out of his home turf—promoted out of where, despite what the city had wrought, he had found some semblance of happiness. From that point forward, the unfinished business galore in the Forest City and area would have to be investigated by him off the books—and from a distance. He was about to become the first telecommuting homicide detective.

## VICTIM: MARY HICKS, AGE 21

The story of Lynda White rightfully horrified Londoners, but it was easy for some to delude themselves into thinking that the discovery of her skeleton was a holdover from the city's dark period in the late 1960s and that order had since been restored. It was also easier for some to think about the whole affair as a Norfolk County problem, nearly two hours outside the city. In reality, within just a few months of Lynda finally being properly buried in her hometown of Burlington, a new murderous force, unlike anything the city had seen, was already in the offing. It would be years before the city and its police had any clue he existed, and just as long before Londoners knew what hit them.

Sometime overnight on October 18th, 1973, a stranger made his way into the bedroom of Mary Hicks while she slept in her Talbot Street apartment in downtown London. Standing over her in the darkened bedroom, he watched her in her bed, utterly transfixed on how peaceful she looked while fast asleep. He vowed to himself that he would make sure she stayed that way forever.

The next morning, Mary's roommate tried to wake her up in vain, finding her tucked in tight under her sheets with her face partially covered by her pillow. When the roommate finally clued-in that she wasn't breathing, she called the police and paramedics. They were of no assistance; Mary had already been dead for some time.

The attending officers from the London PD did exactly what her killer had hoped they would do. With nothing in the seemingly peaceful circumstances of her passing to suggest otherwise, they wrote it up as an unexplained death, notified the right people, and ensured that the body of the 21-year-old woman in good health was sent for an autopsy. There was no sign of a break-in or a struggle, no violence to the body, and nothing suspicious either seen or heard. The autopsy yielded an equally innocuous conclusion: death was accidental, an unforeseen reaction to prescription drugs leading to accidental suffocation from the pillow over her face. It was the perfect beginning for an aspiring serial killer and a seemingly undetectable, tailor-made MO. If you commit a murder and no one knows it, no one comes looking. By the time anyone actually came looking, he had already become the worst serial killer in Ontario history.

# THE GORE

On May 26th, 1974, just over a year after Lynda White's skeleton had been found posed across from the unheard-of hamlet of Forestville's historic Hillcrest Cemetery, there was another unlikely but disturbingly similar find: the body of Soroya O'Connell. Partially concealed beneath some brush and bark that had fallen from some nearby trees, her skeletonized remains were found by an aimless junk picker looking for old bottles. The dump itself was located in what was then called—at least in Dennis Alsop's reports—as The Gore of Downie in Perth County, now known as simply Downie Township, located about five miles from the historic town of Stratford where an annual Shakespeare-themed festival draws theatre buffs and celebrities from across North America. As with Lynda White before her, once Soroya's skeleton was discovered, her identity also needing to be verified through dental records, Downie went from being unknown to most outsiders to a place that very quickly attracted widespread morbid curiosity. Also similar to Forestville, Downie was located a considerable distance away from where Soroya was last seen alive; in this case, over 30 miles northeast of the drop-in centre in London Township.

OPP detectives—this time from Perth County—knowing nothing of the find in Norfolk County with respect to Lynda White, were not exactly sure what to make of what they had. Once again, true to form, was no proper archaeological excavation or anthropological consultation to aid the investigation. When Dennis, for most of the time now chained to a desk two hours east of London in Toronto got wind of the details, he instinctively knew that Soroya's body was the missing link between at least two other cases—Lynda White and Jackie English—and possibly others.

Like in the White and English murders, Soroya had been transported over a comparatively large distance, although whether alive or not is unknown. As with White and English, the body had also been stripped of clothing, none of it recovered in this case. She was also a teenaged girl last seen walking alone at night, as were the other two. Then there were some additional specific points in common between Soroya and Jackie English alone. Like in Jackie's case, Soroya's jewellery—which included a watch and a chain with pendant—had all been taken save her earrings, which had been removed but then deposited near the body as a type of macabre calling card. Soroya's skeleton was fully intact but, like Lynda White, she appeared to have been placed there in the summer. At face value, this would seem to make sense given that she vanished in the late summer of '70, other than for an observation made by the attending chief pathologist who conducted the autopsy—a different examiner than in the case of Lynda White. The post-mortem examination, although unable to confirm a cause of death, did suggest what should have been properly noted in Lynda White's autopsy—that the victim had *not* been at the site during the full period in which she was missing. Soroya had been gone for nearly four years, yet the state of the skeleton suggested that she had only been at the site for at most three years, likely deposited there—at the latest—sometime in the summer of '71. Like the other girls, Lynda and Jackie, Soroya had also been transported a considerable distance and concealed but the state of her remains was inconsistent with her having been left at the recovery site immediately after her disappearance. The question that remains and which dogged Dennis Alsop until the day he died was where exactly had all three girls been during those periods, and with whom?

Today, an even more disturbing observation reveals itself in light of our improved understanding of the elaborate necrophilic posing seen in the White and O'Connell slayings in particular. It reflects a newly proposed paraphilia known as necronopositophilia, a tongue twister coinage set to appear in forthcoming forensic literature, and which appropriately describes the devious process of arranging bodies for display as part of a killer's internal narrative—to fulfil, often with the assistance of photographs and even painting or sketching, his need to create lasting visuals and material artefacts of his crimes. Such a compulsion would be limited to killers who also have a variety of other and pre-existing necrophilic interests and behaviours. With respect to both placophilia and taphophilia as known predictors of such necrophilic compulsions, we predictably find another unsettling and very specific point in common between the White and O'Connell cases. Not only were both victims driven a great distance, stripped of clothing and jewellery, posed in isolated rural settings, not found for several years, and not deposited at these locations for several years, but Soroya's last known location and Lynda's recovery site are also very close to some of the region's most historic cemeteries.

While Lynda White was found concealed parallel to the pioneer era Hillcrest Cemetery, the drop-in centre where Soroya was last seen alive was located at 1455 Fanshawe Park Road, just across the street from the Siloam Cemetery—also pioneer-era graveyard. Soroya was in fact last seen walking eastbound past this same graveyard when she was last seen alive. Most interestingly, the CNR rail line at the time—now an Amtrak route—also ran right past it before continuing on, north-by-northeast, past the Canadian Baseball Hall of Fame in St. Mary's and ultimately into Downie, adjacent to where Soroya's posed skeleton was ultimately discovered. None of this was of course known at the time and of course no one but Dennis ever went looking.

## VICTIM: JUDITH BARKSEY, AGE 19

In 1974, the town of Strathroy was to London what Downie was to Stratford: a suburb separated by a contiguous stretch of farms spanning only a few miles. Part of the same Middlesex County as the Forest City, and squarely within London's CMA, Strathroy remains a place today where many Londoners prefer to live or work. It is an earnest and good-natured place where people still call movie theatres "the show." The town was and remains extolled as "Strath Vegas" among some—a social destination and place to cut loose on the cheap, and in large groups, without worry. But by March of 1974, the scourge of London—its unrelenting serial sex killer problem—had officially made its way west to the small and peaceful exurb.

On the morning of March 3rd, following an unseasonably and bitterly cold series of days, a man cutting across the property of a warehouse next to the town railway station had been on his way to post a letter when he stumbled across the frozen body of 19-year-old nursing aid Judith Barksey lying on the pavement with her throat slashed. Nearby, the man found a blood spattered pizza box, some pop bottles, and chocolate bars strewn across the ground, in effect creating a trail leading back to a nearby Bell telephone booth with its door open and receiver off the hook. The man also found one of the girl's shoes, apparently having slipped off as she started running from someone.

The Strathroy Police, a small, independent contingent of officers who—as they still do today—often hailed from larger neighbouring departments and transferred there in search of a slower small-town pace, were caught entirely off guard when they arrived at the scene. It was a winter's morning portrait of the final terrifying seconds of a young girl's life. These types of events had by then become commonplace a few minutes down the road in London, but Strathroy had always prided itself in its *not* being London. That was, until the morning of March 3rd, 1974. It had only been a matter of time, after all, before the townships immediately surrounding the Forest City became officially cross-contaminated.

The early murder investigation soon revealed that Judith was last seen alive leaving a nearby pizzeria, where she had apparently gone to pick up some comfort food in preparation for a cold night indoors. Off the main road, and with the realization that she was being followed, she then ran to a nearby phone booth to presumably call the police—a call that was never completed. A reconstruction of events suggests that Judith likely ran when the murder weapon came into view, literally running out of her shoes and dropping her food as she fled for her life. In short order, however, the assailant caught her and slashed her throat. As she bled to death, he unfastened her pants before then taking the change from her purchases out of her pockets. That was on the night of March 1st. She would lie there on the warehouse parking lot pavement, undiscovered, for nearly two days.

## VICTIM: ELEANOR HARTWICK, AGE 27

Back in Forest City, the murder of Mary Hicks in her own bed hadn't only gone unsolved but also entirely unnoticed. The day after Judith Barksey's frozen body was found in a vacant and frozen-over Strathroy parking lot, the morning of March 4th, 27-year-old Eleanor Hartwick was found dead inside the bedroom of her Westlake Street apartment in London. It was a near replica of the Mary Hicks scene. The young woman was found tucked neatly beneath her sheets, peaceful as if still fast asleep. The mass market paperback she had been reading while in bed was still in her hand, as though she had dozed off while flipping through the flimsy creme pages. The killer's methods were evolving, the narrative created by the scene he was staging becoming more methodical yet also unapologetically theatrical.

The same police protocol was followed as in the case of Mary Hicks. The London PD attended the scene, canvassed the neighbours, and called all the right people. The coroner attended and confirmed death and helped arrange the removal of the body for a thorough autopsy. Once again, the story was the same when the results of the post-mortem examination came back: accidental death resulting from an adverse reaction to prescription drugs. We can only guess today what might have happened if both Mary Hicks and Eleanor Hartwick hadn't by sheer coincidence been on similar medications. We can only wonder if these first two crimes would have not then been properly identified as homicides, if a serial murder investigation might have started sooner, and if the lives of subsequent victims might have been saved. But in 1974, no one saw fit to challenge a pathologist's report, least of all a police officer concerned about rocking the boat—in other words, committing career suicide. The Mary Hicks and Eleanor Hartwick suffocations certainly had no clues at the scene to justify any objections to the official findings, and no cop in his or her right mind was looking to unnecessarily add more murders to the ballooning list if they didn't have to. Dennis Alsop was by then also sequestered away in Toronto, and operations in London and area were at that point, for the most part, on autopilot.

## MURDER CITY

# VICTIM: SUZANNE MILLER, AGE 26

On the afternoon of Saturday, October 12th, 1974, the body of 26-year-old Suzanne Miller was found in a forested area in the town of Thorndale, not far from where Scott Leishman was last seen alive during the spring break of 1968. Suzanne, a mother of three who had been living on Gammage Street in London near the city's army barracks, was last seen nearly a month earlier, on September 15th, leaving her apartment parking lot driving her unmistakable blue Datsun. That same car was then found abandoned eight days later, September 23rd, in the parking lot of the Argyle Mall, located near the city's eastern boundary. By way of eerie coincidence, Suzanne—like Jackie English before her—was also working at a Metropolitan Store at the time of her death.

Early on, a missing person file was opened by the city cops but soon vaporized when, as usual, the woman's body turned up in the brush out in the counties. Officially, it would now be an OPP case. The cause of death, again reminiscent of the Jackie English murder, was determined to be severe head trauma from some type of tool or other metal instrument, with one key exception: the body was clothed and there was no indication of sexual assault. All evidence was that Suzanne had been killed elsewhere and then transported to the brush solely to be concealed there—to postpone its inevitable discovery. A forensic examination of the victim's Datsun came back clean and confirmed that there was another crime scene somewhere else, likely in another car. With the absence of a sexual component suggesting that her murder was likely a personal-cause homicide, the investigation rightfully turned—as with all personal-cause killings—to motive. The problem was that no one could find a remotely plausible reason anyone would want to kill the young mother who, as with so many of the other London victims, appeared—on the surface at least—to be an unlikely target. Then, at a funeral home back in London the day before Suzanne was scheduled to be buried, there appeared to be a new lead.

On the afternoon of October 20th, a dishevelled-looking wretch walked into the Evans Funeral Home on Hamilton Road in East London and signed the condolence register. There was something inherently unusual, and even suspicious about his uneasy presence, not to mention the fact that no one recognized him. The balding man, with a drawn-out and time-worn face and reeking of Southern Comfort, stood pensively over the casket and then left $20 in cash as a donation towards flowers for the funeral service. As he was shuffling out through the lobby, a mourner approached and made a comment to him about the sizeable donation. The mystery visitor, against an ambient soundtrack of pre-recorded organ music, claimed to be a friend of Suzanne's before then disappearing onto the street. When Suzanne's family checked the register, the only clue to the man's identity left in writing mirrored the brief words uttered at the visitation. He had signed the register as simply, "a friend."

The next day, investigators from the OPP and London PD Persons Squad attended the funeral service and tried blending into the small crowd, hoping the same man, now considered a person of interest, would return and could be formally interviewed and his details checked out—he failed to show. The man, it was thought, could have been a friend as he stated and merely chosen not to leave his name. He could have also been something more. A month after Suzanne's body had been discovered, and two weeks after she had been buried, the OPP nonetheless elected to go public with a reward of $5000 and a newly created composite drawing of the mystery visitor to the funeral parlour. The reward posted in Suzanne's case, like the many thousands of dollars in reward money still unclaimed in other London and region cold cases, sat idle in escrow for years before eventually being retracted. The composite drawing also failed to yield any substantive tips and today exists only in the *London Free Press* archives or in various online versions uploaded by historical collectors and armchair sleuths. Perhaps he was in fact a friend as stated; perhaps he was somehow involved in Suzanne's murder. Then again, perhaps he was one of the countless taphophiliacs hiding in plain sight in London at the time, one who decided, for whatever reason, to crash the visitation but not the funeral proper. No one will ever know for certain.

## VICTIM: IRENE GIBBONS, AGE 66

By the summer of '75, Dennis Alsop, now a *Chief* Inspector in Toronto, was tasked with personnel issues, drafting memos, and putting out public relations fires all over the province—but he was still working his old London files in secrecy. For many years, Dennis had been accustomed to working with the London Police and its ranks of detectives, especially after inheriting most of the city's unsolved sex murders post-1963. Following his having been parachuted into an office in Toronto and taken out of the rotation he was still teletyping decent leads to the Strathroy Police-OPP task-force working the Barksey job. The first name that Dennis offered up for further investigation—rightfully so given the severe nature of the mutilations—was David Pullin. It turned out that Pullin, like the Neighbour and other Londoners before him, was at the time of the Barksey murder actually enjoying the perks of the province's drive-thru psychiatric rehabilitation system in order to avoid police questioning on unrelated matters, and by a pure fluke had an iron-clad alibi for the night in question. Watching from a distance, but still personally invested—if not consumed—Dennis had of course seen this all happen before, down the road in London. Even with Pullin ruled out, he knew that Barksey was likely just the beginning, and that other murders would soon follow. He knew that the Barksey murder had opened the floodgates. He was right, again.

On the hazy morning of Thursday, July 31st, 1975, 66-year-old lifelong Strathroy resident Irene (Frances) Gibbons walked from her modest red bungalow on Keefe Street, where she lived alone, to the local Foodland grocery store on nearby Front Street to complete her weekly shopping. Making use of a long-since bygone service, Irene selected the groceries to be picked from the shelf and later delivered to her door for free by the store's attentive staff. She arrived home from the store just after noon that same day and spoke briefly to a friend on the telephone. After that, no one knows what happened.

Within the hour, a Foodland grocery boy attended her home as per usual and rang the bell to hand Irene her week's supply of goods. After not getting an answer at the door, the boy left the paper bag of meat and produce on the stoop and headed back to the store. The following Monday, August 3rd, a newspaper delivery girl attended the same door only to find the fly and ant-ridden Foodland grocery bag oozing out onto the concrete stop. The bag had been untouched since being left there. Inside, Irene's dog howled relentlessly. The delivery girl alerted the local police who, given Irene's age and the fact that she lived alone, rightfully thought that some kind of medical distress might have befallen the reserved woman. With the front door to the home subsequently forced open, the uniformed officers on scene entered to find something they had only read about in the London media reports of the Tissue Slayer from the previous decade.

The modest home of Irene Gibbons as it appeared in August, 1975 following the discovery of her body bound and gagged inside, her apparently having been ambushed and killed within minutes of returning home from a mid-day grocery errand. Courtesy: Western University Archives.

Lying posed on her back on the linoleum floor of the kitchen, Irene had been dead since the previous Thursday afternoon. Her eyes were still open and a wad of rags, stockings, and other fabric was jammed into her mouth and down her throat. There was no evidence of forced entry. The victim was still fully clothed, and there was no sign of a struggle whatsoever. Whoever did this, investigators soon realized, either talked their way in through a back door or—more disturbingly and probable—was already waiting inside the house when she arrived home from the grocery store. Her killer had applied restraints made from expandable nylon to her limbs, not unlike the same stockings found in her mouth. The fastenings around her wrists and ankles weren't simple granny knots, as one might expect from a panicked burglar or drugged-out amateur; they were elaborate and tightly fastened restraints made by someone who no doubt had done this before. As the equivalent of handcuffs and manacles fashioned from synthetic fabric, the ligatures would have completely incapacitated the terrified woman who, it seems, had otherwise complied with the intruder's demands. He had no doubt told her, as the police later speculated, that the motive was robbery. Her killer likely explained to her—as Dennis Rader, the "Bind-Torture-Kill (BTK) Strangler" told his unsuspecting victims around that same time in Wichita, Kansas—that he needed to bind her, take some money, and be gone. Like most trapper-oriented killers, the BTK Strangler included, this was merely step one of a more sadistic plan.

At some point after tying up and rendering Irene helpless, the killer then fastened another piece of nylon around her throat and tightened it like a tourniquet until her airway was slowly closed-off. The ligature, tied tight with its own elaborate knot, was still bound around her throat when police found her. The stockings stuffed into her mouth, it seems, were placed there while being strangled—overkill to the point of its being more expressive and paraphilic than functional to the crime. The scene as a whole was indicative of a process-focused offender rather than an act-focused one. We can thus better understand today, despite the absence of an *obvious* sexual assault, that the home invasion murder of Irene Gibbons has all the markings of a sadistic sexual homicide. It is one that, minus what most closely fits a category 3 rape, is remarkably similar not just to the MO of the BTK Killer but also that of Carlton Gary, "the Stocking Strangler," who used pantyhose to strangle elderly women in their homes in Columbus, Ohio in the fall of '77. While there is no indication that Gary ever travelled to Canada, the elaborate procedure and specificity of the MO and signature in the Gibbons murder, from the unforced entry to the precise fastening of the bindings and paraphilic use of the gags, suggests that in the intervening forty years some variation of this crime has repeated itself somewhere—has been carried out in some other city by this same killer. In other words, Carlton Gary is likely not the only "Stocking Strangler" with an elderly preferred victim to have gone serial in the late 1970s. To this day, Irene's murder remains open, unsolved, and officially inactive.

## VICTIM: LOUISE JENNER, AGE 19

In the fall of '75, now over eighteen months after the murder of Judith Barksey, and a little over one month after the home invasion slaying of Irene Gibbons, tiny Strathroy would get rocked again. On the afternoon of October 20th—a year to the day after Suzanne Miller's funeral visitation and the appearance of the mystery mourner who was never identified—19-year-old homemaker and new mother Louise Jenner heard a knock at her front door. What happened next remains unclear, but it would seem that, unlike Judith Barksey, Louise was specifically targeted and knew her attacker.

At 5:00 p.m. that evening, Louise's husband came home to find his young wife lying in a pool of blood on the kitchen floor and their baby daughter upstairs crying in her crib. Whoever Louise let in to the house had quickly overpowered her, raped her, and then, it seems, allowed her to redress herself. It was apparently little more than a ruse to make her think that she might be spared. In reality, the assailant was simply using the additional time to plan what to do next. Impulsively, he pulled out his boot-lace, slipping it like a noose around her neck and strangling her unconscious. As she lay on the kitchen floor defenceless, much as he had done with Judith Barksey, the intruder proceeded to slash her throat from ear to ear with a jackknife. As quickly as he managed to complete the task, he was gone. No evidence was left behind, and there were no suspects. Again.

# HUNTER'S MOON

The third week of October 1975 was a period coinciding with what's known as the Hunter's Moon. The Hunter's Moon is a full moon, appearing in October following the autumn harvest and after the fields have been reaped, associated in myth and lore with everything from lunacy to lycanthropy—the reported appearance of werewolves. As events of the previous couple of years had either shown—or were about to show—there were also two new hunters operating simultaneously in London's metropolitan area, albeit with different tactics. This was, of course, in addition to the (at least) four other contemporaneous killers, based on current linkages, who were still at large at the time. Just as with some of the city's previous serial offenders, including the two or more killers who, for years, were erroneously linked as a single "Tissue Slayer," it seemed as though each man was keenly aware of the other's existence.

As police—London PD, OPP, and now also the Strathroy cops—were all largely without the direct assistance of Dennis Alsop, they did their best as a combined force to close ranks. They soon realized that, at the very least, many if not all of the Strathroy slayings were connected. What they didn't yet know of was the even larger threat that was looming back in downtown London. One of the two hunters was what is now known as a hedonistic-lust killer, based on the current Holmes and Holmes (previously the Holmes and De Burger) serial offender classification system. The other was an unprecedented visionary-lust killer who, by the fall of '75, was also beginning to experiment with necrophilia. With both still at large and unidentified, the late 1970s in London and across Middlesex County would mirror the same horror and confusion of the second half of the previous decade. Unfortunately, it would take many more victims before the most recent set of killers began to slip up and make the necessary mistakes that ensured their eventual capture. It didn't help that medical experts were misreading murders and that police forces, while ostensibly cooperating on joint investigations, were still not always showing all their cards. It might be fair to say that no one really knew, had much interest in knowing, or had the necessary tools to know what was really going on in London's backyard at the time. It was a debilitating alloy of apathy and denial unique to the Forest City which allowed both killers to simultaneously experiment and escalate with relative impunity. Within the next year, "The Mad Slasher" and "The Bedroom Strangler" would become the greater Forest City's modern iterations of the ancient lycanthropic myths—the real werewolves of London.

# -CHAPTER 7-
# THE SLASHER AND THE STRANGLER: 1976-79

"All of a sudden I am climbing balconies. I have strength beyond me… if I lose my grip, it doesn't matter."
–Confession of Russell Maurice Johnson, "The Bedroom Strangler"

# MOVING THE NEEDLE

It wouldn't be until the mid-1980s, in the wake of the abhorrent child murders committed by Clifford Olson, known as the "Beast of British Columbia," that talk of an integrated database for tracking serial homicides and other violent crimes started to gain traction in Canada. The idea of a centralized system that could flag potentially connected crimes across multiple jurisdictions through a standardized process of signature analysis was first conceived in the United States and was initially inspired by the investigation of Harvey Glatman as far back as the late 1950s. By 1982, the Violent Criminal Apprehension Program (ViCAP) was in development by the FBI and went live in 1985, with the hope that a standardized system of objective scientific analysis could do what individual cops scattered across the country, and looking only at their own files, could not: identify multiple murderers and connect their crimes as they roamed from city to city or from state to state. Since that time, every homicide or other violent crime that occurs in the United States requires that a corresponding checklist of victim, crime scene, and offender characteristics be submitted to the database in the event that individuating variables show up between two or more cases and can in turn reveal previously unknown connections. By way of comparison, Canada's equivalent database, the Violent Crime Linkage Analysis System (ViCLAS), didn't undergo any real development efforts until 1991, and it wasn't until several years later that a fully functional version was eventually rolled out piecemeal on the initiative of a single RCMP investigator, Inspector Ron MacKay, who returned from the FBI Academy aghast at the state of Canadian offender tracking systems.

Today, very little is known—even amongst law enforcement personnel—about the actual successes achieved and linkages made through either the Canadian ViCLAS system or its American antecedent, ViCAP. There are any number of "big fish" stories told in cop bars and at conferences across both countries citing the effectiveness of these systems but, particularly in Canada, there are comparatively few corroborated accounts of crimes being solved or offenders being collared based on prerequisite knowledge gleaned from the system. There are indeed a handful of successes that have been made public knowledge, but not enough it would seem to counter the system's inveterate cynics and critics. This unfortunately includes police skeptics who often treat the completion of the questionnaire as a last-minute and perfunctory exercise, and who still don't recognize its merits. Another reason why police investigators and ViCLAS administrators remain silent on how often it really works, is that to cite even a single success story made as a result of the system would be to allow the public and by extension criminals to peek behind the curtain. To reveal how matches are made and who has been apprehended would allow any enterprising person with an Internet connection or library card to determine, from the available literature, which types of characteristics relating to MO, signature, organization, and criminal paraphilia the police document as part of the 262-question checklist used to feed the system. For would-be offenders, to learn how the information is documented and uploaded to the database by police investigators would be to learn how to defeat it. For this same reason, the RCMP and other police agencies have also refused freedom of information and court disclosure requests from the media and lawyers regarding the questionnaire that investigators are required to complete. ViCLAS is also, like all databases, a garbage-in/garbage-out system where the information uploaded and stored is only as good as the thoroughness of the information entered at source by investigators. Many of these same investigators aren't properly trained on how to look for the information the questions are designed to catalogue, and are in some cases disinterested in learning this same information, treating ViCLAS as an afterthought or additional form of nuisance paperwork rather than as a key investigative tool.

But back in 1976, ViCLAS, for all of its criticisms and input compliance deficiencies, would nonetheless have come in handy. By that time, the London Police were certainly aware of a sexual sadist attacking and mutilating women down the road in neighbouring Strathroy, and that many if not all of these crimes were related, but they lacked an accepted system with which to quantify these linkages. Amongst a number of London officers living in Strathroy or Strathroy cops living in London, the word about a serial killer in London's bedroom community was also the latest water cooler talk at 601 Dundas Street—the new location of London Police headquarters as of January of 1975. The city of Guelph, on the other hand, 75 miles to the east down Highway 401, was well out of earshot. It was, however, well within reach of the man who soon became known as London's "Bedroom Strangler": Russell Maurice Johnson.

By the end of 1975, Johnson had claimed victims in both London and his hometown of Guelph using precisely the same MO. In both cities, all of his murders were declared deaths by natural or accidental causes, ranging from pharmacological anomalies resulting in asphyxiation in London to hardened arteries and a pulmonary edema in Guelph. All of the victims were females who lived alone in low to medium-rise apartment buildings, and all of them were off the police books in just a few days. Only with the discovery of the body of Diane Beitz, in her Drew Street apartment in Guelph on New Year's Eve, 1974, did it dawn on anyone that a motivated killer, as seemingly impossible as it was to imagine, might be able to gain access through an apartment balcony after scaling the building's exterior. Found naked with her brassiere fastened around her throat and hands bound, it was the first time that Johnson had truly lost control and not been able to meticulously stage the scene to throw off police investigators and forensic pathologists. Something had gone off inside him while in Guelph, and there would be no more containing it. By 1976, he would bring those same insatiable compulsions back to London with him.

## VICTIM: SUSAN SCHOLES, AGE 15

As Johnson was safely holed up in his London apartment and putting time and distance between himself and the uncharacteristically chaotic Beitz murder in Guelph, his equally twisted offshoot stalking Strathroy—a mop-haired and mutton-chopped psychotic named Christian Magee—had already come under police suspicion. He was hauled in for questioning by a consortium of Strathroy and OPP detectives in October of 1975 after cops realized that he knew both Judith Barksey and Louise Jenner. But absent a confession, his being a common denominator in a small town where everyone was three degrees of separation from everyone else was all they had, and he was soon free to go. Unfazed by the interrogation, on November 3rd, 1975, he picked up a 19-year-old hitchhiker whom he drove to a remote location, raped, and strangled unconscious before fracturing her skull and leaving her for dead in a ditch. Incredibly, the girl survived and for the first time the police had a description of the man the media and locals had dubbed the "Mad Slasher" of Strathroy.

Learning from his November 3rd attack, Magee escalated his brutality when he picked up 15-year-old Susan Scholes seven months later, on June 15th, 1976. His interrogation by the police had taught him two things: pick random strangers rather than acquaintances as victims, and be sure to never leave witnesses. On that afternoon, Susan was hitchhiking from Strathroy to her family cottage in the town of Hillsboro Beach on Lake Huron. At 1:30 p.m., she was seen by a forklift driver, standing on the side of a county road outside of town with her thumb out. Just over 24 hours later, a farmhand found her partially naked body in a nearby field. Her throat had been cut and she had multiple stab and slash wounds to her chest. She had also had her abdomen cut open in a clear case of erotophonophilic lust murder and what was the most savage mutilation of his victims to date. In Magee's twisted mind, the girl was far enough removed from him and was found far enough outside of town that there was no way the police would look his way this time. He might have been right had the same forklift driver who was the last to see the girl alive not made a quick shoulder check after driving past her. Chugging down the county road at only a few miles per hour, he was able to look back and watch as the girl got into a '75 Ford pickup that he recognized as belonging to a Strathroy man who held the contract for collecting area roadkill. A stop by the man's home-based business by police turned up the truck with the animal filleting knife curiously missing from the vehicle's inventory. The proprietor remembered the name of the man he had hired the previous day to pick up the dead animals, and remembered that he seemed to like the gruesome job a little too much. The man in question was a local down-and-outer named Christian. It was a name that resonated with detectives, and in next to no time the Mad Slasher was in custody. It was the first serial job in London and region to go from the red column to the black column—from open/unsolved to closed/cleared—and while the case was wrapped in record time, it ended somewhat anti-climatically. The Slasher was no criminal mastermind; in fact, he was just the opposite.

## VICTIM: LUELLA GEORGE, AGE 23

As Magee languished in the newly opened Elgin Middlesex Detention Centre in London, awaiting the start of his trial in the spring of '77 for the murders of Barksey, Jenner, and Scholes—as well as the attempted murder of the teen-aged hitchhiker and another attack in 1975—Russell Johnson had once again resurfaced. Already responsible for five apartment murders, and with only one of these murders on the books as a homicide, new victims and an evolving MO would allow Johnson's signature to soon come to the surface and reveal him for what he was.

In April of that year, a 23-year-old, wide-eyed and restless country girl named Luella George was working as a snack bar cashier at Victoria Hospital in London. She had been drawn to the Forest City, like so many others, because of what was often touted as the Goldilocks Effect—not too big, not too small—that for years had made London seem like the perfect way to try out urban living for new generations of agrarian girls looking to reinvent and resituate themselves. Like so many others, Luella also had no idea about just how dangerous the city still was for young women at that time. Less than a year after landing a job and a new life in London, including a loving fiancée, Luella was found dead in the bedroom of her top floor one-bedroom apartment. Like most of Johnson's other murders, he had scaled the exterior of the building with almost super human strength, agility, and fearlessness before slipping in through the unlocked balcony door while his victim slept. With Luella's murder, he had also replicated the MO of his first two London victims, tucking her tightly into bed and staging a peaceful, non-violent scene to conceal what really happened. But once again, he was unable to maintain complete control and felt compelled to help himself to the girl's undergarments before leaving. Had he not surrendered to his compulsions and taken souvenirs of his crime, it might have easily been his fifth kill to go entirely undetected. But when Luella's intimates turned up in a trash can several blocks away, the death was immediately flagged as suspicious and a more thorough autopsy finally revealed the precision of the Strangler's MO, until now overlooked by countless experts.

When Luella's death was confirmed as a methodically executed homicide, a police-issued public warning went out about a nighttime intruder, along with the usual list of safety precautions. Despite this, a connection had yet to be made to the earlier London apartment deaths initially dismissed as accidental, and which had all been near replicas of the latest case. Even with just one *confirmed* victim in London to date, by the summer of '77, the public details were provocative enough to make the Bedroom Strangler the latest London boogeyman, his essentially holding the Forest City to ransom for months. South of the border, that same summer similarly became known as the "Summer of Sam" as New York City lived in continuous fear of serial killer David Berkowitz, the "Son of Sam." An equally psychotic loner on par with Johnson, Berkowitz killed couples in their cars at close range with a .44 calibre revolver because, as he claimed, his neighbour's dog was channelling a demonic entity that told him to. From May to August of 1977, London, like New York City, was a place immersed in justifiable paranoia as its people endured countless hot summer nights with their windows tightly fastened. This included those living on the upper levels of apartment buildings—people who had always thought that they were safe, the walls of their buildings unscaleable by anyone other than a cat burglar or a superhero, and neither of which London had in any great supply. But while Berkowitz revelled in the public panic he had created, and even sent taunting letters to the NYPD and local newspapers in the vein of the Zodiac Killer before him, the media spectacle in London only seemed to enrage and unravel Johnson even further. Before long, the intervals between his attacks became shorter, his nocturnal intrusions more careless. Like Magee, under pressure his compulsions only overwhelmed him further. Before long, he just became sloppy.

## VICTIM: DONNA VELDBOOM, AGE 22

Between May and July of 1977, Johnson gained access to three more apartments, attacking, raping, and either strangling or suffocating women alone in their beds as they slept. But in all three of these cases, the women survived and were able to describe the sequence of events for investigators for the first time. Another three women awoke before they were attacked to find a massive shadowy figure standing above their beds before suddenly vanishing back out through the balcony door and into the night. Others reported waking up in the morning with items in their bedroom moved and the balcony door open, despite its having been closed when they went to sleep. By mid-July, Johnson, in looking to change his point of entry, even tried buzzing one intended victim through her apartment lobby intercom while posing as a London police officer. Sceptical, the woman rang the front desk at the LPD's new digs on Dundas Street and confirmed that no officer had been dispatched there and that no officer of the name provided was even on police payroll. By the time she hung up and buzzed the lobby speaker back to challenge the self-proclaimed cop, her nighttime caller was already gone. Johnson was spiralling out of control and getting reckless. On the night of July 15th, it came to a final climax.

Donna Veldboom, like Luella George, was a country girl with city dreams, and London was the perfect stopover as she made the move from New Brunswick to Ontario in the fall of '76. She quickly found a job as a clerk at the Union Gas building on Commissioners Road and a quaint little one-bedroom apartment in a building on nearby Orchard Street, by eerie coincidence also not too far from the same bus stop where Jacqueline Dunleavy was last seen alive in January of 1968. She had been working at her job and enjoying it for nearly a year when the unthinkable happened.

On the morning of July 16th, 1977, when a consistently punctual Donna failed to show for work, her co-workers got worried and immediately called police. LPD officers were dispatched to her Orchard Street apartment and, on letting themselves in, found a bizarre and ghastly scene. Donna was naked in her bed and had been strangled like all of the others, but the difference this time was that police saw something they might have expected to find from Christian Magee—Donna's having been slashed across the chest in frenzied fashion. Beyond this escalation in violence, it was soon discovered that her killer, after strangling the young blonde, had also taken the time to meticulously and dotingly bathe her corpse in the tub before posing her back in the bed. It later also became evident that the young woman's apartment was cleaner than it ever had been, and that her killer had spent an inordinate amount of time at the scene both polishing and disinfecting the entire premises following the murder. This was more than an attempt to destroy evidence, as the killer, by cleaning rooms and surfaces with which he had never even come into contact, actually introduced rather than eliminated physical evidence. Instead, the deep-cleaning, like the posing and staging, was part of the larger signature—an intrinsic compulsion that the police thought might present itself in other ways during the course of the killer's daily life and relationships, and which might help identify their man.

The prolonged time spent by the killer at the scene also suggested something else to the city detectives who caught the Veldboom file—that only someone familiar with the building and exploiting this geographical awareness would be so cavalier. In a piece of stellar detective work, the cops immediately pulled the building's list of current tenants, and in seeing Johnson's name on the register, recognized it as a name that had also appeared on a list of previous tenants renting in Luella George's building. They dug deeper. It turned out that Johnson was an assembly line worker at the local Ford automotive plant and was recently separated from his wife—a potential psychological trigger for what had been preparatory paraphilias quickly escalating to the attack variety. An amateur weightlifter obsessed with his physique, Johnson trained at the London franchise of the now defunct Vic Tanny's Gym where he was known only as "good ol' Russ." The truth is that Johnson's obsessive-compulsive cleanliness issues had also given way to increasingly violent and intrusive sexual thoughts, with his—at one point—going so far as admitting himself to the London Psychiatric Hospital out of concern that he might act on those thoughts. But like so many others in London and area, once he was supplied with some medications and deemed cured, he was sent on his merry way.

The kicker came when London detectives phoned down to Guelph—Johnson's hometown—and happened to speak with the lead investigator on the Diane Beitz murder, providing him with Johnson's name as a newly revealed person of interest. A check of Guelph PD's records later confirmed that on the night of the Beitz murder, Johnson had been careless enough to report a break-in to his car to the local police. The location where the vehicle was parked turned out to be just around the corner from Beitz's apartment, its window being smashed by some unknown local vagrant while Johnson was raping and murdering Beitz in her apartment a block away. With Johnson being a current or former resident of the buildings occupied by the last two London victims and having parked his car walking distance of the last Guelph victim, located nearly a two-hour drive from his own apartment back in the Forest City, the London Persons Squad had what it needed to make their move.

# THE RIDGE

On the morning of July 28th, 1977, Johnson voluntarily accompanied London city officers downtown for an interview. Within minutes, he broke down and confessed to everything, including the first four murders—two in London, two in Guelph—which the police still had no idea were deaths by anything but natural causes. Johnson also admitted that he had cleaned the apartments of all of his victims so they wouldn't be "mad" at him and that, in all of the murders, the sexual assaults took place after the victims were already dead. In some cases, including in the slaying of Donna Veldboom, he would lie in bed with the sleeping women before he decided to kill them. Sometimes, he would even spoon with their corpses for hours afterwards. Even in a city like London, which had seen more homicidal perversion, paraphilic homicides, and serial killer activity over a compressed time-line than anywhere else in Canada, Johnson was an aberration the city was entirely unprepared to confront.

Like their crimes that shook the London region, the trials of the Slasher and the Strangler occurred in near immediate succession. In 1977, Magee was found not guilty by reason of insanity and sent to the same Oak Ridge facility that had once briefly housed nighttime intruder Sandor Fulep, located in the maximum-security wing of the Waypoint Centre for Mental Health in Penetanguishene. In 1978, Johnson followed suit, being certified insane and sent to the same imposing stone structure, reminiscent of the fictional, Gothic-inspired Arkham Asylum from the Batman franchise. Having terrorized metropolitan London together for so many years, the paths of Magee and Johnson would refuse to diverge, and they would go on to spend the rest of their days together behind the walls of "the Ridge" along with some of Ontario's most infamous sexual predators and serial killers. Magee has since then taken to building baby cribs and preaching the word of God, happily agreeing to meet with researchers, victim advocates, and anyone who will listen. Johnson, on the other hand, has kept a comparatively low profile.

As recently as 2010, the applications of both the Slasher and the Strangler to transfer to medium security have been denied. A 2004 psychiatric re-assessment of Magee confirmed that he still harbours deep-seated erotophonophilic and necrophilic fantasies, which now also include cannibalistic impulses. Johnson remains under control only through the use of Lupron, a potent testosterone-regulating drug that was first designed for testicular cancer patients and is now used to keep sexual psychopaths at bay. Through his long-term commitment to repetitive assembly line work and vintage 1970s Nautilus weight machines, Johnson is also an interesting but often overlooked Canadian case study with respect to mechanophilia, or repetitive "machine fixation" occupations and leisure activities as their own type of preparatory paraphilia. Machine fixation as an occupational and social force in a person's life has also since been shown to be strongly linked with necrophilia—a finding later corroborated through interviews with infamous necrophilic serial killer and cannibal Jeffrey Dahmer nearly twenty years after Johnson's trial. Once again, it would seem as though London set the precedent for what are now considered significant findings in the behavioural sciences and paraphilic research across the world, doing so well ahead of some better known case studies like Dahmer and Gary Ridgway, previously mentioned. With their latest bids for security transfers having been rejected, it seems certain that both Magee and Johnson will die behind the walls of the Ridge—the one place where it seems that "life" really means life. Had they not been declared insane by the courts in 1977 and 1978 respectively, and had instead been convicted of murder and sent to federal prison, both the Slasher and the Strangler would no doubt be on parole and back walking the streets of the Forest City today—no doubt deemed rehabilitated.

## VICTIM: IRENE MACDONALD, AGE 31

By Labour Day of 1978, both Magee and Johnson were safely locked away a three to four hour's drive from London. But while London's protracted equivalent of the Summer of Sam had come and gone, the era was far from over.

That same weekend, 31-year-old Irene MacDonald and her husband Donald Spindler, a bus driver with the London Transit Commission, got into a heated argument, and Irene is said to have stormed out of their London home in anger. The story was suspiciously similar to the one offered by Margaret Sheeler's husband back in the winter of '63, the difference being that this was Donald's second marriage and yet another union that seemed to be going south fast. As in the Sheeler case, once the token 24 hours had elapsed on September 5th, Donald reported his wife missing to the London Police.

In near identical fashion to what played out in the Sheeler townhouse on the Bridle Path nearly a full fifteen years earlier, the police arrived and took a largely perfunctory report regarding Donald's missing wife. Names of some places where Irene might be staying or people to whom she might have reached out quickly led nowhere. As with Glenda Tedball, the months and years began to go by without a word from a woman with no history of running away or erratic behaviour. There were no sightings, no financial activity, and no body to be found. It was yet another London vanishing with no logical explanation—except foul play.

# CORPUS DELICTI

The presence of a body, whether at the time of a reported incident or sometime later, even years later, is not the only proof required to suggest that a missing person or death is inherently suspicious. Although the case of Irene MacDonald is not a case of serial homicide, it usefully demonstrates that a body it not always required for someone to be elevated from a missing person to a murder victim, nor for a prosecution to be initiated.

*Corpus delicti* is a Latin term for "body of crime"—the "body" in this case being the sum of facts and evidence indicating that a crime has actually occurred. Contrary to popular belief, in murder cases it does not indicate the actual recovery of a human body. Although the best evidence in such cases would be the physical presence of a body, the body of available evidence—circumstantial or otherwise—may be sufficient to convince a trier of fact beyond a reasonable doubt that someone is guilty of murder, even though no victim has been found. A frequently cited example would be the presence, at a missing person's home, of that person's identifiable blood in such a quantity that what's known as exsanguination (severe blood loss to the point of death) is the only reasonable inference to draw. The remaining facts and evidence in aggregate, *corpus delicti*, would subsequently determine, in light of such a find, if a homicide prosecution of a particular individual would be warranted.

Admittedly, although a rare occurrence, it is clearly not without precedent to see a murder conviction without the remains of a victim or victims being recovered and identified. John George Haigh, the so-called "Acid Bath

Murderer" of West Sussex in England, was likely the first killer to learn this reality the hard way.

Haigh was a British serial killer who murdered between four and nine victims, always for profit and identity theft purposes. Haigh's MO was to then dissolve the bodies of his victims in oil drums filled with sulphuric acid, believing that, without a body to confirm the offence of murder, he was untouchable. In Haigh's case, the *corpus delicti* made it clear that the victims had been murdered and their assets stolen, even with the bodies obliterated. In August of 1949, Haigh was executed by hanging after being found guilty of murder in just a matter of minutes.

## THREE DECADES ON

That was then. Fast-forward to a cold and grey Friday evening in 2001 when, while working the afternoon watch as a young patrol officer in London, I was tasked with attending the city courthouse underground lock-up to single-handedly relieve the prisoner security team guarding the building's lone remaining inmate. It was an unusual detail for an unusual scenario. The jury in a murder trial was still sequestered and a verdict was expected at any time. Until the verdict was reached, the accused needed to remain under constant guard in the bowels of the building awaiting his fate, but the overtime tab into the weekend for his usual security team was considered too costly. So the decision was made, as it often is in policing, to rob Peter to pay Paul, as they say. In these cases, police departments will often strip a patrol beat staffed by a junior officer and use him or her as a pinch hitter to save on overtime costs by seizing them with a task that is, in theory, still within their job description. Turns out that on this particular date, I was up.

So there I sat, watching the inmate eat his last meal as a free man—a McDonald's Quarter-Pounder combo, brought to him by a lawyer working her first ever murder trial—before his being sentenced to life in prison a short time later. The man was Donald Spindler, his victim Irene MacDonald. The names meant nothing to me at the time—I was an infant when news broadcasts about Irene's disappearance would have first gone to air—but sitting outside Spindler's cell that night, as we waited for the jury to come back, it would mark the beginning of my foray into London's dark history. It would serve as the case that first piqued my curiosity about why and how, so many decades on, the murder was finally being resolved. More interestingly, I would later determine what was *not* yet resolved.

In 1998, after a series of "witnesses" had come forward citing statements allegedly made by Spindler over the previous twenty years regarding what really happened to his wife after their argument—that he had murdered her, poured either lye or acid on the body, and then thrown it in Lake Huron near Southampton—he was arrested for Irene's murder in what would become one of the few cold cases from London's past to ever receive any type of official closure. After the night he and I were first acquainted, Spindler would be convicted for that same crime, in spite of the fact that there was no corpse and only a *corpus delicti* that proved sufficient to convince a jury of his guilt.

George Haigh, the acid bath murderer, found out his fate from the jury following just a few minutes of deliberation. Spindler's jury took much longer—over a day—and as of 2009, the Innocence Project at Osgoode Hall Law School, one of the leading Canadian societies for the wrongfully convicted, has agreed to take on Spindler's case and pursue it to the Supreme Court of Canada. Time will tell what happens next. In London, it always does.

# -CHAPTER 8-
# EBB TIDE: THE 1980s

"There was *another* young London woman murdered, and *still* police are looking for her killer."
–London AM Radio Broadcast, October 14th, 1983

# A NEW ERA

In December of 1979, Dennis Alsop—by that point an acting Detective Superintendent—called it quits. After thirty-four years with the OPP, he had shouldered the burden of investigating countless London area slayings when victims had been either taken or disposed of in his jurisdiction—crimes that in many cases had no precedent in Canada at the time. He also inherited cases that were officially London PD files and which he ran with on his own time—cases he knew were connected to countless others. By the end of his career, he had personally chased at least a dozen killers, including a minimum of five of the as many as nine of the city's serial murderers, and had been chased back. Beginning with the Lynne Harper murder in 1959, and ending with the discovery of Lynda White's remains in 1973—his last official London case—he had been in the trenches for nearly twenty years. He didn't have another decade in him, and he knew—as so few cops do before it's too late—that it was simply time to go. He had incredibly made it out alive and with his health, mind, and original marriage intact. He had beaten the odds and then some—*fait accompli*.

The irony is that Dennis would end his now celebrated career by being left out of the investigations that successfully netted London's last two serial killers of the era—Magee and Johnson—with his being sidelined in Toronto and out of the field rotation. He had initially recommended David Pullin's name to lead investigators in the Barksey murder, given the over-the-top mutilations, but in the end, he knew he had to let his men run their own cases. He also knew there was nothing more in terms of "hands-on" work that he could do while assigned to his final detail, driving a desk in a corner office in some anonymous government tower. The names that had haunted him for so long—names like Jackie English, Frankie Jensen, and Lynda White as his last official investigation—had already become footnotes in history. Police investigative tactics were changing, and the job was no longer what it once was. As police departments were set to become police "services" over the next generation, case men like Dennis were soon to become a comparatively rare breed. As 1979 became 1980, for the first time since 1959 life actually began for Dennis Alsop. It was simultaneously the end of two eras: Dennis's storied life as a cop's cop and after a while, the reign in terror that had dominated London for the last two decades.

As a new decade came into focus and Dennis Alsop began his retirement, the world as a whole had become a very dangerous place—not just in the Forest City. Between cold wars and wars on drugs, high-profile airline hijackings, the rise of mass shootings, the emergence of crack cocaine, and skyrocketing violent crime in all major cities, the entire Western hemisphere was on perpetual edge. In Canada, the national crime rate and crime severity index both began upward swings in the 1980s, cresting in the early 1990s before entering a continuing period of steady decline. Hollywood films certainly didn't help abate people's sense of anxiety at the time—with a burgeoning industry of "splatter" and "slasher" film franchises linking sex and murder (*Friday the 13th*, *Halloween*, *Nightmare on Elm Street*, *Prom Night*, etc.) that came of age in the 1980s all reflecting a new fascination with what was not only a new breed of public enemy but also a new culture industry: the serial killer.

The term serial killer is murky in its origins, but was most likely first coined in German as *sireinmörder* (serial murderer) in the 1930s to retroactively describe the investigation and subsequent arrest, conviction, and execution of Peter Kürten, the so-called "Vampire of Düsseldorf." Kürten was a sadistic sex killer who murdered between nine and sixty victims between 1913 and 1929, eventually making his way to the guillotine in 1931. He was beheaded in Cologne the same year that his biopic, the German film *M*—generally considered the first serial killer film and one modelled on Kürten's crimes—was released in theatres across Europe. It would be another forty years before the term serial killer would enter the Canadian or American imagination, and another fifty years before it had become a standard film-making formula used to perpetuate both fear and fascination.

The first use of the term in English likely showed up in print in 1966, in the obscure book *The Meaning of Murder* as "serial homicide," though FBI special agent and early profiler Robert Ressler, a colleague of Howard Teten referenced earlier in this book, is believed to have begun using the term "serial" in an investigative context in the 1970s. By the summer of '77—the infamous Summer of Sam in New York City—the terms serial murderer and serial killer were both being thrown around interchangeably to refer to the gun-wielding predator later identified as David Berkowitz. Seven years later, by 1984, the FBI publicly announced that serial killers were one of the major domestic threats facing America, and asked the U.S. Senate for special funding to help combat this growing epidemic, which the Bureau claimed at the time was responsible for upwards of 5000 deaths a year in America. Where exactly FBI lobbyists obtained these figures was never clear, but the rhetoric alone, along with some timely and grisly case studies, horrified the Senate and the American public to the point that the requested funding was ponied-up no questions asked. From that moment on, serial killers were a prime mandate of the FBI, and the Bureau henceforth assumed control of the nomenclature and narrative surrounding serial killers, including how to catch them. Hollywood, in turn, assumed control of contouring the public image of serial murder, with the number of major motion pictures depicting serial or sexual homicide as the main plot device produced annually since 1984 having increased in excess of two-hundred percent.

Whether through the FBI's publicity machine, the proliferation of tabloid magazine shows, or the rise of the slasher film, the 1980s was the decade when it seemed the world woke up to the existence of serial killers. As names like Allan Legere and Clifford Olson soon became synonymous with Canadian serial homicide, the reality is that London had been living a reality that the rest of the country—and world—was just finally coming to accept. But as the serial killer "epidemic," as the FBI described it, seemed to be cresting in cities across the continent, in London things finally seemed to ebbing. Yet again, the Forest City seemed to be in retrograde motion against the rest of the nation, forever bucking dominant trends. While London had been a fertile laboratory for largely undocumented criminal paraphilias and a national progenitor to the serial killer phenomenon as later seen in cities like Vancouver and Edmonton, by the time the word "serial killer" became a household term, the city's time in the pole position was curiously coming to an end. But it was a streak that would not end quietly.

MICHAEL ARNTFIELD

# VICTIM: DONNA JEAN AWCOCK, AGE 17

With the onslaught of bizarre sex killings targeting young mothers, teens, and children from the 1960s and 1970s having subsided as suddenly and mysteriously as it began, it seemed London was finally shaking its tragic and horrific twenty-year reign. The early 1980s certainly didn't bring the end of violence to the Forest City, but the murder rate seemed to have stabilized. The London Police and OPP also seemed to be doing a better job at catching killers, which in the early 1980s consisted largely of domestic homicides and team murders—two or more killers operating in league—that all managed to get solved and which saw some degree of public confidence in the safety of the city being restored.

The morning of Thursday, October 13th, 1983 would shatter that confidence. On the previous evening, 17-year-old Donna Jean Awcock had left her ground-floor apartment at 88 Cheyenne Avenue, located at the boundary of the city's eastern limits. Donna, the youngest of four sisters living in a three-bedroom efficiency-style apartment, had kissed her mother Carol goodbye as she usually did before leaving. In fact, everything seemed to be predictably unfolding according to normal that night, including Donna, the preferred babysitter for many local residents, heading out for one of her usual assignments. On that fateful night, she was babysitting for a woman named Michelle who lived on the second floor of the three-story walk-up located just one building to the north of Donna's home. Michelle's balcony and the ground floor patio outside Donna's living room offered a direct sight-line—Carol could literally look out the window and watch over her youngest daughter while she minded Michelle's children. It was through this sight-line that Carol last saw her daughter alive.

Autumn in London, especially October, is a crap-shoot in terms of weather. The city's humid continental climate and lake effect weather can produce remarkable Indian Summers one week followed by freezing torrential downpours the next. On that particular night, the balmy fall weather had been squeezed out by a cold front that brought in temperatures near zero, howling winds, and a driving rain. The normally active apartment complex teeming with tailgaters, children playing in the common greenspace, and residents socializing on balconies had been rendered eerily quiet as people were forced indoors. The sole exception seemed to be Michelle. Wednesdays were, regardless of the weather, her preferred night to attend a local watering hole called the Town & Country Tavern—colloquially known as the T&C.

In the fall of '83, the T&C was rough trade—a honky tonk, kick-n-stab saloon where Michelle was right in her element as a Wednesday night habitué. But while Donna was a hit with the neighbourhood children, Michelle's selection of Donna as her babysitter on Wednesdays was really more a matter of convenience and affordability. Donna lived in the building next door and wouldn't haggle over money—assuming she got paid at all. True to form, shortly after 9:00 p.m. on October 12$^{th}$, Michelle left her sleeping children in Donna's care and boarded a London Transit Commission bus to head to the T&C. When she arrived at the bar, the band was already on stage and Michelle gravitated to a table where she saw some familiar faces through the haze of smoke, including another regular she knew only as Joanne. Michelle quickly ordered her usual poison—rye and water—and then another. Before long, Michelle was half cut and cozying up to a man seated at the round barroom table whom no one else recognized. Michelle assumed he was there with Joanne, while Joanne assumed he was there with the other people at the table. In reality he was there with no one. The stranger turned out to be just that—an unknown troller who somehow made his way to the bar that night and ingratiated himself with the group. Like most of Michelle's suitors, she would never need to know his name or likely worry about seeing him again. He would do for the night. Before long, she was fawning over him while the rest of the table remained unfazed and the band played on.

Back at the Cheyenne Apartments, shortly after 11:00 p.m., Donna stepped out onto Michelle's second-story balcony and made herself visible to her mother Carol across the greenspace that separated the two buildings. No words were exchanged. Donna simply blew her mother a kiss goodnight. Carol reciprocated and went back inside to watch television before turning in for the evening. That was the last time Carol would see her youngest daughter alive. Within the next two hours, what began as a routine night of harmless babysitting would turn into a night of unspeakable horror for the Awcock family, and plunge the neighbourhood, and all of London, into mass hysteria—again.

By 1:00 a.m., Michelle was barely able to walk herself out of the T&C un assisted, the stranger back-strapping her across a floor blanketed in crushed-out cigarettes and bootsauce. The unknown loner, who hadn't exchanged so much as a word with anyone else at the table, also happened to have a car parked directly in front of the bar—a car conveniently available to take Michelle home in her drunken state. To secure such a coveted parking spot on a busy night, the stranger would have had to have arrived at the bar much earlier than anyone else, yet no one ever seemed to take note of the make or model as they saw him pulling away with Michelle riding shotgun. Exchanging drunken small talk, they drove to a nearby pizzeria and the stranger bought a full pie with half a dozen slices. The clerk who served them, like the patrons at the bar and Michelle herself, also never noticed anything memorable about the man or his car. Nothing stood out—not then, not now.

Upon their arrival back at the Cheyenne Apartments around 1:30 a.m., what exactly happened has remained the fodder of local folklore for decades. Michelle would later claim that she told the nameless suitor to wait in the car while she relieved her babysitter, and that she would later signal him to come in. The reasoning behind this is puzzling, as Michelle had no sterling reputation to preserve. To conceal from Donna that she had brought home a man from a local bar was not in keeping with Michelle's usually shameless behaviour. Michelle would later insist that she returned to the apartment alone and that she last saw the stranger in his car as it sat idling in the parking lot outside. Michelle would also later claim that she and Donna had sat and talked for upwards of thirty minutes, finishing what remained of the pizza and smoking the last of Michelle's cigarettes. She even claimed that, at one point, the stranger knocked on her door, antsy for an update on the status of their hook-up. How the stranger would have known what unit to find her at, given that she never told him her apartment number, was never explained. When challenged by police about this bizarre and largely unbelievable sequence of events, Michelle agreed to a polygraph examination that in 1983 yielded inconclusive results. A follow-up polygraph test in 2013, as part of the research for this book confirmed that Michelle was in fact being truthful, including with respect to what happened next.

Within minutes of the stranger apparently moping his way back to his car in the drizzle outside, Michelle made one more request of Donna before she paid her for the night. She handed Donna a ten-dollar bill and asked her to pick up a new pack of cigarettes at the variety store in a nearby commercial plaza—one that was located less than 100 metres away, effectively within the apartment complex itself. Most teenagers, at now nearly 2:00 a.m. on a school night, would reject such an idea, but Donna was a pleaser. She dutifully took the money, left Michelle's apartment, and descended the stairs to exit out the east door of the building into the common greenspace. She walked directly past her own ground-floor apartment, by then shrouded in darkness, to the 24-hour convenience store located just a stone's throw away. The path taken also brought her directly past the parking lot for the building, where Michelle had left the stranger and where, based on her account, he had returned just minutes earlier after she shooed him away. Whether the stranger or any other person had any contact with Donna over this 100-metre stretch remains a mystery, but it was later confirmed by the store clerk that Donna made it to the shop to purchase the cigarettes. A second witness in the store—one who knew Donna by name—would later describe her as looking terrified and as though she had been crying. When asked if she was all right, Donna just stared blankly at the witness before walking back out into the rain.

Back at Michelle's apartment, neither Donna nor the stranger from the bar ever returned. Michelle passed the time by drunk dialling some people on her rotary phone, but eventually grew tired of waiting for her beloved smokes. She then made the trip to the store herself, using the money that should have been Donna's babysitting wages to buy a fresh pack of menthols. Assuming that she had simply changed her mind and gone home, Michelle planned on taking the matter up with Donna the next time she saw her. The truth is that, by the time Michelle was staggering her way to the convenience store to buy the cigarettes herself, Donna was already dead.

At dawn, Carol went to Donna's room to wake her for school, but on this particular morning, she found the bed ominously vacant. She then roused a still half-drunk Michelle by pounding on her apartment door to see if perhaps Donna had spent the night there. When Michelle told Donna's mother about the unfinished errand run, Carol's motherly intuition told her that something had gone horribly wrong. In trying to report Donna missing to the London Police, the Awcocks received the same retort that so many London families had before: Donna needed to be missing for 24 hours before she was *technically* missing. Like the White family did back in 1968, the Awcocks took matters into their own hands and organized a search party from within their own East London community. Parents for whom Donna had babysat, and their children who loved Donna, all pitched in and scoured the area, checking every nook and cranny of the neighbourhood. Two boys knew better. They knew exactly where to find Donna, though there have been varying accounts as to why.

In 1983, what is now Kilally Road in the City of London was at the time the 4th Concession Road in London Township—the same rural area where Robert Stapylton's body was found in the summer of '69 and from where Soroya O'Connell had vanished the next year. The concession butted-up against Clarke Road as the city's eastern boundary and was actually the closest main road to Donna's apartment complex. At the dead end of this concession in 1983, the paved road ended and turned into a private dirt lane leading to a clearing at the base of one of three dams located along the city's iconic Thames River. On any given day, the clearing where that path ended served a hodgepodge of purposes, all of which classify it as a known vice location by current criminological standards: an illegal dumping ground, a rendezvous point for extramarital assignations and prostitutes to turn tricks, and a refuge for reefer madness. There is no evidence that Donna, as a perpetual homebody, ever travelled to the site, but the boys who ventured there looking for her claimed she had been there previously, a reason that drew them to the location as part of their search. Using a dog owned by one of the boys, they proceeded to the clearing but found no sign of Donna, just the usual rubbish left there by trespassers. But then the dog started to act up and pull on its lead.

The dog led the boys about halfway down a steep embankment leading to a man-made lake, where they could see a solitary figure, pale and motionless amidst the tall grass and weeds in the autumn twilight. They had found what they had come for. While the body was face down, the boys recognized Donna's strawberry blond hair and noted that her pants were removed. While it looked as though the body had been thrown or rolled down the embankment with the intent of its ending up in the lake below, it had become hung up on some brush about halfway down. The trio ran to a nearby farmhouse where the police were called. Both the area residents and the police would later claim that the boys simply found Donna's body "too fast" and that they must have somehow known where to look—must have somehow been involved. The boys were, for a period, considered strong persons of interest for this very reason, later being cleared as suspects only after providing voluntary DNA samples once the technology became available. While they may not have killed Donna, there are some who still believe that the boys had been counselled as to where to find the body and told to go there before anyone else did. But while the teens seemed to find Donna's remains with suspicious swiftness and efficiency, it would be some time before police showed up, with the body recovery site going unguarded and unsecured for hours.

Police search the tall grass along the London city boundary of Clarke Road following the disappearance of Donna Awcock on October 13th, 1983. Donna was later found dead in a nearby ravine immediately to the east, once again in OPP jurisdiction. Courtesy: Western University Archives.

## HOT POTATO

While in the 1960s and 1970s, most of London's victims who were deposited outside the city and in the jurisdiction of the provincial police were well outside the city proper and immediately became part of Dennis Alsop's workflow, Donna's body was left in what might be best described as the disputed zone. Located only a few hundred metres beyond the city's eastern boundary—about three times the distance Donna walked to the convenience store just hours earlier—securing the crime scene would be delayed as brass with the London Police and OPP bickered over exactly whose case it was. The truth is that neither wanted it, but there was no clear policy in place to help conciliate the dispute. Donna had been reported missing to the city police but no official report had been taken, and while technically found in OPP territory, it would be logistically easier for the London Police to attend in order to at least maintain continuity of the body and any potential evidence. But London bosses knew that it wouldn't be that simple, and that attendance at murder scenes couldn't be done in half measures—if you were in for a penny you were in for a pound. As the two forces played hot potato with the case, Donna's family waited with unspeakable anguish for confirmation of the body's identity as the autumn rain returned with a vengeance and began to wash away the evidence.

The debate over which agency would take the lead in recovering Donna's body and assume carriage of the investigation would serve as an omen for the way the case would slip through the cracks for years to come. It would also serve as an early example of the type of bureaucratic bickering over jurisdiction in hopes of dodging unwanted cases that endures to this day between the two departments. Suicide jumpers, for instance, who leap to their death from an overpass located within the city, like the one Jackie English never made it over in 1969, and then land on the highway below are a common example. The overpass that serves as their platform is located in London's jurisdiction, but the impact that kills them is located in the OPP's jurisdiction. If the intent is made in one jurisdiction and the effect realized only seconds later in another, who lands the unwanted and messy investigation? It seems like a question suitable for a law school exam or philosophy dissertation, but in reality, the answer still seems to vary depending on the day. On October 13th, 1983, it was at last decided that it was the OPP's turn, and sometime before midnight, officers were finally on scene to take ownership.

Despite many initial oversights in the investigation, considering the time elapsed and challenges of the outdoor scene and inclement weather, the forensic work done in Donna's case was truly exceptional, even by today's standards. It's unfortunate that few other areas of the investigation managed to show the same level of commitment or diligence. For one, no neighbourhood canvass was conducted to determine who might have seen Donna along that fateful 100-metre walk back to Michelle's apartment or who might have been lurking in the parking lot when she exited the store. Had proper neighbourhood interviews been conducted, investigators might have realized that the man living across the hall from Michelle, and who was drinking with Michelle's delinquent brother that same night, was a fugitive sex killer from Tennessee on the FBI's most wanted list. Operating under the alias Joe Tripp, Michelle's neighbour was actually Joseph Alvin Shepherd, on the run since breaking out of a county jail in 1978 where he was being held on murder charges for the sex slayings of two teenaged girls. It wasn't until the premiere episode of the

NBC series *Unsolved Mysteries* in 1988 that a Cheyenne Apartments resident recognized him and called authorities. Initially a promising lead, Shepherd was later extradited back to Tennessee by U.S. Marshals where a DNA sample eventually ruled him out as a suspect in Donna's death.

Even Michelle herself wasn't tracked down by the OPP until a full six days after Donna's murder, by which time she was claiming that she had no recollection of the man who brought her home. Nonetheless, she was made to meet with a police sketch artist—the Identi-Kit having been shelved in favour of a hand drawn facsimile in this case—in hopes that it might help identify and locate the stranger as the lone person of interest. Michelle in turn played a game in which she provided an elaborate description to the sketch artist, a description she would later confirm she "just made up" as she went along, since she had been too blackout drunk to remember what the stranger actually looked like. The same sketch artist also met with Joanne, the comparatively sober T&C regular who was at the same table that night and who had a very clear recollection of the man. The descriptions—one genuine, one fabricated—were so dramatically different that investigators decided to create a mash-up drawing with features taken at random from the contradictory descriptions. Michelle's description of the hair would be used, Joanne's description of the nose would be used and so on. The process used in determining whose description of what identifying features would be consolidated in the final version was never clarified and the OPP have refused comment on this otherwise unheard-of tactic of going public with a mash-up composite. Not surprisingly, when the image was disseminated as an accurate likeness of the "Mystery Man" in an attempt to solicit tips, nothing materialized. The sketch was not of the Mystery Man or even of a real person; it was an artistic alloy drawn from divergent descriptions, one of which was later admitted to be pure fiction.

Left: The 1983 blended composite drawing of the "Mystery Man" last seen outside the Cheyenne Apartments on the night of Donna's murder. Right: The revised 2013 version created from the recollection of the lone sober and credible eyewitness using contemporary digital technologies. Courtesy: Ocean Entertainment.

Over thirty years later, the Mystery Man, like "The Degenerate" wanted in connection with Susan Cadieux's 1956 slaying, has never been identified and seems to have vanished without having ever resurfaced. Referring to the case as "very frustrating," the OPP—four years post-Dennis Alsop—were initially very contrite in publicly stating that their experiment with the sketch hadn't yielded any substantive tips. In spite of the physical evidence at the crime scene—a semen sample, a partial fingerprint, and some fairly clear discriminators in terms of disorganized offender characteristics that included stealing the cigarettes Donna bought at the store—the case went cold relatively quickly. By the time Halloween rolled around, just over two weeks later, other stories were eclipsing news of Donna's case. Soon her once-recurring photo, as well as the sketch of the Mystery Man, was pushed below the fold and eventually to the back pages of *The London Free Press* as the case fizzled and new crimes took centre stage.

## "WHO KILLED ME?"

In recovering Donna's battered body, once an OPP forensic team was able to erect a tent over the scene and bring flood lighting equipment down the slippery embankment, they began the methodical process of examining the girl's remains for evidence. Donna's body had come to rest in an awkward position, with one arm tucked beneath her torso, one arm at her side, and her legs together. Her shoes were removed, but her ankle socks remained intact. Her face had been battered and she had been manually strangled, either during or immediately following the act of forced intercourse. While the recovery of her body was in itself horrific, once Donna's body was turned over, investigators saw something truly startling.

Still protruding from Donna's mouth was an orange synthetic object that crime scene investigators soon realized was a plastic Halloween bag, presumably designed for use by a smaller child for trick-or-treating. With Halloween just over two weeks away, and given that the killer had access to a car, one needs to ask a simple question: what grown man would have a children's trick-or-treat bag stowed in his vehicle two weeks before Halloween? It remains, along with the crime scene behaviours, one of the best non-biological leads in the case.

Investigators at the time were also able to recover a partial patent fingerprint, believed to be that of the killer, from the portion of the bag visible outside of Donna's mouth, though it's unclear if recent advances in what is known as vacuum metal deposition (VMD), have been applied to the same exhibit, still in the custody of the OPP. Such a procedure could in theory enhance that partial print so that it could be searched against the Regional Automated Fingerprint Identification Access System (RAFIAS), Canada's dominant digital fingerprint database. What is also unclear is why the bag was left protruding from her mouth when Donna's body was finally moved from the ravine dump-site to a metal table at the morgue for her family to identify her. When the lead investigators and pathologist pulled back the white sheet to reveal the body of his youngest daughter, Donna's father was forced to see the plastic bag still stuffed in her mouth. Almost every night for the following years, and until his death at an unusually young age from a combination of illnesses, Donna's father would wake up in the middle of the night screaming "It's her!" as he relived that morgue identification process again and again as part of a recurring nightmare.

Investigators had promised Donna's father, while still tormented by these dreams, that they would solve his daughter's murder before he died. They failed. In the years after his death, Donna's older sister Tammy has followed his lead and has remained relentless in keeping the story in the public eye, by circulating the composite of the Mystery Man, taking out ads in the newspaper and on London and area billboards, and circulating bumper stickers bearing Donna's photograph and emblazoned with a simple appeal: "My name's Donna Jean

Awcock, do you know who killed me?" Over the years, a variety of OPP lead investigators, who assured Tammy like her father before her that the investigation was still active, would come and go, but there was never any news—good or otherwise. At one point, Tammy was unable to get a phone call returned for upwards of nine years until a shuffling of management led to some renewed enthusiasm in the years after 2000. By then, the advances in DNA and an increasing public interest in cold cases (largely the result of some television programs and the way the Internet and social media began connecting people like Tammy with the families of other victims) also renewed public interest in the case; so did the offer of a $50,000 reward that, like so many others in London's history, remains unclaimed.

## TIES THAT BIND

The recovery site of Donna's body, near a local lovers' lane but with crime scene behaviours that suggest the killer isn't properly socialized and thus wouldn't have normally frequented such a location with a consensual participant, tells us a great deal about his mindset. It suggests that Donna's murderer—like so many other offenders in London and elsewhere who instinctively bring victims to known vice locations—was likely a scopophiliac accustomed to watching others at these same types of areas. The decision to transport Donna to such a spot—in much the same way that David Bodemer had transported Georgia Jackson to the Boxtown switchback—instead of a more secluded and anonymous site suggests that this location offered some specific intrinsic value to the killer. This is, in fact, the same way that David Berkowitz, the Son of Sam, routinely prowled for his victims in areas of Queens and the Bronx known to be preferred make-out spots. The MO also bears a strong resemblance to the officially unsolved crimes of the Zodiac Killer and the Monster of Florence, both of whom similarly ambushed victims in known vice locations scouted ahead of time. There are also some clear consistencies between the Awcock murder and the slaying of Jacqueline Dunleavy fifteen years earlier, based solely on surface disposal method at or near known vice locations that reflect preparatory paraphilias that include both exhibitionism and Peeping Tom activity. In simplest terms, anytime you have a killer with a car, and who has the luxury of making decisions about where to transport a victim, these types of locations need to be understood as *never* being random.

Of course, what we all know from cases like the Son of Sam, the Zodiac Killer, and other murderers who target these locations is that they are obsessed with media coverage of their crimes and are also very much aware of the behaviours of other murderers, many of whom they seek to emulate. For this same reason, the other connections between the Awcock slaying and earlier London murders seem artificially engineered. The placement of the plastic Halloween bag in Donna's throat—not unlike the MO and apparent signatures used in the earlier Dunleavy, Jensen, and Gibbons murders—quickly rekindled talk of the Tissue Slayer from over two decades earlier. To this day, rumours still swirl about the same multi-generational killer returning to the city to find new victims and insert items in their mouths post-mortem. Statistically speaking, it would seem to make sense.

With fewer than one percent of all recorded homicides in U.S. history—the nation with by far the highest murder rate and violent crime severity index in the developed world—involving anything being placed in the mouths of victims, whether for instrumental or expressive reasons, the recurrence of the same signature in so many cases in London over such a compressed period would certainly seem to point to a common offender. The truth is, however, that the legend of the Tissue Slayer has actually been more dangerous and detrimental to ongoing investigations than any one murderer, all of it dating back to a single police leak in January of 1968. The Awcock slaying is thus yet another one off, as verified by signature analysis, blood typing, and later DNA profiling, all of which confirm Donna Awcock and Jacqueline Dunleavy's murderers as being two different offenders, albeit with similar preparatory paraphilias and a mixed level of organization.

But in the years after Donna's murder, as some semblance of calm was being restored in London in the late 1980s and its serial killer problem seemed to be diffusing across the rest of the country, there emerged an even more disturbing case of crime scene mimicry that cannot be attributed to any leak or compromise in a hold-back evidence policy. There endures such an obvious case of homicidal tutelage—not so much copycatting as outright instruction and sadistic mentorship—with respect to the sexual murders of boys and male teens, that it is clear that all roads, even after 1984, would lead back to London.

On August 12th, 1989, the body of 16-year-old Jason Franklin was pulled from the waters of Big Otter Creek outside Tillsonburg, just under twenty years since Jackie English's naked body was located by duck hunters at the same location, and just over twenty-one years since Scott Leishman was found there under literally identical circumstances. Like Scott Leishman—remarkably similar in age and general appearance—Jason Franklin had gone in the water fully clothed, other than that his pants were disarranged with the zipper left undone. The cause of the boy's death was also determined to be drowning after he was strangled unconscious and then thrown into the water while still alive but choked out cold. The MO, victimology, and bizarre signature, consisting of the pants being loosely re-fastened and the zipper left down, all matched with remarkable precision what was done to 15-year-old Scott Leishman by the Neighbour in March of 1968, as well as to Frankie Jensen in February of that same year. But unlike in the murders of the previous boys, that were linked to a mysterious white car analogous to the one owned by the Neighbour, this time the 16-year-old victim was last seen on the back of a distinctive motorcycle. It turned out that the driver of that motorcycle had been hunting along the main strip in the nearby beach town of Turkey Point on Lake Erie and down Highway 3 into nearby Port Dover, looking to entice teenagers at random—boys and girls alike—to go for a ride on the back of his Honda touring bike. Jason was a hard-working boy who held a part-time job at Callahan's Beach House on Walker Street in Port Dover, and had somehow ended up at the now defunct Robin's Donuts at the edge of town after work on the evening of August 11th. How the driver of the motorcycle and Jason first made contact, and how the driver convinced Jason to leave behind his own bicycle and get on the Honda to be driven to his death, remains unclear. It didn't take long before police had a name to go with the motorcycle: 55-year-old Robert Maclean Henderson, more commonly known as Robert Bridgewater.

Following Bridgewater's arrest for the murder of the Franklin boy, a twisted and puzzling criminal background came into focus that defied the general understanding of a "sociopath" as Bridgewater was called by a purported expert witness at his 1990 trial. Charged with the first degree murder of Jason Franklin, Bridgewater was also described by forensic psychiatrists as "dull witted," which for much of his life no doubt made him seem less threatening—not unlike David Bodemer, who was once upon a time dismissed as being "not too intelligent" by CNR investigators. In other words, for much of his parasitic existence, Bridgewater was the beneficiary of a perfect cover story that seemed to have everyone convinced he was dumb as rocks but otherwise harmless. Like his contemporary Alexander Kalichuk, he was the proverbial wolf in ass's clothing. By way of disturbing coincidence, Bridgewater also grew up in Aylmer just a few blocks from where Bodemer was living at the time he killed Georgia Jackson, and was for a time similarly able to blend in with conventional society, at one point even being married and fathering a daughter. But following his irreversible onset of offending with children in the late 1950s, Bridgewater—often being convicted under the surname Henderson—would spend the rest of his life either in prison or back living with his adoptive parents. In 1957, he was convicted for sexual assault on a female under fourteen after he lured a small girl into his car. He served four years and then re-offended within just weeks of his release, this time targeting a female over fourteen—a crime that earned him a slightly lesser sentence. In 1965, he attacked another girl, and upon being released in 1970, apparently had no intention of leaving witnesses alive the next time.

On the cold and blustery afternoon of February 23$^{rd}$, 1970, Bridgewater was marauding along some rural roads in Norfolk County near the Hillcrest Cemetery—where Lynda White's remains were later recovered—when he spotted a teenaged girl disembarking from a school bus. He had been hunting the area around Turkey Point and neighbouring Port Dover—his home turf when not otherwise in prison—knowing that after area schools had let out for the day, nearby students would eagerly welcome a ride from a Good Samaritan rather than endure the bitterly cold walk home along blustery rural routes. It was an MO similar to the one used by the Neighbour to lure Frankie Jensen into the car just three years earlier, and on this particular day, a 16-year-old girl got into Bridgewater's warm car for the quick jaunt up the road, thinking he seemed harmless enough. She was wrong. Within seconds of the door closing, Bridgewater produced a knife taken from his stepmother's kitchen and held it to her throat. What Bridgewater was certainly not expecting, given his history of targeting defenceless children, is what came next. The feisty teen smacked the ruddy deviant upside the head and tried to wrestle the knife from him as the car veered out of control on the snowy road. During the struggle, the girl tore part of the horn off the steering wheel and then jumped from the moving car, barrel rolling into an icy culvert, and barely escaping with her life.

When the incident was reported to Norfolk County OPP, a BOLO (Be On the Look Out) alert as it's known was sent out to all patrol officers, asking them to keep their eyes peeled for an older-model sedan with a missing section of steering wheel. The girl also met with a police sketch artist and helped create a hand-drawn composite that went out to the local media. A month later, a keen-eyed OPP patrolman responding to a fight at a nearby tavern happened upon a drunk and disorderly Bridgewater. The officer recognized him from the composite and later saw that his car, found parked nearby, had a missing horn piece. Bridgewater was quickly in custody and later tried and convicted for the Turkey Point kidnapping. Following a June 1971 trial, where his purported girlfriend at the time—a woman named Linda Terry—perjured herself in a futile attempt to alibi him, Bridgewater was sentenced to life in prison.

Left: A 1970 OPP composite drawing of Robert Bridgewater (Henderson) that was circulated following the knife-point abduction of a 16-year-old Turkey Point girl. Right: An aged Bridgewater being escorted from court to prison following his 1990 conviction for what turned out to be, much to the indignation of nearly everyone, second-degree murder in the sexual assault and drowning death of 16-year-old Jason Franklin. It was a crime that recalled the 1968 murders of both Frankie Jensen and Scott Leishman with remarkable and disturbing precision. Courtesy: Western University Archives.

But in 1971, even for high-risk serial sexual predators and sadistic pedophiles with nearly a half-dozen previous rape convictions like Bridgewater, life in prison was yet again little more than a misnomer. So in 1985, he was back on the streets and deemed "corrected" by self-proclaimed experts and patronage appointed officials. True to form, between 1985 and 1989 and while on parole, Bridgewater showed the same type of tremendous criminal versatility accounted for by the PCL-R when assessing clinical psychopaths—all of it going unnoticed by those charged with ensuring public safety at the time. Bridgewater sought to re-brand himself by experimenting with disparate offences that were, for the first time, not always sexual in nature. The result was, when he actually got arrested for crimes such as forgery, theft, and impaired driving, he managed to avoid federal prison time. All the while, it seems as though Bridgewater was just biding his time to commit an attack that had been conceptualized years before, and a collaborative fantasy that dated to the mid-60s or even earlier.

At his latest parole hearing in 2013, Bridgewater—then nearly 81 years old—tried to explain that the murder of Jason Franklin, and the bizarre but individuating signature that matched the murders of the Jensen and Leishman boys over two decades earlier, had been induced by a combination of cocaine use and his affiliation with outlaw motorcycle gangs. It was an absurd attempt at what is known in criminology and penology as "neutralization" that was rejected outright by the parole board, whose members were no doubt also aware that biker gangs loathe sex offenders as much as anybody else—not to mention that their members ride Harleys and not Hondas. In reality, Bridgewater, based on his previous prison stints following attacks on female children, appears to have adopted a practise of sexual polymorphism while in federal custody, not unlike infamous teen and child killer Clifford Olson. In other words, he emerged from prison declared corrected but had really only evolved insofar as his being willing to experiment with secondary victims—boy or girl, adult or child—depending on the opportunity. That said, where exactly Bridgewater learned the customized MO and signature that forever connects his murder of Jason Franklin to the deaths of Frankie Jensen and Scott Leishman in the London area—and other probable murders in the Toronto area—was, for a long time, the real burning question. The answer is now clear. The common denominator is the summer-cottage town of Turkey Point.

Bridgewater kidnapped both Jason Franklin and his 1970 female victim in the general vicinity of Turkey Point and when not in prison, spent much of the time—when he kept a fixed address—living with his stepparents in the nearby town of Simcoe. In February and March of 1968, Bridgewater was still in prison on a 1965 sexual assault conviction when Frankie Jensen and Scott Leishman's bodies turned up in the water—Frankie with his pants unfastened and later removed by debris in the water and Scott with his pants refastened and zipper pulled down. None of these details were, by 1989, public knowledge or printed in any newspaper. It is simply too specific a signature—too paraphilic, iconographic, and even ritualized—to be a coincidence that young Jason Franklin was found precisely in the same way as Leishman in particular, and in precisely the same body of water. Indeed, it turns out that Bridgewater and the Neighbour who killed the Jensen and Leishman boys, and apparently others, had a shared fondness for offending in the teen-friendly beach towns of Port Dover and Turkey Point, the latter in particular. In the summer of '64, the Neighbour, while ostensibly travelling on business, ended up in Turkey Point and was arrested for exposing himself and masturbating in front of a group of children at the beach. That same summer, Bridgewater was briefly out of prison before he was arrested for sexual assault in 1965. While Bridgewater was sent back to the penitentiary, charges against the Neighbour were later dropped for reasons that are still not entirely clear and for which records no longer exist. How the Neighbour ended up in Turkey Point, and how he and Bridgewater might have come to meet and discuss their mutual interests, is a secret he took to his grave with him, and one he was never questioned about. Beyond the Turkey Point connection, remember that when Dennis Alsop went to interrogate the Neighbour in August of 1968, he too was living in Simcoe, immediately near the Bridgewater family home. Before moving to the Toronto area, the Neighbour was still in Simcoe—at the time a town of under 10,000 residents—when Bridgewater was released from prison and had settled back at his family home there. It was all no coincidence.

The Neighbour and Bridgewater, as mutually serial offending, homicidal pedophiles with the sedate Ontario towns of Turkey Point and Simcoe as apparent points of mutual departure and shared intersection suggests that whether in the summer of '64 or at some other place and time thereafter, the signature seen across all three London area murders of Jensen, Leishman, and Franklin was somehow hatched between both men. Given that the Neighbour was never sent to prison for any previous offences rules out their having met while serving time together, as some team killers and other murderous accomplices often do. It's also unclear whether Bridgewater ever made his way to London to offend independently of the Neighbour. Dennis Alsop actually—and rightfully—listed Bridgewater as an early suspect in the murder of Lynda White, once her remains turned up near where Bridgewater had picked up the Turkey Point schoolgirl in the winter of '70. It turned out that dates failed to line up, Bridgewater still being in federal custody on the 1965 "kiddie rape" at the time. Otherwise, it was a good hunch.

With the Neighbour long since dead and buried, I have naturally made repeated attempts to visit Bridgewater at the medium-security "Club Fed" Warkworth Institution near Campbellville, Ontario which he has called home since 1990. I have sought to ask him about his affiliation with the Neighbour, as well as where and with whom the shared signature seen in the Frankie Jensen, Scott Leishman, and Jason Franklin crimes first originated—and what it symbolizes. I have also sought to ask him about the apparent linkages between the unsolved Erik Larsfolk, John McCormack, Simon Wilson, and Tracey Bruney child murders that overlap with this same signature, albeit in the Toronto area. He has refused all of my requests to meet and is, of course, not compelled to accept. After all, unlike his victims, he has absolute privacy rights—as the prison administration likes to remind me. Management at Warkworth has actually gone to extraordinary lengths to keep me away from Bridgewater and shield him from these same questions. As recently as November 2014, I've been placed on the institution's so-called "cancelled" visitor list which disallows me from either visiting him or attending his future parole hearings—in spite of their ostensibly being "public" sessions. Now 82 years old, soon the secret of the water murders and the accompanying signature will be buried with Bridgewater, just as it was with the Neighbour before him. This is the simultaneously haunting and infuriating finality to the Bridgewater-Neighbour saga. Protected by the system to the bitter end just as the Neighbour was, there is bound to be no acceptable closure to this dark era in Canadian crime—one that transcends the boundaries of the Forest City where it all first began.

## - CHAPTER 9 -
# AFTERSHOCKS

"The only thing we learn from history is that we learn nothing from history."
 –Georg W. F. Hegel

# TYPECAST

The Forest City's first official serial killer, the "Lambeth Poisoner," Thomas Neill Cream, claimed his first victim in London, Ontario before moving to London, England and carrying on from there. He also—albeit somewhat conveniently—admitted to being Jack the Ripper just prior to being hanged at the infamous Newgate Prison 1892. Whether his being the Ripper is fact or fiction, Cream's London-to-London connection, in terms of serial homicide, is at the very least a disturbing coincidence. It would in some sense prefigure a future trend, one in which London either drew in or spit out serial offenders of national and even international distinction.

The year 1984, however, was one defined by the city's dubious reign as the serial-killer capital drawing to a close. This is, in part, why Donna Awcock's slaying still resonates with so many today. To some extent, it endures as the punctuation mark on the city's darkest hour. Yet, for years afterwards, London remained an unlikely but sought-after destination for killers, as its reputation—one forged perhaps as far back at the Lambeth Poisoner—continued to linger. Even with a brief respite from the torrent of paraphilic violence that had defined the London of the previous quarter century, 1984 onward saw a number of unusual crimes that live on in infamy. For instance, the slaying of Hanna Buxbaum at a staged roadside breakdown that same year engendered one of the most sensational investigations and trials since the prosecution of Glen Fryer in July 1970. It was ultimately revealed that Hanna's multimillionaire husband, Helmuth Buxbaum, a nursing home magnate with a sweet tooth for hard drugs and prostitutes, had grown restless amid the 1980s divorce boom. His solution was a murder-for-hire scheme orchestrated to look like a botched roadside carjacking. It was the type of contrived murder plot one would expect to find in any number of the Cohen brothers' darkly satirical films about crime, betrayal, and ineptitude. But before long, even the Buxbaum job—on the surface a non-sequitur to the last three decades in London—was yesterday's news and a seemingly renewed trend in random attacks on the city and region's young was resuming.

## REINDEER GAMES

By March of 1988, someone had the bright idea of letting two convicted triple murderers team up while on day passes from the St. Thomas Psychiatric Hospital (now the Southwest Centre for Forensic Mental Care) just south of London. Serial sex killer Paul Cecil Gillis had raped and murdered two teenaged hitchhikers in British Columbia and then another young girl near Midland, Ontario before being apprehended and declared NCR. Some people, including Carleton University historian and freelance journalist Mark Bourrie, who authored the book *By Reason of Insanity*, puts Gillis's unofficial but more accurate body count at closer to nine victims. At the psychiatric hospital, Gillis's new best friend turned out to be Robert Abel, a certified psychotic in custody for slaughtering his wife and two children. On the afternoon of March 31$^{st}$, while still declared criminally insane and yet also somehow working together in unsupervised community placement positions, the two killers hit the road no questions asked. With a sexual serial killer and mass-murdering family slayer teamed up for the first time, they would immediately head to where their murderous colleagues had told them, through the jungle telegraph, the hunting was good: the Forest City. Drinking in the car the whole way, they drove to London to go on a human safari. At around 6:45 p.m., they found a 14-year-old girl sitting atop a Canada Post relay box and waiting for a bus in the same Old North neighbourhood where Robert Stapylton once lived. They quickly snatched the young teen and told her that if she complied and didn't put up a fight they wouldn't hurt her. They were lying.

The two killers transported the girl back to their community placement job-site, where Gillis proceeded to rape her in variously inventive and cruel ways in a darkened office before taking her back to the car where Abel was passed out drunk. The two then drove the girl, barely alive, to the nearby town of Sparta where Gillis roughed her up a little more and then threw her off a bridge into the water below, leaving her for dead. Running late to sign in back at the mental hospital, they peeled off without verifying that she was done for. Unbeknownst to the two men, their victim was revived by the impact with the water, swam to shore, and then summoned the will to crawl over a mile to the closest farmhouse where she broke in and collapsed on the floor. The owners returned after dark to find the young teen in the front parlour, crumpled up and caked in blood, but alive, and called the police. The case was not a tough one to piece together, especially after Gillis turned himself in on the morning of April Fool's Day and confessed. In 1989, both men were finally sent to the penitentiary and in June of that year, Gillis was declared a dangerous offender under what was then seldom-used legislation and jailed indefinitely. Neither killer was from London, nor had they ever lived in London, but both were drawn down the highway by something elusive but infectious—drawn there to hunt and to kill. After 1989, neither one would see the likes of London again, although neither Gillis nor Abel would be the last convicted multiple murderers to follow the trail to the Forest City.

# LONDON CALLING

The very next year it happened again. Like Lynda White in November of 1968, the disappearance of 19-year-old Western student Lynda Shaw on Easter Weekend of 1990 involved the writing of an exam. Also like Lynda White, the Western community was the first to know something was afoul, with word of the disappearance quickly spreading across campus.

Lynda's last confirmed whereabouts, prior to her disappearance, were at a roadside service centre just east of London, along the same stretch of Highway 401 travelled by so many of London's killers before. Travelling back to London from her native town of Huttonville after the Easter holiday weekend to write an engineering exam, Lynda stopped for a fast-food meal sometime around dusk. While inside for only a few minutes, it would seem that Lynda attracted the attention of a sadistic and impulsive mass murderer named Allan Craig MacDonald. Having already been paroled for the thrill murders of a police officer and taxi driver committed in Dartmouth, Nova Scotia thirteen years earlier, MacDonald's release into society and his ability to move largely unsupervised to Southern Ontario again epitomizes the irreparable design of Canada's federal prison and parole system. How and why MacDonald was able to hunt for lone female motorists at rest stops and service stations near London, while living at a halfway house in the city of Brantford, and what initially drew him there that night will never be known. What is known for certain is that MacDonald put a slow leak in Lynda's car tire while she was ordering her last meal at the centre's Burger King kiosk, sabotaging her return home and forcing her into his depraved trap. Lynda's Dodge Shadow was later found by the OPP at the roadside with a flat tire, her bag of food left untouched on the front seat.

In a previously unpublished photograph, classmates from Lynda Shaw's engineering program at Western University wait anxiously at her London apartment for word of her whereabouts after she was reported missing on April 16th, 1990. Courtesy: Western University Archives.

Six days after her vehicle was recovered, Lynda's remains—raped, beaten, tortured, and burned—were located in a wood lot near a gravel road off the highway. The dumpsite, like in the Donna Awcock slaying seven years earlier and the Georgia Jackson slaying in the winter of '66, was a notorious lovers' lane that again reflects a geo-spatial relationship between where offenders indulge their preparatory paraphilias and where they dispose of their victims to fulfil sadistic fantasies cultivated in those same places. Also, as in the case of the Awcock slaying, DNA was left at the scene. Had MacDonald not been in the penitentiary in 1983, he might have actually been a viable suspect in the Awcock case, given the similarities between the impulsive but process-focused MOs and surprise attacks seen in both cases.

In the fall of 1990, after cross-referencing the location of Lynda's murder to paroled sex offenders and convicted murderers in the area, OPP detectives actually stopped in to the halfway house to visit the 300-pound MacDonald who offered an alibi for the night of Lynda's murder. He even volunteered a strand of his scraggly hair for comparison to the physical evidence at the crime scene. Given the nascent state of DNA profiling at the time, and the fact that MacDonald's previous double murder—a cop killing no less—hadn't been sexual in nature, he was bumped to the bottom of the list and the hair never tested as the police moved on in their fruitless search.

But by January of 1994, MacDonald's luck was running out and he found himself up on impaired driving and theft charges relating to a stolen vehicle and subsequent police chase. Looking at the certainty of returning to prison, he elected to take the easy way out and blow his own head off with a shotgun in a Brantford phone booth. Over the following years, the OPP investigated new leads and made public pleas for tips, releasing vetted versions of hold-back information and offering sizeable rewards for anything leading to an arrest. The whole time, the bright co-ed's killer lay six feet underground and the evidence linking him to the crime lay long since forgotten in a drawer in some nondescript OPP detachment office. Then, in 2005 and largely on a whim, the hair was entered into the National DNA Data Bank for comparison, resulting in confirmation of MacDonald as Lynda's killer. Sadly, it would take Lynda's mother leaking MacDonald's name to a reporter with the *Toronto Star* in order for the public to find out. The OPP had provided her with the name of the man who raped, murdered, and set the body of her daughter on fire reluctantly and in confidence, but refused to publicly announce it, citing what they erroneously interpreted to be MacDonald's posthumous privacy rights. The debacle around withholding the name in such an enormous investigation continues to raise questions about the viability of post-mortem *ex parte* trials for those implicated by DNA following their deaths. To this day, everyone in London knows the case of Lynda Shaw, but many people, in part because of MacDonald's name being *officially* withheld, are still unaware that the case has actually been solved.

MICHAEL ARNTFIELD

# PROJECT ANGEL

While it took until 2005 for investigators in the Lynda Shaw case to make full use of the National DNA Data Bank, by the time the legislation that would later become the *National DNA Identification Act* of 1998 was in preliminary discussion, investigators and scientists alike were looking to London as a natural starting point for using new inroads made with respect to genetic profiling. This included how new technologies and biological evidence could be used to solve cold cases. By the mid-1990s, no one had linked Bridgewater and the Neighbour in terms of their identical crime scene behaviours, yet both men would very soon be two of nearly a hundred known offenders or sexual deviants hailing from the London area to come under the microscope of a joint London Police-OPP cold case task force dubbed Project Angel.

The early successes of the Human Genome Project, along with the first successful DNA profile being reported as early as 1984, soon became the driving force behind a combined effort to clear the backlog of unsolved sex slayings from the city's past. Project Angel would require an odd-couple pairing between the two departments that had handled and often fought over cases the first time around—the London PD and the OPP—as cold cases from the city and region were shortlisted based on their perceived solvability. From the 60s to the 80s, most of these crimes on the OPP side were investigated by Dennis Alsop and him alone. In London the cases were officially investigated by rotations of detectives working in the now extinct Persons Squad, but many were also investigated by Dennis off the books. By the mid-1990s, Dennis was long-since retired and Persons was rebranded as the Major Crimes Section—a new speciality unit complete with its own subculture, embroidered crest, and even its own credo: "Don't forget, we work for God!" The naming of Project Angel was no doubt inspired by the same ideology that London investigators were, in some shape or form, the new disciples and doing the work of angels. In reality, the task force was far from deified when it officially began operations in January 1997.

From the outset, there were differing opinions as to which officers were qualified for temporary re-assignment to the project. London still had a number of *current* murders that they were burdened with addressing, so liquidating their existing complement of skilled homicide investigators for secondment to the task force was not an option. Instead, investigators were drawn from a variety of operational and investigative units—sex crimes, intelligence, and even patrol—and were selected for their suitability to work complex cases and conduct investigative interviews, often with what were, by that point, very elderly witnesses. On the OPP side, Project Angel was the perfect clearinghouse for malcontents and a place to hide organizational pariahs from across the province. While some of the provincial imports were certainly motivated and earnest investigators, others who were sent kicking and screaming to the task force included an officer recently off suspension for discharging their service pistol into a bedroom wall while off-duty, an officer assigned to a desk job in Toronto who had never even made a single arrest or investigated so much as a shoplifting case, and a hodgepodge of others who were uprooted from their current assignments and living arrangements for up to three years, and diverted to London by bosses who wanted to be rid of them. It seemed that even before the project got off the ground, the London Police and the OPP could not agree on what quality of officer merited being assigned to such a sensitive and high-profile initiative, one that was in theory breaking new ground in terms of the exploitation of new DNA technology. Project Angel was also competing with Project Millennium for the lion's share of the OPP's talent, the latter being a much larger initiative that examined nearly 200 unsolved murders throughout the remainder of the province, and which netted some high-profile arrests that included cop-turned-serial killer Ronald Glenn West, previously known as the ".22 Calibre Killer."

But in London, with Project Angel serving as a sanded-down version of Project Millennium, and with a mismatched assortment of investigators in terms of skill and experience, DNA (rather than crack detective work) became the focal point of the task force. Eliminating the usual suspects using this new miracle technology not surprisingly became the main objective of the project as the 1990s wound down and the task force officially disbanded in the summer of 2000. Following an initial pie in the sky executive briefing in 1997, eventually only cases with viable DNA samples were prioritized, since after four years of dedicated resources and investigators, clearing books rather than laying charges took precedence. The low hanging fruit—cases where biological evidence was preserved and uncorrupted and could be submitted for DNA testing—seemed the one sure way for the project to yield something to justify its time and expense. In the end, only two of nearly twenty cases were ever cleared by DNA—the killers long since dead and buried.

It was DNA that definitively linked Gerald Thomas Archer to the murder of hotel housekeeper Jane Wooley. The Chambermaid Slayer had previously confessed to the murder of Edith Authier prior to his own death, according to his estranged family, but it was DNA extracted from cigarette butts left at the Wooley crime scene that confirmed that Archer *was* who he claimed to be. After obtaining a court order to exhume the body of Sandor Fulep in Toronto's historic Mt. Pleasant Cemetery, Project Angel detectives were also able to confirm that the out-of-work dishwasher had in fact killed Victoria Mayo—just as he confessed to doing in 1967 when he turned himself over to police in Toronto. It took an announcement by London Police brass in February 2000, in the final days of Project Angel, to confirm that Fulep was right when he said he had stalked and then stabbed the 32-year-old single mother in her sleep over a dozen times in August of 1964. It was curious then that, five years later, when a similarly deceased Allan Craig MacDonald's DNA was matched to the equally brutal murder of Lynda Shaw, the public was kept in the dark about the link. It may have been that Project Angel gambled that any possible rebuke by the Privacy Commissioner was worth the risk to showcase their work to the public. Maybe, in 2005, non-disclosure in the Shaw homicide was a reflection of the fact that, with Lynda Shaw's mother privately notified, the OPP had hoped the rest of the public would have forgotten about the case. Or, at least, that the public would not have to learn of their failure to submit MacDonald's hair sample for medulla testing as far back as 1990, and that it could still be swept under the rug. Maybe it was both.

Strangely, the only London cold cases with living suspects who were charged and prosecuted for any dated murders were tried without any supporting DNA evidence or, for that matter, the bodies of any victims. Besides the arrest of Donald Spindler in 1998 for the murder of his wife, Irene MacDonald, there was the even stranger arrest of a 66-year-old Londoner named Edward Gratton, a friend of the Tedball family when Glenda vanished on the morning of Halloween of 1967. Gratton, a 34-year-old and twice the age of the farmer's daughter when she vanished without a trace, had reportedly also impregnated her—a problem he needed make go away.

Like so many cold cases, it turns out that it would take a deathbed confession to finally reignite interest in Glenda's disappearance, for years rumoured to be the work of some Wiccan cult as part of some Halloween ritual. In fact, when Project Angel began in 1997, Glenda's dusty missing person file didn't even make the short list of cases cherry-picked for re-investigation. But in 1999, when Glenda's mother Norma Poore died, Glenda's father approached police with new information, apparently disclosed in Norma's final days. Before long, Gratton was in custody and charged with statutory rape and culpable murder, crimes retroactively relying on the wordings that were on the books at the time of the initial investigation. Even without a body or a living witness to establish the *corpus delicti*, Gratton himself later corroborated what it seems Norma Poore waited until the last possible opportunity in her life to reveal by way of dying declaration, the most notable exception to the hearsay evidence rule.

The mildly delayed 34-year-old Gratton had apparently been carrying on a secret relationship with Glenda, and her mother discovered the secret of the affair and pregnancy sometime in the fall of '67. Infuriated as well as terrified at the potential public embarrassment in the tiny village, Norma sought an immediate remedy. Gratton was summoned to the farmhouse on October 31st, and in the dimly lit, dirt-floor basement, he bound and gagged his teen lover while Glenda's mother used a coat hanger to conduct a home abortion. The procedure was quickly botched, and when Glenda died from blood loss and shock, Norma's solution was to claim Glenda had disappeared—allegedly having last been seen wandering off into the woods. In truth, by the time police and volunteers were combing those woods, and the local legends had begun to swirl, Norma had buried her daughter's body beneath the basement's dirt floor. For over thirty years, Norma withheld this grim truth from her husband, who woke up every day hoping that, maybe, that would be the day Glenda was found safe. All the while, she apparently lay beneath the family's home until it suspiciously burned to the ground. The cause of the fire and whether this was also part of Norma's plan was never revealed.

Following up on Gratton's account, an excavation of the site where the Tedball homestead had once stood failed to turn up any sign of the girl's remains. The body was not where it was supposed to be and has yet to be found. In November 2000, with no murder having been substantively proven, Gratton pleaded guilty to illegally procuring an abortion and received a conditional sentence to be served in the community. Following the conviction and sentence, a handful of people were outraged and made the usual—and often justified—pontifications about the toothless Canadian justice system and its saddening lack of respect for victims. But the sadder reality is that Glenda's case wasn't even confirmed as a homicide until most people had already forgotten about it. By that point, the happenstance killer—Glenda's own mother—was also dead. For Project Angel investigators, it was a bottom-of-the-ninth win and they would take it, conditional sentence or not—case closed, books cleared, an arrest made, and a guilty plea entered on the record.

With Gratton's copping to his role in Glenda Tedball's death, and with Spindler's conviction in the murder of Irene MacDonald following a year later, Project Angel's work had officially come to a close. Of the original twenty cases selectively earmarked for new investigation, sixteen remained unsolved and uncleared—and still do. Many of the more puzzling cases, with either highly paraphilic or serial identifiers—Jacqueline Dunleavy, Frankie Jensen, Scott Leishman, Lynda White, Soroya O'Connell, Patricia Bovin, Jackie English, Priscilla Merle, Irene Gibbons, and more—weren't examined in any real detail over the course of the project, and many not at all. Using a variety of furtive and innovative tactics, investigators were able to collect a DNA sample from the Neighbour, in hopes that they could also match him to the Dunleavy case (the first "Tissue Slaying"), but they could not. Project Angel detectives even managed to get a sample from Robert Bridgewater while in the penitentiary, using a tactic that is not my place to reveal. Glen Fryer, thought to be the infamous Porn Man, had his DNA collected through public discard without his knowledge, and was once and for all cleared as a suspect for just about everything Londoners ever thought he had done. David Bodemer, on parole for fifteen years by that point for the murder of Georgia Jackson, was never questioned or had his DNA compared to any scene. He was by that time driving a commercial rig all over the country—and doing who knows what else. By the time the lids were put back on the boxes for these cases, once and for all, only about one quarter had been entered in the ViCLAS system that had been running since the early 1990s. None of the cases for which the OPP still had exclusive carriage—Dennis Alsop's career worth of work—had been computerized or placed into the Powercase system, the provincial standard since 1996 for both current and historical homicides. Most still haven't.

# UNLOCKING THE PAST

In examining the twenty-five-year period in which the Forest City became Murder City, through the lens of the current research and our knowledge about relational paraphilic attachments, signatures, and victimology, the linkages that Dennis Alsop once speculated about can now be plotted in black and white and are as plain as day. The victims and related incidents can be consolidated by offender typology based on what's known as the Holmes and Holmes offender classification index, and which has already been referenced in passing in earlier chapters. This taxonomy, while not perfect, provides us with the most effective method for breaking down the era's unprecedented serial violence into categories that reflect the psychological make-up and motivations of London's killers. While at least six serial killers appear to have been stalking London either simultaneously or in immediate succession over the period in question—roughly ten percent of the total number of serial killers in Canadian history—a more detailed review of these linkages also suggests that, whether in London or elsewhere, at least three other killers also went serial following their crimes in the Forest City. This suggests that between the period of 1959-1984, up to *nine* serial murderers either hailed from London or killed at least one victim each there before moving on, as Thomas Neill Cream once did.

## Grouping 1 – Hedonist-Thrill Murders

| Victim & Year | Age/Gender | Offender Organization | Offender Focus | Contact Method | Attack Paraphilia(s) | Preparatory Paraphilia(s) | Rape Category | Offender ID | Other Victims/Serial Indicators |
|---|---|---|---|---|---|---|---|---|---|
| Wooley - 1969 | 62/F | Mixed | Process | Ruse | Sadism | Unknown | 3 | Confirmed | Yes |
| Authier - 1970 | 57/F | Mixed | Process | Ruse | Sadism | Unknown | 3 | Confirmed | Yes |
| Russell - 1970 | 57/F | Mixed | Act | Surprise | Sadism | Unknown | N/A | Confirmed | Yes |

This category reflects the murders of Gerard Thomas Archer that, while containing a sexual component in two of the three cases, were ultimately motivated by the fact that he, like many angry psychopaths, was fixated on using another human to fulfil a pleasure-seeking drive (hedonism) through what he saw as adventurous stimulation (thrill). An interview with Texas hedonist-thrill killer Tommy Sells, after his 2000 arrest for the murders of over 22 people, sums up this typology's motivation most accurately: "I didn't do it for the power; I didn't do it for the sex … like a shot of dope, I did it for the rush."

## Grouping 2 – Hedonist-Lust Murders

| Victim & Year | Age/Gender | Offender Organization | Offender Focus | Contact Method | Attack Paraphilia(s) | Preparatory Paraphilia(s) | Rape Category | Offender ID | Other Victims/Serial Indicators |
|---|---|---|---|---|---|---|---|---|---|
| Mayo – 1963 | 32/F | Mixed | Act | Surprise | Erotophonophilia, Amokoscisia | Crytoscopophilia | 2 | Confirmed | Yes |
| Jackson – 1966 | 20/F | Organized | Act | Ruse | Necrosadism, Odaxelagnia | Exhibitionism, Crytoscopophilia, Partialism | 1 | Confirmed | Yes |
| White – 1968 | 19/F | Organized | Unknown | Ruse | Necrosadism Necrophilia | Exhibitionism Partialism Taphophilia Placophilia | Unknown | Unconfirmed | Yes |
| Bovin – 1969 | 22/F | Mixed | Act | Surprise | Erotophonophilia, Amokoscisia | Crytoscopophilia | 2 | Unconfirmed | Yes |
| English – 1969 | 15/F | Organized | Act | Ruse | Necrophilia | Exhibitionism, Crytoscopophilia, Blastolagnia | 1 | Unconfirmed | Yes |
| O'Connell – 1970 | 15/F | Organized | Unknown | Ruse | Necrophilia | Exhibitionism, Crytoscopophilia, Blastolagnia, Placophilia, Taphophilia | Unknown | Unconfirmed | Yes |
| Merle – 1972 | 21/F | Organized | Unknown | Surprise | Necrosadism | Partialism | Unknown | Unconfirmed | Yes |
| Barksey – 1974 | 19/F | Mixed | Act | Blitz | Erotophonophilia, Amokoscisia, Sadism | Blastolagnia, Crytoscopophilia | 1 | Confirmed | Yes |
| Jenner – 1975 | 19/F | Mixed | Act | Surprise | Erotophonophilia, Amokoscisia, Sadism | Blastolagnia Crytoscopophilia | 1 | Confirmed | Yes |
| Scholes – 1976 | 15/F | Mixed | Act | Ruse | Erotophonophilia, Amokoscisia, Sadism | Blastolagnia, Crytoscopophilia | 2 | Confirmed | Yes |

This category of offender is the most prevalent in London's history, with every crime furnishing behavioural evidence of either previous or future serial offending—whether confirmed or unconfirmed but suspected. This category is closely affiliated with the power-control typology (Grouping 3 to follow), the primary difference being that the hedonist-lust killer is driven by compulsive and overwhelming attack paraphilias, as well as intrusive violent fantasies that inevitably require killing in order to satisfy. The intention from first contact is therefore to murder the victim. The paraphilias tabled here include preparatory acts that are either known to be correlated with the attack paraphilias seen with respect to the murders themselves, or which reflect either known or suspected earlier behaviours of specific individuals.

## Grouping 3 – Power-Control Murders

| Victim & Year | Age/Gender | Offender Organization | Offender Focus | Contact Method | Attack Paraphilia(s) | Preparatory Paraphilia(s) | Rape Category | Offender ID | Other Victims/ Serial Indicators |
|---|---|---|---|---|---|---|---|---|---|
| Harper - 1959 | 12/F | Disorganized | Process | Ruse | Sadism | Blastolagnia, Pedophilia | 1 | Unconfirmed | Yes |
| Dunleavy - 1968 | 15/F | Mixed | Process | Ruse | Sadism, Necrophilia, Necrosadism | Blastolagnia, Exhibitionism, Scopophilia | 5 | Unknown | Yes |
| Jensen - 1968 | 9/M | Organized | Process | Ruse | Sadism, Pedophilia | Exhibitionism | 4 | Unconfirmed | Yes |
| Leishman - 1968 | 16/M | Organized | Process | Ruse | Sadism, Pedophilia | Exhibitionism | 4 | Unconfirmed | Yes |
| Beer - 1968 | 32/F | Disorganized | Process | Surprise | Sadism | Unknown | 1 | Unconfirmed | Yes |
| Gibbons - 1975 | 66/F | Organized | Process | Surprise | Sadism | Crytoscopophilia | 2/3 | Unknown | Yes |
| Awcock - 1983 | 17/F | Mixed | Process | Surprise | Sadism | Blastolagnia, Scopophilia | 1 | Unknown | No |

This category of serial killer is, like the hedonist-lust killer, dominated by aberrant sexual practises, the difference being that sex acts are often incidental to the act of murder or are simply a means to an end. The power-control killer's sexual practises tend to be either more conventional forms of forced intercourse or are entirely absent—the act of killing itself serving a sexually and emotionally gratifying purpose. Without exception, killers in this category are the most sadistic and seek to possess, dominate, and elicit responses of pain and terror from their victims, with or without an accompanying sex act. It is therefore not surprising that, in every case, these offenders do not simply stop after one murder. They *cannot* stop.

Once again, the paraphilias tabled here include preparatory acts that are either known to be correlated with the attack paraphilias seen with respect to the murders themselves or which reflect either known or suspected earlier behaviours of specific individuals. In other words, these are behaviours that will present themselves in varying, non-homicidal forms throughout these killers' day-to-day functioning and will hopefully assist in identifying them. While Lynne Harper's murder occurred some distance outside of London, it is nonetheless being included here as a canonical London victim given the similarities to subsequent London victims, as well as its saliency with respect to the methods of investigation and case management practises used in London and region in following years.

Grouping 4 – Visionary-Lust Murders

| Victim & Year | Age/Gender | Offender Organization | Offender Focus | Contact Method | Attack Paraphilia(s) | Preparatory Paraphilia(s) | Rape Category | Offender ID | Other Victims/Serial Indicators |
|---|---|---|---|---|---|---|---|---|---|
| Hicks – 1973 | 21/F | Organized | Act | Surprise | Necrophilia | Crytoscopophilia, Mechanophilia | 4 | Confirmed | Yes |
| Hartwick – 1974 | 27/F | Organized | Act | Surprise | Necrophilia | Crytoscopophilia, Mechanophilia | 4 | Confirmed | Yes |
| George – 1977 | 23/F | Organized | Act | Surprise | Necrophilia | Crytoscopophilia, Mechanophilia | 4 | Confirmed | Yes |
| Veldboom – 1977 | 22/F | Organized | Act | Surprise | Necrophilia, Necrosadism, Erotophonophilia | Crytoscopophilia, Mechanophilia | 4 | Confirmed | Yes |

This category reflects the murders of Russell Johnson, Ontario's worst serial killer and an offender who is the outlier of outliers, even for a city like London. The sub-category of "lust" and the umbrella category of "visionary" in the Holmes and Holmes system cannot normally be combined. By definition, a visionary serial killer is an offender who is psychotic and who is following a calling that presents itself through some form of delusion or hallucination. Herbert Mullin murdered 13 people at random in California in the early 1970s to try to stop earthquakes from occurring; a few years later, and in the same state, Richard Chase, known as "The Vampire Killer" murdered women in their homes and drank their blood because he thought that his own blood was turning to dust as a result of alien experiments. Normally, these delusions preclude any sexual motivation given the specific nature of the psychosis. In Johnson's case, however, we see a broad spectrum of delusions that went unrecognized when he first surrendered himself to psychiatric "experts," delusions at the same time accompanied by extraordinary sexual compulsions involving necrophilia. After extensive peer review and collaboration with other experts, it has been concluded that Johnson—in this book for the first time on record—can be said to fit an otherwise atypical classification of visionary-lust.

# MICHAEL ARNTFIELD

| Grouping 5 – Unclassified Murders | | | | | | | | | |
|---|---|---|---|---|---|---|---|---|---|
| Victim | Age/Gender | Offender Organization | Offender Focus | Contact Method | Attack Paraphilia(s) | Preparatory Paraphilia(s) | Rape Category | Offender ID | Other Victims/ Serial Indicators |
| Sheeler - 1963 | 20/F | Mixed | Act | Unknown | Unknown | Unknown | 5 | Unconfirmed | No |
| Tedball - 1967 | 16/F | Unknown | Unknown | Unknown | Unknown | Unknown | Unknown | Confirmed | No |
| Stapylton - 1969 | 11/M | Mixed | Unknown | Unknown | Pedophilia | Unknown | Unknown | Unconfirmed | Unknown |
| Miller - 1974 | 26/F | Mixed | Act | Unknown | Unknown | Unknown | N/A | Unknown | No |
| MacDonald - 1978 | 31/F | Unknown | Unknown | Unknown | Unknown | Unknown | Unknown | Confirmed | No |

The murders in this fifth and final category represent cases for which there is insufficient data to render a Holmes and Holmes classification. Several of the cases suggest isolated incidents that are more accurately coded as personal cause homicides rather than sexual murders, thereby diminishing the likelihood of serial activity. While some personal cause motives can conform to a specific serial classification, such as the hedonist-comfort killer who is motivated by acquiring wealth or status rather than being driven by psychosis or some paraphilic compulsion, only the case of Robert Stapylton indicates *potential* evidence of one of either paraphilic activity or arbitrary violence of some intrinsic purpose that might be repeated again elsewhere. The fact that all of the cases also involve either staging or inconclusive causes of death, coupled with prolonged periods before recovery (no bodies being recovered in two of these cases), only further complicates the attempt to discern motive, contact method, or the nature of any paraphilic component.

# A BETTER MOUSETRAP

The most common question that arises from these classifications is why, with offender DNA being on file in three of these cases (Awcock, English, and Dunleavy, as well as the 1956 murder of Susan Cadieux not tabled here), these offenders have not been matched to later crime scenes. Part of the answer rests in the fact that, despite many missteps in some of these investigations, police in London and region, the London PD in particular, were rather prescient in recognizing the potential future value of items containing biological evidence, with everything from cigarette butts to bloody sheets and outerwear being preserved and properly stored for decades. This same practise has unfortunately not been regularly applied across Canada over the last fifty years, a deficit which has ensured problems with respect to DNA sample consistency. Another limitation is the design of the National DNA Data Bank itself, which, as seen in some unusual cases internationally, is not foolproof.

Take for instance the case of the so-called "Time Travel Murder" where, in London, England in 1997, a woman was found murdered on the street, with skin and other biological material beneath her fingernails, apparently from when she clawed her attacker while trying to fight for her life. Fingernail scrapings were later taken by forensic technicians and submitted to the fledgling British National DNA Database where a match was quickly made. The problem was that the automated match (known as a DNA hit), and which was made against another sample already on file in the database, confirmed that the skin beneath the victim's fingernails belonged not to a perpetrator but to a woman who was herself murdered three weeks earlier. What seemed on the surface to be the fodder of some far-fetched crime thriller was actually the result of what is known as a false positive, or a hit made in error as a result of some procedural error. In the case of the Time Travel Murder, the cause of the error was revealed to be an unsanitized set of nail clippers used to collect scrapings from both victims, resulting in the cross-contamination of the second sample with the first victim's DNA, which was still on the clippers.

A similar fiasco recently unfolded in Germany, as police found themselves searching for the so-called "Phantom of Heilbronn," a female serial killer who left DNA at the scenes of 14 murders (including one police officer) committed between 1993 and 2009. A reward of €300,000 ($425,000 in Canadian dollars) was eventually offered and a multi-national task force assembled with police from three countries, since the same DNA profile ended turning up at crime scenes as far away as Austria and France. It later turned out, through a proper meta-analysis of the cases, that the female "serial killer" was in fact an employee at the factory in Eastern Europe that manufactured the cotton swabs used by police forensic units in every case, the materials having been contaminated during the production process. Like London's Tissue Slayer, the Phantom of Heilbronn was fiction, and most or all of the murders had separate perpetrators. There was no single killer, just a colossal screw up that underscored the fact that as mathematically certain as DNA can be, the human component will always present some degree of risk for error.

Such laboratory errors are, fortunately, rather rare, with famed Caltech physicist and probability expert Leonard Mlodinow suggesting an error rate as a result of laboratory contamination of around only one to three percent globally. But when an error is made, it can prove costly, not just with respect to false positives that have resulted in wrongful convictions and suspect misidentifications—what acclaimed Canadian crime writer Kirk Makin calls the "dark side of DNA"—but also, and just as importantly, with respect to false *negatives*, with offender hits being missed entirely. The most obvious example in recent years relates to the murders of the Boston Strangler, with only the body of his last victim, in January of 1964 (19-year-old Mary Sullivan) furnishing a usable DNA profile of the offender. Albert DeSalvo, having confessed to the Strangler's crimes in October of 1964, was posthumously cleared as the suspect when DNA testing was first completed in 2001. A new industry then quickly sprung up, with experts and armchair detectives trying to determine who the real killer of Mary Sullivan, and likely the other Strangler victims, might have been. This trend persisted until a second more sophisticated test was conducted at a more sophisticated *private* lab in 2013. The second test confirmed that DeSalvo was in fact the actual killer after all, the first result being a false negative for reasons that were never satisfactorily explained.

If a false negative can occur when DNA is being compared using what we could refer to as an apples-to-apples test—a single crime scene sample to a single offender sample drawn from DeSalvo's exhumed corpse—then it raises serious questions about the prevalence of false negatives when the comparisons are being made while tests are being conducted on auto-pilot and without any direct oversight. In Canada, the National DNA Data Bank is made up of two separate databases that operate in this fashion. The *crime scene index* contains samples obtained from blood, semen, hair, and other biological materials left by offenders at crime scenes, while the *convicted offender index* reflects samples obtained from perpetrators following their conviction for any violent crime. Both databases unite to form what is known as the Combined DNA Index System (CODIS), which runs an automated test every 24 hours to compare offender samples to crime scene samples, as well as to compare separate crime scene samples in an effort to link multiple offences to a common perpetrator. Unbeknownst to most Canadians, the system and its software was developed and is owned by the U.S. Justice Department and is provided to the RCMP, by the FBI, free-of-charge in exchange for access to the data. Crime scene samples are uploaded to CODIS and administered by a number of regional labs scattered across Canada, including the Ontario Centre of Forensic Sciences, while offender samples are administered by the RCMP in Ottawa. As of 2014, there are over 300,000 convicted offender DNA samples on file in CODIS, with at least 500 new samples coming in every week—murderers, rapists, child molesters, burglars, Peeping Toms, and run-of-the mill violent criminals—but automated matches between offender and crime scene samples, known as "cold hits," with respect to historical and unsolved homicides simply aren't being made to the degree which one would expect, nor in the number that other "peer nations" with similar databases are making them. The question is simple, presuming the system is operating as it should: how can repeated false negatives be occurring on a daily basis?

With just under ten percent of the Canadian population having their DNA in CODIS and roughly twenty percent of the nation's male population on file (90.3% of convicted offender samples have been taken from males as of the end of 2014), since the year 2001 it's unclear exactly how many cold hits have been made between newly uploaded offender profiles and crime scene samples left at the scenes of unsolved homicides. The National DNA Data Bank has "assisted" with a total of just over two thousand murder investigations by, as was done in the Boston Strangler case, either clearing or implicating suspects based on specifically requested one-to-one comparisons. Why the rest aren't being matched using the automated system is anyone's guess. It suggests that for the murderers of girls like Jacqueline Dunleavy (employing highly specific and sadistic methods of killing that are indicative of significant future offending) not to be matched to any other crime scenes, one would have to believe that at no time since 2001 has the killer been arrested for any violent or sexual offence, nor has he ever served prison time for any similar offences committed prior to then. Apart from the London cases, consider the countless other sex slayings across Canada committed into the 1980s and 1990s that reflect any or all of the Holmes and Holmes typologies—Christine Jessop, Leah Sousa, the linked Susan Tice and Erin Gilmour murders in Toronto—all with samples loaded into the crime scene index of CODIS. These names reflect the victims of horrifically sadistic and highly specific murders that suggest their killers should have been caught for at least some other DNA qualifying crime since committing these murders—not even necessarily another sex killing—and should therefore be in the convicted-offender index. Yet, it seems, they are not.

When police brass are asked on the anniversaries of these still unsolved murders why a cold hit still hasn't been made in spite of so many offender DNA samples now being in the Data Bank, it's always the same list of suppositions: the killer moved out of the country; the killer died, or the killer simply stopped killing—cold turkey. Maybe in one or two cases, but when looking at the vast numbers of offenders on file with CODIS, and the corresponding number of open/unsolved sexual homicides with paraphilic serial indicators *and* where DNA was left at the scene, it simply doesn't compute. One explanation may be that Canada is the only Western nation whose legislation negates the ability to lower the "stringency" criteria of the automated comparisons to also screen for familial matches to offenders, doing so sparingly and only on a case-by-case basis. This same method, both in the U.S. and the U.K., has been used to solve a number of high-profile sexual homicides and has helped catch killers before they could strike again. This most recently includes "Grim Sleeper" Lonnie Franklin Jr. in Los Angeles, arrested in 2010 after a familial DNA search linked some of the crime scenes to the partial profile of his son, and cops followed the trail from there. In Canada, however, where the "biological privacy" of killers trumps the need to catch them, legislation, through no fault of the RCMP or the regional labs, makes this method impossible, or at least illegal. While on the surface this would seem to be logical and equitable, consider that a hit of any kind doesn't mean the DNA donor is immediately jailed—a thorough validation process must first occur to ensure it's not a false positive. Further, because DNA samples are today taken and stored under conditions that are greatly improved over the Data Bank's early years, it's unclear whether some of these early samples (either crime scene or offender samples) have degraded or been compromised, thus being artificially screened out under Canada's pedantic stringency standards when in fact a manual comparison—like in DeSalvo's most recent test—would actually confirm a match. Most importantly, recent research has confirmed that DNA methylation (the evolving biochemical composition of cells) changes as people age. Of particular significance to cold cases, this could theoretically mean, as some scientists have suggested in studies conducted as recently as 2013, a crime scene sample left by an offender in the 1960s wouldn't look the same to the system for comparison purposes as that same suspect's DNA would today, especially under high stringency standards. In other words, a sample taken from a killer's blood, semen, or hair from a murder scene forty years ago, and then compared to a sample from that same killer taken today would likely *not* result in an automated CODIS match—at least not based on how the system is currently programmed.

In the fall of 2014, to gain better insight on these apparent critical issues and to address these questions using independent experts, members of my Cold Case Society at Western filed a federal *Access to Information Act* request with the National DNA Data Bank requesting clarification surrounding CODIS, including what version of the software first coded in 1999 is currently being used in Canada. The key questions were simple: firstly, beyond the RCMP's published "success stories" of *convicted offender samples* being automatically matched by the system to historical homicides, how many of the other cases in which Data Bank staff claim to have "assisted" local law enforcement actually represent cold hits as the system is designed to make? Secondly, how many of the roughly 100,000 *crime scene samples* with no known suspect represent samples taken from the scenes of unsolved homicides? The figures would, in theory, have allowed us to calculate both a long-term match rate and error probability range for CODIS in Canada.

Within a few weeks, we received a response informing us that the Data Bank staff didn't have answers to some parts of these questions. It was suggested that if we could find someone who could write "a special computer searching script" in order to conduct a thorough search of the Data Bank for the information requested, and *if* we got the FBI's approval to do so, they *might* be able to answer more of our questions. Translation: the current DNA system in Canada is far from the silver bullet people think it is. Conclusion: it might be time to hit the reset button.

## -CONCLUSION-
# LONDON REIGN

"The truth is incontrovertible. Malice may attack it, ignorance may deride it, but in the end, there it is."
-Winston Churchill

# CRIMES OF OPPORTUNITY

There is no denying the unrivalled rarity of what happened once upon a time in the perceptively sedate Forest City, the question is *why*? As previously stated, this book has detailed a specific dark chapter in the city of London, Ontario's otherwise venerable and peaceful history, and today, while not necessarily perfect—no city ever is—London has recovered and moved on. However, the fact that over a discernible twenty-five year period, the city produced or otherwise hosted at least six and as many as nine serial killers based on the current definition—roughly ten percent of all serial killers in Canadian history in one place at one time—demands that the nagging question of "why London?" be addressed. There is, of course, no single factor, only a constellation of circumstances that, added together, seem to have created the perfect storm. But of all of the contributing factors—the Truscott hangover, the awkward jurisdictional issues and communication limitations, the deficiencies of police technologies and training—there emerge two key determinants that require addressing head on: geography and demography.

# BLACKTOP

The Ontario 400 Series (King's) Highway system was thought for many years to have mimicked the "success" of the U.S. Interstate system. The reality is that the Ontario model pre-dated American highway construction by several years. It would actually serve as the forebear of not only the Interstate network as the world now knows it but also the Interstate violence and serial offender transience that still accompanies it.

The first of the three sequentially numbered King's highways, the 400, the 401, and 402, were unveiled and opened to vehicular traffic in 1952, almost a full four years before the *US Federal-Aid Highway Act* of 1956 came into effect. While long-distance roads had, to some degree, previously existed throughout the United States, such as the famed Route 66 which was known as the "Mainstreet of America," the reality is that the 400 series prefigured the idea of the urban-rural controlled-access highway in North America as it now exists, with workers dropping asphalt along various corridors throughout Southern Ontario while Americans were still just discussing the idea. Like the Cretan Labyrinth of Greek folklore, the Ontario highway system soon wove London into a maze-like paradigm of roads, routes, and interchanges into which Minotaurs and other monsters of mythical proportion would soon be unleashed, and for which the city, still believing itself to be safe in its little forested cocoon, was in no way prepared.

The King's Highway network, namely the number 401 and 402 routes, were progenitors to the U.S. Interstate system and connected London to outlying towns by 1952, and with little to no monitoring or police presence. Courtesy: Western University Archives.

South of the 49th parallel, Americans knew early on that urban-rural highways, for all their purported conveniences, could mean big trouble. A number of groups, including scholars, behavioural scientists, journalists, and lobbyists united at the outset of Interstate development to warn that blacktop—the composite material used to make highway asphalt—could literally pave the road to perdition. While much of this initial outcry was dismissed as rhetoric and the propaganda of socialists opposed to post-war capital projects, a 1972 Massachusetts Institute of Technology (MIT) think-tank paper, titled *The Limits of Growth,* provided definitive and cogent evidence—collected by globally respected experts—that interstate highways were antithetical to community development and consistently placed convenience and the commercial interests of moving freight ahead of public safety. In many senses, interstates seem to have actually been designed to favour individualism, isolation, and alienation—the hallmarks of what we now understand to be the commuter killer. The MIT policy paper really just stated the obvious: highways had the power to change the cultural and criminal landscape of cities, counties, and even entire states, and not for the better.

By the early 1960s, offenders like Charles Starkweather and his low-functioning girlfriend, Caril Ann Fugate, served as case studies on the appeal of newly-laid highways to multiple murderers. As the Interstate's first confirmed serial killers, Starkweather and Fugate were enabled by the anonymity and apparent immunity of the highway network and its ability to exploit loopholes in police jurisdictions—not unlike what was seen in London and area at the same time. While Starkweather and Fugate—whose murders of eleven people in 1958 served as direct inspiration for the 1973 Terrence Malik film *Badlands*, as well as indirectly influencing the more controversial 1994 film *Natural Born Killers*—are considered the U.S. Interstate's first serial killers, all evidence points to London's highway network, nearly twenty years before Clifford Olson trolled the Trans Canada Highway, as having spawned Canada's first commuter serial killers. In the United States, the link between the Interstate system and serial homicide, in the wake of Starkweather and Fugate, prompted the creation of the FBI's Highway Serial Killing Initiative (HSKI), a task force focusing specifically on historical Interstate-related slayings with apparent linkages. In Canada, aside from the RCMP's E-PANA task-force that has focused on a specific stretch of highway in British Columbia—the infamous route between Prince George and Prince Rupert known as "The Highway of Tears"—no such initiatives have ever been spearheaded.

The continued work being done by the HSKI indicates that, based on the occurrence of commuter murders in relation to when highways are built, there is a causal relationship between not just highways and homicide but also—and more specifically—highway newness and violence. All evidence points to homicidal occurrences cresting at the beginning of a given highway's life and then ebbing as the route becomes more regularly travelled and familiar to routine commuters and lawful users. In what is arguably one of the definitive works commercially available on the subject, journalist Ginger Strand's book, *Killer on the Road,* examines spikes in serial homicides in Mexico, China, India, and elsewhere across the world in the context of when highways are first constructed and opened to traffic. In each of her national case studies, the data collected and interpreted by Strand points to a clear interconnection between newly laid blacktop and murder rates in areas previously removed from mass vehicular traffic. Not just traffic, in fact, but everything that comes with it: truck stops, hitchhikers, breakdowns, motels, anonymous passers through, and the types of known vice locations referenced throughout this book. As murder rates seem to peak during the formative years of a highway's existence on a global scale, regardless of locale or external socioeconomic, legal, or political factors, it would seem that—like so many things in life—timing is everything. It is therefore not so much the spatial impact of highways as much as their social impact that begets new trends in violent crime.

# GENERICA

A well-respected historian and Dean at Western University in London once referred to the Forest City as the still centre of a moving universe. For decades, there were many Londoners who revelled in this very idea and who extolled London's unchanging "small town feel" that many outside observers simply described as banality. In time, London's somewhat odd and vacuum-sealed culture would be consecrated as its defining feature amongst some of the world's biggest corporations.

No one is entirely sure exactly when it first started or why. Perhaps it was the highway access, with all roads seeming to lead to (or at least through) London. Perhaps it was the *Mr. and Mrs. Average Canadian Consumer* nature of the place. Regardless of the actual genesis, sometime in the 1960s—and largely out of nowhere—London emerged as the preferred consumer test market city in Canada. By the end of the decade, as North American culture began to change dramatically and views on consumerism, politics, and sexuality were being revolutionized, London was ground zero for the way experts would calibrate the status quo and celebrate the "average." In time, London came to be seen as a social experiment that could help determine the future of consumer product testing and merchandising across the whole of the Western world.

By 1968—the same year the purported "Tissue Slayer" began killing the city's teens and children—what was then only the second McDonald's Restaurant to be opened outside of the United States began operations on Oxford Street in West London, just a few miles due east of the spot where Jacqueline Dunleavy's corpse was deposited a few months earlier. While the first Canadian location opened in Richmond, British Columbia a year prior, the London McDonald's marked the first attempt east of the Rockies to pilot a non-American version of what would later become a global phenomenon. Soon after, other major restaurants, retailers, and various corporations ranging from media conglomerates to cosmetic companies—and many with an international presence—followed suit and saw London as the ideal test market community. The logic was that if a company, product, or service could make it in London, it could make it anywhere. In time, well-known chains such as Toys 'R' Us, Denny's Restaurants, and other multinational corporations saw London as a controlled experiment in social engineering and consumer influence. Soon after, chartered banks used London to pilot now common conveniences such as automated teller machines, point-of-sale debit transactions, weekend retail banking, and customer-reward programs.

Many business analysts now look to London's diverse social and economic subdivisions as key determinants for why marketers, advertisers, and large, multinational corporations have historically considered the Forest City to be the acid test of a product or service's long-term viability. They frequently tout London's divided nature as enabling what is now known as life stage-based consumer segmentation. This is a term coined by marketers to describe the phenomenon of a number of people living in the same area, yet all of whom have highly variable lifestyle characteristics and stratified spending habits. The thought is that this type of concentrated socioeconomic mosaic can approximate the larger national market and serve as a microcosm for the demographic makeup of the country as a whole. In London, this certainly makes sense. The city offers white collar and blue-collar neighbourhoods, wealthy enclaves, and transitional, low-income housing, as well as a plenitude of families plus a near equal number of young and single or widowed residents. There are students there temporarily and retirees who have been there for their entire lives. There are healthcare, government, manufacturing, and industrial employers, and over time, a fairly sizeable immigrant population developed. All in all, these identifiable groups have allowed a snapshot of an entire country to come into focus—a municipal Noah's Ark filled with every imaginable demographic group, and with all of them shoehorned into one city walled-off from the outside.

Beyond business metrics and consumer analytics, such a designation, for any city, is something of a cross to bear. Being designated as a consumer test market city—much less the *preferred* one—signifies that a city is at once everywhere, and by extension, nowhere at all. Philosophically speaking, if London's main contribution to the world was, for many years, solely to calibrate which brand of coffee, breakfast cereal, or bath soap people like best, and as a Londoner the only reason you mattered to the outside world is by being a participant in this capitalist game, there is a certain moral deflation that no doubt accompanies such a realization. The city having for so long been defined, along with its citizens, by its generic nature also coincided with the slow decline of postwar prosperity across the nation. As the disparity between social classes in the 1960s, which had been camouflaged by the inflated economy of the 1950s slowly began to reveal itself, London soon became a rainmaker for marketers and corporate decision makers who began looking to the city as what was often called "Generica"—a nameless, faceless biosphere where time stands still and one whose inhabitants could be effectively used in experiments to project national and international sales, especially during economic downturns.

The fact that London's initial designation as a test market city overlapped and occurred contemporaneously with its unparallelled spike in serial and sexual homicides is not a coincidence. This unsettling nexus is rooted in the very reason that first made London the preferred place to engage in these sorts of commercial experiments in the first place—geographic and demographic isolation. Take for instance other consumer test market municipalities across the United States. Cities such as Richmond in Virginia, Muncie in Indiana and Greensboro in North Carolina all have comparable population bases and limited population growth, but most importantly they are socially and culturally islanded from other major urban centres. These cities, like London, are sought out because of their walled-off design and alienation from larger corporate and media centres that might skew the results of consumer market tests. The cities all offer the socioeconomic and cultural segmentation on one hand, and geographic and demographic isolation on the other. All these centres are in some ways one big Generica City. They also are indicative of eerily similar trends in crime. These cities, like London, do not necessarily have statistically elevated crime rates overall as much as they do a disproportionate number of anomalous incidents seldom seen even in larger and stereotypically more "dangerous" cities—incidents that on the surface suggest that consumer test markets, for the same reasons that make them attractive to marketers, are inherently predisposed to certain trends in paraphilia and serial offending. All evidence suggests that this predisposition to (or at least correlation with) serial violence and criminal paraphilia is rooted in the same geographic and demographic factors that earmark them for product piloting and beta testing in the first place. Moreover, the fact that the national murder rates in both Canada and the United States have been steadily declining since the 1990s—Canada being at a fifty-year low in 2014—confirms a link between demography and homicide in more general terms. With an aging population and the declining number of males between the ages of 15 and 24 per 100,000 (the identified prime age for the onset of violent and sexual offending) being understood by criminologists as the main correlate with respect to the falling homicide rate, it is interesting to note that test market cities such as London have historically been dependent on a local and stable number of males within this same age range in order to account for market diversification.

## SISTER CITIES & SERIAL MURDER

Of all of the cities in North America classified as consumer test market centres, the one that would seem to be the most evenly matched with London in terms of its criminal history is actually Rochester, New York. Over the course of the 1970s, Rochester had several points of distinction that, for a city of its size—and as was the case in the then similarly sized London—seemed to defy explanation in terms of trends in serial homicide. They were points of disturbing notoriety that put Rochester on the national map in the U.S., and for all the wrong reasons. First, Rochester produced and ultimately spit out serial killer cousins Angelo Buono Jr. and Kenneth Bianchi, better known today as the "Hillside Stranglers," who may or may not have killed in Rochester before moving to California. During that same period, Rochester was also reeling from a string of horrific child slayings over a two-year period between 1971 and 1973.

The mythologized "Alphabet Murders" in Rochester over that same two-year period denote the sequential sex slayings of 10-year-old Carmen Colon, 11-year-old Wanda Walkowitz, and 11-year-old Michelle Maenza, all of whom were abducted in broad daylight in (perceived) safe areas only to turn up, much as was the case in London, dumped outside the city proper. All of the victims had alliterated names—first and last names beginning with the same letter—and were apparently targeted for this same reason. Then in 1973, as suddenly as they started, the killings stopped.

Then in 1977, four years after the last Alphabet Murder, a second female named Carmen Colon—same name and spelling as the first of the three Rochester victims back in 1971—was found murdered in a ditch outside of Fairfax, California, over 2700 miles away. As happened in Rochester when the first Carmen Colon was murdered in 1971, the Fairfax murder touched off a series of slayings in which all of the victims had the same first and last initial: Roxane Roggash, Pamela Parson, and finally Tracey Tofoya in 1994. Police in two states were left with two sets of victims, separated by decades and thousands of miles, but with the same MO and signature—all white females, all sexually assaulted and strangled, all dumped outdoors near main roads, and all having alliterated first and last names.

Fast-forward to 2011 when the dogged sleuthing of a probation officer in Reno, Nevada, conducting an otherwise routine home visit to senior citizen and Rochester native Joseph Naso, determined that he had travelled regularly between Rochester and California from the 1970s to the 1990s. By 2011, Naso was on probation for a grand larceny conviction in California. The probation officer's search of Naso's hoarder home turned up some necrophilic pornography—photographs of victims, known and unknown—which appeared to have been snapped after the girls were dead and posed in sexual positions. Naso had also compiled press clippings that detailed the California double-initial killings. Also found was a stash of dismembered female mannequins in varying states of undress and a suitcase full of plastic legs with pantyhose and garters. Knowing what we do now about the role played by partialism, specifically the use of mannequins in necrophilic fantasy development, this chilling discovery—especially in the context of the photographs—all but confirmed Naso as a homicidal necrophile, with the lens of his camera having been little more than a window into much darker obsessions.

In June 2013, Naso was convicted of the California double-initial murders that mirrored the earlier Rochester child killings, and was sentenced to death. Recent DNA testing has, however, cleared him of the first set of Alphabet Murders back in his hometown of Rochester. This revelation means that Naso, a part-time Rochester resident, was committing double-initial murders in California immediately following yet independent of the 1971-73 Rochester child killings, with the first set still being unsolved and Naso—as had happened years earlier in London—being a copycat killer.

In addition to the two sets of Alphabet Murders and the spawning of the Hillside Strangler killings, Rochester was of course also home to Arthur Shawcross, known both as the Rochester Strangler and the Genesee River Cannibal. After being convicted of the sexual murders of two children—one boy and one girl—in 1972, Shawcross was paroled in 1987 and immediately resumed killing by committing and being convicted of 11 more murders over a two-year period. Unlike the other Rochester serial killers, however, Shawcross had never moved away but simply picked up where he left off right in his own backyard.

As twisted, frightening, and seemingly rare as the Rochester case studies seem on their face, the reality is that it is precisely this rarity that connects Rochester and London in terms of city-specific trends in serial homicide, trends that contradict data collected internationally and which indicate a statistically disproportionate number of paraphilic serial killers—including copycats and otherwise rare necrophiles—relative to the mean population. The similar social histories of both cities and their non-coincidental designation as preferred consumer test market locations aside, both cities exhibit criminal cycles that appear to have no known precedent, and no known successor. London, however, during this same period had the additional distinction of not just harbouring or attracting a large number of sex offenders, serial killers, and violent criminals with a wide array of criminal paraphilias—all at the same time no less—but also doing so for a period that far exceeds the specific interval witnessed in the 1970s in Rochester. Spanning a period of more than two decades, London has a number of key characteristics that separate it from its sister city, Rochester, and place it in a league all its own.

## - POSTFACE -
# THE LAST DETECTIVE

"Every person born into this world, their work is born with them."
-James Russell Lowell

Dennis Alsop was not the last detective—he was the first. Who the last detective is on these cases remains to be seen, but it is hoped, with time running out, that this book can serve as a vehicle to connect those who have the knowledge with those who have the will to act. For this reason, it is most likely to be the last detectives—plural—that this book will flesh out, and who will finally allow the Forest City to get right with its past.

With so many of the murders detailed here still unsolved, the killers are in many cases still out there: predators who have never been identified and whose other crimes have yet to be linked. There is little question—as verified by everyone who has peer-reviewed this book and the linkages made herein—that Jacqueline Dunleavy's killer went serial. The same scenario is also probable with Helga Beer and Irene Gibbons, the difference being that these people didn't just kill in London. The Forest City is where they cut their teeth before moving on to prey on other communities, their present whereabouts being an open question. Sandor Fulep didn't just kill Victoria Mayo, but likely also Patricia Bovin and others as he wandered aimlessly around the province targeting young mothers while in and out of revolving-door psychiatric facilities. The case is the same with the Neighbour, who killed the Jensen and Leishman boys in the London area and appears to be good for at least one and as many as four other killings in the Toronto area after moving back there. In the meantime, he taught Bridgewater how to carry on his work. Both Fulep and the Neighbour are now dead and so is Archer, the Chambermaid Slayer. Magee and Johnson still live but will never walk the streets again, for which we can be thankful. But the person who killed Lynda White, Jackie English, and Soroya O'Connell is still out there—and it's the same person who murdered them all. As of now I'm the only one—like Dennis Alsop before me—committed to keeping tabs on him. He has not aged out of his horrific paraphilias; he has simply moved them indoors and found a way to indulge them with people he doesn't have to later kill—at least for now. It's also doubtful that O'Connell was his last victim.

Dennis Alsop knew all of this, and more. What was found in his time capsule and can be legally written has been written in this book, but the surface is barely being scratched. There is more in the box and more that was never written that died with him. Over the years, various cops tried to tap this information while they still could. Some well-intentioned detectives, including Project Angel investigators, would occasionally send him letters or call him up for his insights, but it seems that little if anything was done with that information until now.

This book is a valediction to a bygone era in the city of London, as well as to its legions of victims and to Dennis Alsop, all conjoined in what endures as one of the most painful chapters in national history—a Canadian horror story that no other city can rival. My primary goal in writing this book has been to set the record straight. It was also to advance knowledge on the subject of the social history of crime and violence in Canada, present some new insights into London's dark history, and to enlist the meaningful assistance of others—both experts and laypersons. So when you're done with this book, pass it on and spread the word. Like all recycling efforts, think globally but act locally. Despite the at times graphic and disturbing content, leave it in cafes, waiting rooms, salons, and offices. Donate it to flea markets, thrift shops, and used book stores—create an underground distribution network to ensure that the greatest number of people possible read it and know what happened once upon a time in a place called London, Ontario. Ideally this will help ensure that it never happens anywhere again. Additionally, it will perhaps increase the odds that someone will step up to the plate with his or her knowledge about those killers who have, until now, escaped justice. Perhaps something in these pages will jog something useful in someone's memory. This was Dennis Alsop's final wish. It was the first detective's work that was the creative engine behind this book. The last detective will be someone who has read this book and follows his lead.

# NOTES

## PREFACE

All details with respect to the events of February 18, 1966 cited in this portion are drawn from the same list of materials covered in the notes for Chapters 4 and 6, relating to the murder of Georgia Jackson.

## CHAPTER 1

The information on Canadian cities and homicide rates is gleaned from reports published by Statistics Canada and the Canadian Centre for Justice Statistics, and are publicly available.

The information on homicide classifications, offender organization, offender focus, and MO versus signature is gleaned from the books by Geberth, Hickey, Holmes & Holmes, Mellor, and Petherick, as well as the journal articles by Chan & Heide, Canter & Gregory, and Keppel & Walter.

The information on love-map theory is gleaned from both Money textbooks.

The information on paraphilias is gleaned from both Aggrawal books, the books by Hickey and Holmes & Holmes, manuals from the American Psychiatric Association, as well as Krafft-Ebing's seminal treatise in this area.

The rapist classifications are drawn from Aggrawal's paradigm, which differs slightly from the one used by the FBI.

The information on psychopathy is gleaned from the texts by both Cleckley and Hare as the definitive authorities in the field over the last century.

The information on psychogeography is gleaned from the books by Canter & Youngs, Hickey, and Rossmo, as well as the journal article by Canter & Gregory.

The information on attack preferences is gleaned from the 2014 FBI NCAVC report.

# CHAPTER 2

The information on the Cadieux case is gleaned from consolidated period media reports, specifically from January 1956, as well as the Richardson text and London Police publicity materials. Additional insights have been gleaned from interviews with former area residents and both current and former police officers, as well as citizens posting corroborated information to the online forum UnsolvedCanada as a secondary source.

The information on the Harper case is gleaned from the LeBourdais and Sher books, as well as the 2008 Justice Robins report. Additional insights have been gleaned from Dennis Alsop's personal diaries and crime scene reports as a junior identification officer on the case.

The information on the Teten system and the history of profiling comes from Ressler and Keppel's books, as well as the Hickey, Petherick, Holmes & Holmes, and DeLisi & Conis texts. The information on Metesky and Brussel is gleaned from Brussel's autobiography.

## CHAPTER 3

The information on the history of the London Police is gleaned from the Richardson book and from internal publications and memoranda. The history of the OPC is gleaned from the Richardson text and publications available through the Ministry of Community Safety and Correctional Services, which administers the institution.

The information on the murders of Margaret Sheeler and Victoria Mayo, as well as the confession of Sandor Fulep, is gleaned through interviews with Project Angel investigators and notes from Dennis Alsop's files, as well as consolidated media reports from the period.

The information on the M'Naughten and Durham Rules, as well as the history of insanity defences in Canada, is gleaned from the journal articles by Henn, et al. and Gatowski, et al. and the books by Moran and Porter & Wrightsman. The information on Li and the associated RCMP is gleaned from ongoing media reports.

The information on the murder of Georgia Jackson is gleaned from newspaper reports in both 1966 and 1972, as well as the original 1966 autopsy report and other notations and photographs obtained from Dennis Alsop's personal collection of records.

The information on Glenda Tedball is gleaned from Dennis Alsop's files, additional insights being gleaned from interviews with former area residents and both current and former police officers, as well as citizens posting corroborated information to the online forum UnsolvedCanada as a secondary source.

## CHAPTER 4

Information relating to London weather and cultural activities in 1968 is gleaned from a combination of interviews, high school yearbooks, Environment Canada records and newspaper reports.

Information relating to the murders of Jacqueline Dunleavy, Frankie Jensen, and Scott Leishman is gleaned from Dennis Alsop's original notes, diary entries, photographs and other files, as well as the Project Angel executive briefing notes and conversations with Project Angel investigators. Additional insights and quotes have been gleaned from newspaper articles, interviews with Pia Jensen and Bente Jensen, as well as current and former police officers and citizens posting sourced information to the online forum UnsolvedCanada. All verbatim quotes are from the associated *London Free Press* articles cited in the bibliography and the yearbook information re: Dunleavy is gleaned from the 1968, 1969, and 1970 yearbooks archived at Westminster Secondary School.

Information relating to Joe Clarke's activities and affiliations at the Stanley Variety are gleaned from an interview with a former employee who was also under his employ at the time of the Dunleavy murder and who has asked not to be named. Information relating to his ownership history is gleaned from interviews with this same former employee, as well as newspaper reports published in January 1968.

Information on victimology and the routine-activities theory of crime is gleaned from the Cohen and Felson article that pioneered the idea, as well as the books by Cullen and Agnew and Burgess, et al.

Information on the Neighbourhood Watch program is gleaned from the Richardson book as well as the Block Parent Program of Canada official publicity materials, and with additional insights gleaned from interviews with Pia Jensen.

I have chosen to not name the Neighbour in this case at the request of the surviving Jensen family. I was unable to locate the Leishman family to confirm their wishes on this matter, however I am of the opinion that he should and must eventually be publicly named. Of note, his surviving family has refused my—and the Jensens' requests—to meet and discuss his movements in the Toronto area after leaving London. They too must be held to account for this and what knowledge they likely had of his activities.

Information on the murder of Helga Beer is gleaned from news reports and Dennis Alsop's original notes, diary entries, photographs, and other files.

Information on Det. Guenther's role in the Tate-LaBianca investigations is gleaned from the Ellroy autobiography.

Information on the murder of Lynda White is gleaned from Dennis Alsop's original notes, diary entries, photographs, and other files. Additional insights and quotes are gleaned from interviews with John White and other members of the White family, as well as John White's original investigative notes from 1968 onward. Passages in quotations represent condensed paraphrasing.

# CHAPTER 5

Information on London's mood and the cultural changes of 1969 is gleaned from consolidated media reports and interviews with long-term residents alive at the time. Information relating to etymology of nostalgia is gleaned from the Pickering and Keightley article.

Information on the murder of Jane Wooley is gleaned from the personal files of Dennis Alsop and the Mellor book. Information on the Bovin murder is gleaned from the personal files and notes of Dennis Alsop, as well as interviews with former Project Angel investigators.

Information on the Stapylton murder is gleaned from the notes, reports, and photographs of Dennis Alsop, as well as interviews with former Project Angel investigators and consolidated period media reports. Additional insights have been gleaned from interviews with Pia Jensen, as well as citizens posting sourced information to the online forum UnsolvedCanada.

Information on The Lords of Hellmuth and the activities of Robert Hall is gleaned from the newspaper converge of Hall's trial, including the series by Jane Sims of the *London Free Press* between November 2010 and January 2011, as well as Ontario Court of Justice Superior Division transcripts of Hall's trial and sentencing.

Information on the English murder is gleaned from period news reports, as well as the diaries, notes, reports, and photographs in Dennis Alsop's personal collection. Additional insight has been gleaned through interviews with Anne

English, Pia Jensen, and Dennis Alsop Jr. as well as interviews with former Project Angel investigators, long-term London residents, and Marilyn Hird. "Liz" Alsop is a pseudonym used on request of the family.

Information on general-deterrence theory is gleaned from the Cullen & Agnew text.

# CHAPTER 6

Information on the arrest and trial of Glen Fryer is gleaned from period media reports as well as a follow-up 1992 *Toronto Star* series by Duncanson and Pron suggesting that Fryer was the Porn Man, including the circumstances of the search warrant executed at his home, as well as from the notes and reports in Dennis Alsop's personal collection. Additional insight on the legend of the Porn Man is gleaned through interviews with long-term West London residents, and citizens posting sourced information to the online forum UnsolvedCanada. The information on the two fatal fires on Elgin Street and Elmwood Avenue is gleaned from period media reports as well as Dennis Alsop's personal files. The information on the telephone calls to the Alsop residence is gleaned through interviews with Dennis Alsop Jr. and Dennis Alsop's original notebooks and diaries.

Information on the O'Connell murder and the subsequent discovery of her remains is gleaned from period news reports as well as the diaries, notes, reports, and photographs in Dennis Alsop's personal collection. Additional insight has been gleaned through interviews with former Project Angel investigators and Daphne O'Connell, Soroya's mother, as well as long-term Perth County residents familiar with the areas discussed.

Information on the Authier and Russell murders, and the activities of Gerald Thomas Archer, is gleaned from the Mellor book, as well as the diaries, notes, reports, and photographs in Dennis Alsop's personal collection. Additional insight has been gleaned through interviews with former Project Angel investigators.

Information relating to David Bodemer is gleaned through period news reports, as well as the diaries, notes, reports, and photographs in Dennis Alsop's personal collection. Additional insight has been gleaned through interviews with Dennis Alsop Jr. and an *Access to Information Act* request filed with Corrections Canada.

Information on the Merle murder and the activities of David Pullin is gleaned from the diaries, notes, reports, and photographs in Dennis Alsop's personal collection. Additional insight has been gleaned through interviews with former Project Angel investigators and Lee Mellor's original research.

Information on the discovery of Lynda White's clothing and the location and circumstances surrounding the recovery of her remains is gleaned from the diaries, notes, reports, and photographs in Dennis Alsop's personal collection. Additional insight has been gleaned through interviews with John and Joan White, John White's original investigative notes, archaeological visits to the actual recovery site, and genealogical research at the nearby cemetery, as well as research conducted with the assistance of the Norfolk Historical Society. Soil samples from the disposal site were tested by anthropologist Renee Willmon (Western University) and forensic entomologist Dr. Hélène LeBlanc (University of Ontario Institute of Technology).

Information on the Barksey murder is gleaned from the Mellor book and the diaries, notes, reports, and photographs in Dennis Alsop's personal collection. Information on the Hicks and Hartwick murders is gleaned from the Mellor book and subsequent media reports on the NCR hearing of Russell Johnson.

Information on the murder of Suzanne Miller is gleaned from period media reports and discussions with the victim's family over the course of several years.

Information on the murder of Irene Gibbons is gleaned from period media reports, the diaries, notes, reports, and photographs in Dennis Alsop's personal collection, as well as interviews with Project Angel investigators and members of the Strathroy-Caradoc Police Service. Information on the Strathroy murder of Louise Jenner is gleaned from the Mellor book, as well as interviews with members of the Strathroy-Caradoc Police Service and Dr. Kim Luton at Western University, who had exclusive access to interview Magee at Oak Ridge in 2012.

Information on the historical nexus between the mythography of homicide and lycanthropy, as well as other monster legends, is gleaned from the Ingebresten book and my own personal observations, as well as published research regarding semantic distinctions in the press and public sphere in the aftermath of major crimes.

# CHAPTER 7

Information on the ViCLAS system is gleaned from years' worth of personal experience and a comprehensive review of the associated booklet, as well as data published by the RCMP in their official public communications.

Information on the murders of Scholes, George, and Veldboom is gleaned from the Mellor book, as well as period media reports and coverage of the NCR hearings of Russell Johnson and Christian Magee. Additional insight has been gleaned through interviews with members of the Strathroy-Caradoc Police Service, and Dr. Kim Luton at Western University, who had exclusive access to interview Magee at Oak Ridge in 2012. Observations and insights with respect to Oak Ridge are gleaned through first-hand experience after personally transporting offenders to the site in 2001 and 2002, and through subsequent conversations with inmates and correctional staff.

Information on the MacDonald murder is gleaned from peripheral but personal involvement in the trial, period media reports and follow-up publications by the Innocence Project, and interviews with former Crown prosecutors and Project Angel detectives.

Information on *corpus delicti* and the Haigh "acid bath" murders is gleaned from the Ramsland journal article and the Hickey book.

# CHAPTER 8

Information relating to the background and etymological origins of serial murder is gleaned from the Ressler, Keppel, Leyton, and Fox & Levin texts;

the social context and ensuing mythography of serial murder in the 1980s is gleaned from the Jenkins article and statistics on serial killer films is gleaned from the Hickey text.

Information on the Awcock murder and the subsequent discovery of her remains, and the creation of the composite drawing is gleaned from period news reports, as well as interviews with former Project Angel investigators. Additional insight has been gleaned through interviews with Tammy Dennett (nee Awcock) as well as Carol and Laura Awcock, the boys who discovered Donna's body, long-term residents of the same housing complex, former employees of the convenience store, and former patrons of the Town & Country Tavern, including both "Michelle" and witness "Joanne." The polygraph test was administered by Don O'Connor, OPP (ret.).

Information on the crimes of Robert Bridgewater (Henderson) and the murder of Jason Franklin is gleaned from period media reports, interviews with former OPP investigators, a Franklin family member, and Project Angel detectives, as well as original research conducted by Jeffrey Christian, and as *Access to Information Act* requests filed with Corrections Canada.

# CHAPTER 9

All information and case studies in this chapter are gleaned from an assemblage of sources that include firsthand personal experience and insight, the Mellor book, as well as consolidated media reports and interviews with current and former police officers, prosecutors, and former Project Angel investigators.

The information on the DNA Data Bank in particular is gleaned from both personal/professional experience, the associated Makin piece, the Mlodinow book, published reports authored by the RCMP, the published study by Grskovic, *et al.*, a written response to a 2014 *Access to Information Act* request filed with the RCMP, and an eight month research audit of the DNA Data Bank conducted by the Western Cold Case Society and various independent scientists and subject matter experts consulted in Canada, the U.S. and the U.K. These experts include Dr. Peter Cadieux, a widely respected microbiologist and expert on genetic macroanalysis, as well as the nephew of London murder victim Susan Cadieux.

# CONCLUSION

The information on London's population metrics is gleaned from Statistics Canada Census data.

The information on the King's Highway system is gleaned from the Sewell book and the Ontario Department of Highways reports for 1955-1969.

The information on U.S. Interstate violence is gleaned from the Strand book, and the information on Starkweather and Fugate from the Schmid book.

The additional information on London is primary source in nature, and is gleaned from several hundred interviews with local residents, local historical records (both published and unpublished), as well as personal experience as both a city police officer and resident. More specific data was retrieved from electronic publications and secondary sources, as well as interviews with representatives from McDonald's Canada, the Richard Ivey School of Business at Western, and the London Police Service, as well as the various *London Free Press* articles cited in the bibliography.

The information on cultural and environmental models of crime, including their overlapping with test market criteria, is gleaned from the books by Ferrell, Hayward, & Young; Bohn & Vogel; Cullen & Agnew; Linden, Wortley & Mazerolle; as well as the Bursik article—a foundational study in the field.

Information on Naso, Shawcross, and the other Rochester murders is gleaned from the Hickey book and period media reports.

# SELECTED BIBLIOGRAPHY

Acemoglu, D. & Robinson, J.A. (2012) *Why Nations Fail: The Origins of Power, Prosperity, and Poverty*. New York: Crown.

Aggrawal, A. (2009) *Forensic and Medico-Legal Aspects of Sexual Crimes and Unusual Sexual Practices*. Boca Raton, FL: CRC Press.

Aggrawal, A. (2010) *Necrophilia: Forensic and Medico-Legal Aspects*. Boca Raton, FL: CRC Press.

American Psychiatric Association (1968) *The Diagnostic and Statistical Manual of Mental Disorders, 2nd Edition*. Arlington, VA: American Psychiatric Publishing.

American Psychiatric Association (2013) *The Diagnostic and Statistical Manual of Mental Disorders, 5th Edition*. Arlington, VA: American Psychiatric Publishing.

Bohm, R.M. & Vogel, B.L. (2011) *A Primer on Crime and Delinquency Theory, 3rd Edition*. Belmont, CA: Wadsworth.

Brussel, J. A. (1968) *Casebook of a Crime Psychiatrist*. New York: Bernard Geis Associates.

Burgess, A.W., Regehr, & Roberts, A. (2012) *Victimology: Theories and Applications*. Burlington, MA: Jones & Bartlett.

Bursik, R.J. (1988) Social Disorganization and Theories of Crime and Delinquency: Problems and Prospects. *Criminology*, 26(4). 519-552.

Canter, D. & Gregory, A. (1994) Identifying the Residential Location of Serial Rapists. *Journal of the Forensic Science Society*, 34. 169-175.

Canter, D. & Youngs, D. (2009) *Investigative Psychology: Offender Profiling and the Analysis of Criminal Action*. Hoboken, NJ: Wiley.

Chan, A.C.Y., Beh, P.S.L., & Broadhurst, R.G. (2010) To Flee or Not: Postkilling Responses Among Intimate Partner Homicide Offenders in Hong Kong. *Homicide Studies*, 14(4). 400-418.

Chan, H.C. & Heide, K.M. (2009) Sexual Homicide: A Synthesis of the Literature. *Trauma, Violence, & Abuse*, 10. 31-54.

Cleckley, H. (1941) *The Mask of Sanity: An Attempt to Clarify Some Issues About the So-Called Psychopathic Personality*. Maryland Heights, MO: Mosby. Fifth Edition Facsimile Reprinted in 1988 by Emily Cleckley.

Cohen, L. E. & Felson, M. (1979) Social Change and Crime Rate Trends: A Routine Activity Approach. *American Sociological Review*, 44. 588-608.

Cullen, F.T. & Agnew, R. (Eds.) (2011) *Criminological Theory: Past to Present, 4th Edition*. New York: Oxford University Press.

DeLisi, M. & Conis, P.J. (Eds.) (2012) *Violent Offenders: Theory, Research & Practice, 2nd Edition*. Burlington, MA: Jones & Bartlett.

Douglas, J.E., Burgess, A.W., Burgess, A.G., & Kessler, R.K. (1992) *Crime Classification Manual: A Standard System for Investigating and Classifying Violent Crime*. New York: Lexington Books.

Duncanson, J. & Pron, N. (1992) Elusive Killers Leave Cold Trail for Police. *Toronto Star*. April 2 edition, electronic archive.

Ellroy, J. (1997) *My Dark Places*. New York: Vintage Books.

Fox, J.A. & Levin, J. (2014) *Extreme Killing: Understanding Serial and Mass Murder.* Thousand Oaks, CA: Sage.

Gatowski, S. I., Dobbin, S.A., Richardson, J.T., Ginsburg, G.P., Merlino, M.L., & Dahir, V. (2001) Asking the Gatekeepers: A National Survey of Judges on Judging Expert Evidence in a Post-Daubert World. *Law & Human Behavior*, 25(5). 433-458.

Government of Ontario (2008). Ministry of the Attorney General. *In the Matter of Steven Truscott.* Advisory report by S.L. Robins. Issued March 28, 2008.

Gerbeth, V.J. (1996) *Practical Homicide Investigation, 3rd Edition.* Boca Raton, FL: CRC Press.

Girard, R. (1979) *Violence and the Sacred.* Baltimore: Hopkins Press.

Grskovic, B, Zrnec, D, Vickovic, S, Popovic, M. & Mrsic, G. (2013) DNA Methylation: The Future of Crime Scene Investigation? *Molecular Biology Reports*, 40(1). 4349-4360.

Gunn, L. & Caissie, L.T. (2006) Serial Murder as an Act of Deviant Leisure. *Leisure*, 30. 27-53.

Hare, R. (1970) *Psychopathy: Theory & Research.* New York: Wiley.

Hare, R. (1991) *The Hare Psychopathy Checklist—Revised.* Toronto: Multi-Health Systems.

Hare, R. (1998) *Without Conscience: The Disturbing World of Psychopaths Among Us.* New York: Guilford Press.

Hare, R. (2003) *The Hare Psychopathy Checklist—Revised, 2nd Edition.* Toronto: Multi-Health Systems.

Ferrell, J., Hayward, K., & Young, J. (2008) *Cultural Criminology: An Invitation.* Los Angeles: Sage.

Henn, Fritz A., Merijan Herjanic & Robert H. Vanderpearl (1976) Forensic Psychiatry: Diagnosis of Criminal Responsibility. *Journal of Nervous & Mental Disease*, 162(6). 423-429.

Hentig, H. von (1948) *The Criminal and His Victim: Studies in the Sociobiology of Crime.* New York: Schocken.

Hickey, E.W. (2010) *Serial Murderers and Their Victims, 6th Edition.* Belmont, CA: Wadsworth.

Holmes, R.M. & Holmes, S.T. (2009) *Profiling Violent Crimes: An Investigative Tool, 4th Edition.* Thousand Oaks, CA: Sage.

Ingebresten, E. (2001) *At Stake: Monsters and the Rhetoric of Fear in Public Culture.* Chicago: University of Chicago Press.

Jenkins, P. (1988) Myth and Murder: The Serial Killer Panic of 1983-85. *Criminal Justice Research*, 3(11). 1-7.

Jones, B. (1968) Girl, 16, Found Slain: Gagged Body in London Schoolyard. *The London Free Press.* January 10th edition, page 1.

Jones, B. (1969) Dead Boy, Shack Link Studied. *The London Free Press.* September 25th edition, page 1.

Kelly, S. (2002) *The Boston Stranglers.* New York: Pinnacle.

Keppel, R. & Walter, R. (1999) Profiling Killers: A Revised Classification Model for Understanding Sexual Murder. *International Journal of Offender Therapy and Comparative Criminology*, 43. 417-437.

Keppel, R. (2010) *Riverman: Ted Bundy and I Hunt for the Green River Killer.* New York: Pocket Books.

Krafft-Ebing, R. von (1892) *Psychopathia Sexualis.* Philadelphia & London: F.A. Davis Publishing.

LeBourdais, I. (1966) *The Trial of Steven Truscott.* Philadelphia: J.B. Lippincott.

Leyton, E. (2005) *Hunting Humans: The Rise of the Modern Multiple Murderer.* Toronto: McLeland & Stewart.

Linden, R. (2014) *Criminology: A Canadian Perspective, 8th Edition.* Toronto: Nelson.

Livingston, J. (2004) Murder in the Juárez: Gender, Sexual Violence, and the Global Assembly Line. *Frontiers: A Journal of Women Studies*, 25 (1). 59-76.

Makin, K. (2010) The Dark Side of DNA. *The Globe & Mail*. March 13, 2010 edition, online.

Makin, K. (2007) Truscott Judge Wanted Author Prosecuted. *The Globe & Mail*. January 31, 2007 edition, online.

McGuire, B. & Jones, B. (1968) Girl's Slaying Stymies Police. *The London Evening Free Press*. January 10th edition, page 1.

McGuire, B. (1968) Nearly Nude, Badly Beaten Woman Found Dead in Car. *The London Evening Free Press*. August 6th edition, page 1.

McGuire, B. (1969) Decomposed Body Believed Boy, 11. *The London Free Press*. September 24th edition, page 1.

Mellor, L. (2012) *Cold North Killers: Canadian Serial Murder*. Toronto: Dundurn.

Mlodinow, L. (2009) *The Drunkard's Walk: How Randomness Controls Our Lives*. New York: Vintage.

Money, J. (1986) *Lovemaps*. New York: Irvington Publishers.

Money, J. (1989) *Lovemaps: Clinical Concepts of Sexual/Erotic Health and Pathology*. New York: Prometheus Books.

Moran, R. (1981) *Knowing Right from Wrong: The Insanity Defense of Daniel McNaughton*. New York: The Free Press.

O'Brien, J. (2011) Here For a Good Time or a Long Time? *The London Free Press*. September 6th edition, online.

Ontario Department of Highways (1970) *Annual Average Daily Traffic Reports, 1955-1969*. Ministry of Transportation and Communications: Toronto.

Pantaleo, K. (2010) Gendered Violence: An Analysis of the Maquiladora Murders. *International Criminal Justice Review*, 20(4). 349-365.

Petherick, W. (2009) *Serial Crime: Theoretical and Practical Issues in Behavioral Profiling, Second Edition*. Burlington, MA: Elsevier.

Pickering, M. & Keightley, E. (2006) The Modalities of Nostalgia. *Current Sociology*, 54(6). 919-941.

Porter, S. & Wrightsman, L.W. (2014) *Forensic Psychology, Second Canadian Edition*. Toronto: Nelson Education.

Raban, J. (1974) *Soft City: A Documentary Exploration of Metropolitan Life*. New York: Harvill.

Ramsland, K. (2006) John George Haigh: A Malingerer's Legacy. *The Forensic Examiner*, 15(4). Online edition.

Ressler, R. K., Burgess, A.W. & Douglas, J.E. (1988) *Sexual Homicide*. Lexington, MA: Lexington Books.

Ressler, R. K. & Schachtman, T. (1993) *Whoever Fights Monsters: My Twenty Years Tracking Serial Killers for the FBI*. New York: St. Martin Press.

Richardson, M. (2005) *On the Beat: 150 Years of Policing in London Ontario*. London: Aylmer Express Ltd.

Reasons, C.E., Francis, T. & Kim, D. (2010) The Ideology of Homicide Detectives: A Cross-National Study. *Homicide Studies*, 14(4). 436-452.

Rosman, J. P. & Resnick, P.J. (1989) 'Sexual Attraction to Corpses: A Psychiatric Review of Necrophilia. *Bulletin of the American Academy of Psychiatry and the Law*, 17(2). 153-163.

Rossmo, D. K. (2000) *Geographic Profiling*. Boca Raton, FL: CRC Press.

Ruhl, B. (2014) *A Viable Suspect*. Victoria, BC: FriesenPress.

Schmid, D. (2005) *Natural Born Celebrities: Serial Killers in American Culture*. Chicago: University of Chicago Press.

Sewell, J. (2009) *The Shape of the Suburbs: Understanding Toronto's Sprawl*. Toronto: University of Toronto Press.

Sher, Jonathan. (2013) Injection Drug Use: A Survey Uncovers Grim Numbers in London. *The London Free Press*. November 20th edition, electronic record.

Sher, Julian (2002) *Until You Are Dead: Steven Truscott's Long Ride into History*. Toronto: Vintage Canada.

Silverman, M. (2014) The Strange Case of the "Time Travel Murder." *BBC News*. Science and Environment, April 27th edition, electronic record.

Sims, J. (2010) Fear and Shame 40 Years Later. *The London Free Press*. November 10th edition, electronic record.

Strand, G. (2012) *Killer on the Road: Violence & the American Interstate*. Austin: University of Texas Press.

Uncredited (1968) Police Report New Lead in Jensen Case. *The London Free Press*. April 20th, 1968 edition, page 1.

U.S. Department of Justice (2014). Federal Bureau of Investigation, Behavioral Analysis Unit. *Serial Murder: Pathways for Investigation*. A Report from the National Center for the Analysis of Violent Crime. Quantico, VA.

Weber, A. (2012) London Solidifies its Role as Retailers' Test Market. *The London Free Press*. July 6th edition, electronic record.

Wortley, R. & Mazerolle, L. (Eds.) (2008) *Environmental Criminology and Crime Analysis*. Portland: Willan.

# INDEX

Abduction/kidnapping, 38-40, 74, 82-84, 117-120, 130, 132, 143, 192, 195, 258-260, 266-267, 300,

Abel, Robert, 266-267

Act-focused murders, 22-24, 219, 276-284

Alphabet Murders, the, 300-301

Alsop, Dennis Sr., 14-17, 53-55, 78-81, 84-86, 93-94, 98, 111-123, 129, 136, 139, 145, 151-173, 177-182, 185, 187, 189, 192, 194-199, 201-212, 214, 216-217, 220, 241-242, 250, 253, 261, 270, 274-275, 305-306

Alsop, Dennis Jr., 80, 155, 171

Amokoscisia, 27, 168

Archer, Gerald Thomas, 13, 190-194, 196, 199, 272, 276-277, 305

Authier, Edith, 188-191, 193-194, 272, 276

Autopsies, 23, 46, 77-78, 95, 113, 116, 125, 136, 140, 189, 202, 201, 210-211, 214, 229

Avon, Ontario, 198-199

Awcock, Carol Ann, 245-248

Awcock, Donna Jean, 244-254, 255, 256, 265, 268, 280, 285

Aylmer, Ontario, 3, 5, 46-48, 60, 72-73, 75-76, 149, 194, 198, 258,
  Dairy Bar, 3-5, 72-73, 75,

Police Department, 73, 75-76

Barksey, Judith, 212-213, 214, 217, 219-220, 227, 229, 241, 278
Buxbaum, Hanna, 265
Buxbaum, Helmuth, 265
Bayham Township, Ontario, 157, 206
Bestiality (see Zoophilia)
Beer, Helga, 123-127, 128, 129, 132, 138, 139, 140, 160, 280, 305
Beitz, Diane, 227, 232
Berkowitz, David, 230, 243, 255
Bernardo, Paul, 54, 153
Bezzo, William, 190-191, 193
Bianchi, Kenneth, 299
Big Otter Creek, 115-116, 122, 154-157, 257,
Bite marks (see Odaxelagnia)
*Black Christmas*, 164
Black Donnellys, the, 180
Blastolagnia, 26, 278, 280
Blitz attacks, 33, 278
Block Parent program, 15, 108-109
Blood typing, 66, 95, 126, 156
Bludgeoning, death by, 63, 112-113, 137, 190-191
Bodemer, David, 195-200, 202, 255, 257, 258, 274
Bond, Dr. Thomas, 46
Boston Strangler, the, 96-97, 115, 143, 189, 218, 219, 286-287, 288,
Bovin, Patricia, 138-142, 160, 274, 278, 305
Bradford, Charlie, 39
Brawner Rule, the, 70
Bridgewater, Robert, 257-262, 270, 274, 305
Brooks, Dr. David Hall, 49
Bruney, Tracey, 122
Bryant, Michael, 45, 51
Buono, Angelo Jr., 299
Burlington, Ontario, 128-130, 209
Byron (London subdivision), 92

Cadieux, Susan, 37-39, 47, 50, 59, 126, 154, 253, 285

Campbell Commission, the, 54
Canadian Baseball Hall of Fame, 212
Canadian Broadcasting Corporation (CBC), 44
Canadian National Railway (CNR), 73, 194-195, 206, 212, 257
Canadian Police Information Centre (CPIC), 178
Cannibalism, 27, 71, 80, 196, 233, 234, 301,
Carroll, Chief Finlay, 60
Ceeps Tavern, the, 129
Cemeteries, 26, 206, 210, 212, 258, 272
Chase, Richard, 283
Chatham, Ontario, 188-189, 190-191, 193
Chikatilo, Andrei, 65
Children's Psychiatric Research Institute (CPRI), 106, 178, 179, 180
Clark, Constable David, 93, 94, 100
Clarke, Joe, 90, 92-93, 98, 99, 121, 178
Cleckley, Hervey, 19
Clinton, Ontario, 16, 34, 37, 39, 41-42, 45-49, 52
Colter, Justice W.E., 182
Combined DNA Index System (CODIS), 287-290
Commuter offenders, 31-32, 37, 50, 295-296
Composite sketches, 38-39, 125, 162-164, 169, 178, 216, 252-253, 254, 259
Consumer test markets, 296-299, 301
Cop killers, 38, 267, 286
Copycatting, 96-97, 114-115, 256, 301
*Corpus delicti*, 235-237, 273
Cream, Thomas Neill, 265
Criminal Investigative Analysis, 18, 46, 165
Crocker, Albert, 197
Crytoscopophilia, 26, 67, 278, 280, 282

Dahmer, Jeffrey, 234
DC Snipers, the, 67
Decomposition, 62, 77, 147, 208
Dismemberment, 23, 78, 81, 202, 209
Disposal sites, 24, 41, 54, 64, 67, 76, 78, 95, 111, 113, 121-122, 198, 202, 207, 254-255

DNA, 38-39, 66, 83, 120, 126, 194, 249, 252, 255-256, 268-269, 270-272, 274, 285-290, 301
   National Data Bank, 137, 269-270, 285-290
   *Identification Act*, 193, 270
   Limitations & Inconsistencies, 285-290
Downie Township (see Gore of Downie)
Doyle, Sir Arthur Conan, 17, 175
Drowning, death by, 112-113, 116-117, 122, 257-259
Dunleavy, Jacqueline, 90-103, 104, 106, 110, 111, 113, 115-117, 125,-126, 135, 138, 145, 151, 178, 197, 231, 255, 256, 274, 280, 288, 297, 305
Durham Rule, the, 70

Edmonton, Alberta, 243
Elgin County, Ontario, 74, 115, 189
Elgin-Middlesex Detention Centre, 229
English, Anne, 150-151, 182
English, Jackie, 133, 150-173, 178, 180-181, 182, 184-185, 206, 211, 215, 241, 251, 257, 274, 278, 305
Equivocal death, 145, 146
Erotophonophilia, 27, 65, 141, 202, 228, 233, 278, 282
Erskine, John, 49, 52, 78
Essex County, Ontario, 61
Exhibitionism, 26, 47, 49, 67-68, 76, 96, 98, 119, 164, 195, 205, 255, 278, 280
Exsanguination, 235

Fantasy, 7, 18, 24-31, 67, 76, 81, 117, 167, 260, 300
Fecophilia, 180
Federal Bureau of Investigation (FBI), 12, 46, 66, 67, 225, 242-243, 251, 287, 290, 294
   Behavioral Analysis Unit, 46
   Mindhunter Program, 46
   National Center for the Analysis of Violent Crime, 12
Ferguson, Justice Ronald, 42-43
Fingerprints, 66, 201, 253, 254
Fire, death by, 183-185
Footprints, 66, 100
Foreign object penetration, 30

Forensics, 18, 27, 44, 46, 49, 52-53, 63, 69, 71, 77-80, 83, 95-97, 100, 113, 121, 126, 147, 195, 208, 212, 215, 227, 251, 253, 257, 266, 285-286, 287
  anthropology, 208, 211, 83
  pathology, 46, 49, 63, 77, 96, 113, 147, 156, 207, 211, 214, 227, 254
Forest City, the (see London, Ontario)
Franklin, Jason, 257-262
Franklin, Lonnie Jr., 32, 289
Fryer, Glen, 180-185, 265, 274
Fugate, Caril Ann, 295
*Fugitive, The*, 163
Fulep, Sandor, 68-72, 121, 233, 272, 305

Gacy, John Wayne, 32
Gary, Carlton, 219
Geographic profiling, 32-33
George, Luella, 229-230, 232
Gibbons, Irene, 305, 216-219
Gillis, Paul Cecil, 266-267
Glatman, Harvey, 192, 225
Goderich, Ontario, 42, 50
Gore of Downie, Ontario, 210-212
Graham, Harold, 51-53
Gratton, Edward, 272-274
Guelph, Ontario, 227, 232-233

Haigh, John George, 235-237
Hall, Robert, 147-150
Hanging, execution by, 236, 265
Hare, Dr. Robert, 19-20
Harper, Lynne, 15-16, 39-55, 241, 280-281
Harrison, Elizabeth, 162-173, 178-180, 182-185
Harrison, Verdun, 166, 183-185
Hartwick, Eleanor, 214, 282
Hedonist-comfort killers, 285
Hedonist-lust killers, 22, 278-279, 281
Hedonist-thrill killers, 22, 276-277
Henderson, Robert (see Robert Bridgewater)

Hicks, Mary, 209-210, 214, 282
High-risk victims, 73, 152
Highway of Tears, 295
Highway Serial Killing Initiative (HSKI), 295
Hird, Marilyn, 160-162, 178-179
Hitchhiking, 23, 42, 108, 111, 186, 205, 228,
Hold-back evidence policy, 96-97, 256, 269
Holmes & Holmes classification system, 220, 275, 283, 285, 288
Huron County, Ontario, 47
Huron University College, 119, 129, 131

Identi-Kit, 162-168, 252
Ingersoll, Ontario, 73, 198
Innocence Project, the, 237
Insanity defence, 68-71, 121, 161, 165, 217, 233-234, 266

Jack the Ripper, 27, 46, 265
Jackson, Georgia, 3-8, 72-81, 84-85, 92, 157, 159, 170, 194-200, 255, 258, 268, 274, 278
Jeffrey, Superintendent Herb, 97, 145
Jenner, Louise, 219-220, 227, 229, 278
Jensen, Frankie, 104-123, 125, 129, 131, 132, 136, 143, 146, 153-154, 159, 169-170, 178, 187, 194, 203, 241, 256, 257-261, 274, 280, 305,
Johnson, Russell, 13, 209-210, 214, 220-221, 223, 227-234, 241, 282-283, 305

Kalichuk, Alexander, 45-50, 60, 258
Katherine Harley School, 93, 95, 99
Kemper, Edmund, 23-24, 32
Kent County, Ontario, 189
Keppel, Robert, 67
Kibbe, Roger, 32
King's Highways (400 series), 3-8, 32, 37, 46, 50, 72, 121, 151, 153, 166, 190-191, 227, 251, 267-268, 293-296
Kingdom Hall (Jehovah's Witnesses), 1, 73, 194-198
Kitchener, Ontario, 194, 197-198
Kurten, Peter, 242

Lake Erie, 115, 136, 257
Lake Huron, 228, 237
Larsfolk, Erik, 122, 262
Latin Quarter Restaurant, the, 151
LeBourdais, Isabel, 43-45, 52-54
Leishman, Scott, 110-113, 115-117, 120-123, 125, 129, 132, 136, 146, 154, 159, 169-170, 187, 194, 215, 257, 259-262, 274, 280, 305
Li, Vince, 71
Ligature strangulation, 40, 94, 96-97, 139, 218-219
Linkage blindness, 24, 96, 140-141, 198, 225-226
Lockyer, James, 44
London, Ontario, 4-8, 11-17, 25-27, 29, 31-34, 37-40, 45-50, 53-55, 59-62, 64-66, 68-71, 72-74, 79-86, 89-100, 103, 104, 106-109, 111-115, 118-127, 128-132, 133, 135-140, 142, 150-154, 156-167, 169, 171-173, 178-191, 193, 197, 200-205, 209-217, 220-221, 226-236, 239, 241-242, 244-246, 248, 250-251, 253-256, 260-261, 265-272, 274-275, 279, 281, 283, 285-286, 288, 291, 293-301, 305-306
  City Hall, 85
  Courthouse, 38, 236
  *Free Press*, 39, 91, 97-98, 120, 126, 145, 216, 253
  Hunt and Country Club, 93, 95, 99, 101
  Police (see London Police Department)
  Psychiatric Hospital, 46, 232
  Township, 59, 186, 211, 248
  Transit Commission, 92-93, 234, 245
London Police Department, 38, 54, 59-60, 62, 68, 84-85, 93, 97-99, 100-101, 103, 106-107, 112-113, 117, 126, 128, 139, 145, 149, 160-161, 163-165, 179, 183, 187, 203, 205, 210, 214-216, 220, 226, 231, 234, 241, 244, 248, 250-251, 270-272, 285,
  Association, 93
  Criminal Investigation Division, 117, 140, 149, 165
  Headquarters, 59-60, 85, 118, 124, 132, 187, 226, 231
  Major Crimes Section, 128, 270
  Persons Squad, 128, 216, 232, 270
  Uniformed Division, 65, 93, 102, 120, 160-161, 163-164, 166, 168, 183-184, 236, 271

"Lonesome victim" typology, 192
Lovers lanes, 76, 255-256, 268
Lust murder, 22, 27-28, 65, 202, 220, 228, 278-279, 281, 282-283,
Lycanthropy, 220-221

M'Naughten Rule, the, 70
MacDonald, Allan Craig, 267-269, 270, 272
MacDonald, Irene, 234-237, 272, 274, 284
Magee, Christian, 13, 227-229, 231-233-234, 241, 305
Major Case Management, 54
Malahide Township, Ontario, 7, 157
Manson, Charles, 114
Manual strangulation, 15, 24, 32, 49, 113, 116, 125, 147, 229-232, 254, 257, 299-301
Martin, Michael, 183
Masturbation, 99, 261
Mayo, Victoria, 64-71, 72, 84-85, 121, 125, 132, 136, 139-143, 160, 170, 272, 278, 305
Marauder offenders, 30, 32
McBride, Inspector James, 159-160, 163, 165, 170, 173, 187, 204-205
McCormack, John, 122
Mechanophilia, 26, 234, 282
Media, role of, 21-22, 39, 60, 82, 85, 96-99, 103, 117-118, 128, 138-139, 146, 149, 158, 160, 164-165, 169, 172, 180-182, 184-185, 188, 192-193, 195, 205, 217, 226, 228, 230, 236, 253-256, 259-260, 266, 297-299,
Meirhofer, David, 66
Merle, Priscilla, 200-206, 274, 278
Merlin, Ontario, 188-189, 193
Metropolitan Store, the, 151-152, 157, 161-162, 166, 168, 178, 215,
Middlesex County, Ontario, 79, 81, 144, 157, 164, 183, 189, 212, 221, 229
Miller, Suzanne, 215-216, 219, 284
Missing persons reports, 62-63, 83-84, 93, 106-107, 110-112, 115-117, 132, 143-145, 154, 157, 165, 187, 200, 203, 215, 234-235, 248, 250, 268, 273
Mission-oriented killers, 23
*Modus operandi* (MO), 23-24, 30-33, 96, 116-117, 136, 140, 188-189, 219, 225-227, 229, 236, 255-257, 258, 268, 276, 278, 280, 282, 284, 300

Money, Dr. John, 28-29
Monster of Florence, the, 255
Morden, Dr. John, 119, 129, 170
Mullin, Herbert, 283
Mutilation, 21, 23, 27, 65, 69, 75, 78, 80-81, 84, 168, 180-181, 195, 201, 209, 217, 226, 228, 241, 276, 278, 280, 282, 284

Naso, Joseph, 300-301
Necrophilia, 26-27, 96, 98, 117, 164, 178-180, 196, 207, 212, 221, 233-234, 278, 280, 282-283, 300-301
Necrosadism, 26-27, 96, 126, 278, 280, 282
Norfolk County, Ontario, 189, 206, 208-209, 211, 258
Nostalgia, 135-136
Oak Ridge (institution), 68, 233-234
Oakridge (London subdivision), 93, 106-107, 110, 118, 143, 179
Occult, 82-83, 119, 127, 169
O'Connell, Soroya, 185-188, 210-212, 248, 274, 278, 305
Odaxelagnia, 27, 77, 278
Offender organization level, 18, 20-23, 32, 65, 67, 69, 137, 189, 226, 253, 256, 276, 278, 280, 282, 284
Offender profiling, 22, 46-47, 66-67, 76, 242-243
Old North (London subdivision), 143, 146-148, 266
Old South (London subdivision), 92, 143, 151, 158, 184
Olson, Clifford, 225, 243, 260, 295
Ontario, Province of, 11-12, 14, 22, 34, 37, 42-44, 45-46, 50, 52, 53, 55, 60, 73, 79, 83, 100, 121, 140, 183, 188-189, 191, 193, 198, 208, 210, 231, 233, 261, 265, 266-267, 283, 287, 293-294
   Centre of Forensic Sciences, 100, 287
   Coroner Service, 63, 96, 140, 209, 214
   Fire Marshal, 183
   Police College, 60, 73
   Provincial Police (see Ontario Provincial Police)
Ontario Provincial Police (OPP), 14-17, 41-43, 45, 47-54, 78-81, 84-85, 94, 99, 111, 113, 118, 120, 122, 144-145, 154, 157, 159, 163-165, 169-170, 183, 187, 189, 195, 201, 204-205, 206-209, 215-217, 220, 227, 241, 244, 250-252, 253-255, 258-259, 268-269, 270-274

Detachments, 15, 41-43, 45, 47, 144, 157, 169, 189, 195, 201, 206-209, 217, 220, 227, 258-259, 268-269, 270-274

Forensic Identification Branch, 41-43, 78-81, 253-255

General headquarters, 15, 17, 54, 122, 169-170, 187-188

London office, 17, 84-85, 94, 99, 144, 157, 163-165, 169-170, 183, 215-216, 220, 241, 244, 250-252, 253-255, 270-274

Senior command, 17, 45, 50-55, 122, 169-170, 187-188, 241, 250, 269

Ottawa, Ontario, 13, 287

Paraphilia, 14, 18, 23-34, 45-46, 49, 67, 69-71, 76, 96-98, 116-117, 128, 138, 159, 164-165, 172-173, 177-178, 195, 212, 219, 226, 232-234, 243, 255-256, 265, 268, 274-275, 276, 278-279, 280, 282, 284-285, 288, 299, 301, 305,

Attack, 26-27, 45, 67, 69, 97-98, 116-117, 138, 159, 195, 212, 219, 274-275, 276, 278-279, 280-281, 282, 284, 288, 299, 301

Preparatory, 25-26, 67, 76, 164, 195, 232, 234, 255-256, 268, 276, 278, 280, 282, 284,

Parole, 44, 178, 193, 199, 234, 259-260, 262, 267, 269, 274, 301

Partialism, 26, 78, 278, 300

Pedophilia, 26-27, 38, 45, 49, 106, 117, 119, 147-148, 164, 178, 184, 259, 261, 280, 284

Peeping Tom, 26, 67, 255, 287

Penetanguishene, Ontario, 68, 233

Penistan, Dr. John, 49

Perth County, Ontario, 210-211

Phantom of Heilbronn, the, 286-287

Photographs, 16, 26, 43, 79, 95, 100, 103, 111, 119, 124, 126, 148, 160-161, 172, 178-180, 184, 212, 253-254, 300

Placophilia, 26, 212, 278

Poe, Edgar Allan, 96-97

Police (see London Police Department, OPP)

Polygraph test, 247

Poore, Norma, 83, 273

Pornography, 92, 148, 178-179, 300

Porn Man, the, 177-181, 184-185, 274

Port Dover, Ontario, 257-258, 261

Port Stanley, Ontario, 201-202

Posing, body, 94-95, 99, 104, 111, 207, 210, 212, 218, 300
Power-control killers, 22, 95, 278, 280-281
Process-focused murders, 22-24, 177, 189, 268
Project Angel, 270-274, 306
Project Millennium, 271
Prostitution, 248, 265
Psychogeography, 31
Psychopathy, 18-20, 23, 25-26, 37, 50, 67, 70, 72, 80, 97, 99, 108, 117, 122, 128, 157-158, 165, 170, 172, 177, 205, 234, 259, 277
Psychosis, 18-20, 65, 71, 121, 227, 230, 266, 283
Pullin, David, 202-206, 217, 241

Rader, Dennis, 218
Ramirez, Richard, 21, 32, 67
Rapist typologies, 18, 29-33, 189
Religious mania, 196
Resindez, Angel, 32
Ressler, Robert, 242
Reward money, 75, 169, 216, 255, 269, 286
Robinson, John Edward, 32
Rochester, New York, 299-301
Royal Canadian Air Force (RCAF), 37, 46-48, 52, 60, 78
Royal Canadian Mounted Police (RCMP), 22, 49, 71, 225, 226, 287, 289, 294
Ruse attacks, 8, 33, 38, 74, 96, 192, 220, 276, 278, 280
Russell, Belva, 190-193

Sadism, 23, 27-28, 30-31, 41, 67, 70, 74, 76, 84, 97-99, 115, 116, 159, 165, 167, 169, 190, 192, 195-196, 219, 226, 242, 256, 259, 267, 268, 276, 278, 280-281, 282, 288
San Antonio symposium (2006), 338
Scatologia, 26, 98, 164-165
Scavenger activity, 77-78, 144, 147, 208
Scholes, Susan, 227-229, 278
Sells, Tommy, 277
Serial Murder, 11-15, 17-34, 45, 54, 65, 84, 86, 100, 136, 138-139, 153, 158, 170, 177, 184, 187-188, 190, 195-196, 210, 213-214, 219-220, 225-226,

228, 230, 233-236, 241-243, 256, 261, 265-266, 271, 276, 278, 280, 282, 284-286, 288, 293, 295-296, 298, 299-301, 305, 338
   Defining, 18-29, 338
   Etymology, 24-34, 274, 276, 278, 280, 282, 284-286, 288
   In Film, 18, 143, 164, 242-244
Sexual assault, 18, 29-31, 47, 49, 54, 63, 77, 94, 102, 113, 125, 149, 194-195, 197, 199, 219-220, 227, 259, 261, 266, 268-269, 273, 276, 278, 280, 282, 284, 287
Sexual dysfunction, 21, 31
Sexual homicide, 53, 63, 84, 86, 124, 128, 132, 138, 164, 173, 191, 219, 243, 251, 270, 288-289, 298, 300
Shaw, Lynda, 267-270, 272
Shawcross, Arthur, 301
Sheeler, Margaret, 60-65, 68, 85, 125, 132, 170, 186-187, 234-235, 284
Shepherd, Joseph Alvin, 251-252
Sheppard, Sam Dr., 162-163
Signature, 14, 23-24, 32-34, 65, 69, 96-97, 113-117, 119, 177, 198, 219, 225-226, 229, 231, 256-257, 260-262, 275, 300
   Analysis, 14, 65, 23-24, 32-34, 96-97, 113-117, 198, 219, 225, 229, 256, 260-262, 300
   Linkage, 32-34, 65, 119, 177, 226, 256-257, 262, 300
   Stability, 23-24, 32-34, 96-97, 113-117, 119, 226, 229, 256-257, 260-262,
Simpsons Department Store, 123, 125, 160
Sociopathy, 19-20, 69, 257
South Norfolk Railway, 206
Souvenir taking, 8, 24, 81, 115, 156, 159, 198-199, 229
Speck, Richard, 163
Spindler, Donald, 234-237, 272, 274
St. Thomas, Ontario, 47, 266
   Psychiatric Hospital, 266
Stabbing, death by, 65, 68-69, 140, 142, 147, 272
Staging, crime scene, 63, 67, 207, 214, 229, 231, 265, 285
Stanley Variety, 90-92, 98-99, 143, 178
Stapylton, Robert (Bruce), 142-149, 154, 159, 170, 186-187, 194, 208, 248, 266, 284-285
Starkweather, Charles, 295

Strangulation, death by, 15, 24, 32, 40, 49, 94, 96-97, 113, 116, 125, 139, 147, 218-219, 229-232, 254, 257, 299-301
Strathroy, Ontario, 98, 212-214, 217, 219-221, 226-228
  Police Department, 217, 220, 226, 228
Suffocation, death by, 77, 116, 210, 214, 230
Suicide, 71, 121, 142, 149, 160, 214, 251
Supreme Court of Canada, 44, 237
Surprise attacks, 33, 65, 268, 276, 278, 280, 282

Taphophilia, 26, 211, 216, 278
Tedball, Glenda, 81-85, 111, 127, 132, 145, 154, 158-159, 187, 235, 272-274, 284
Telephone scatologia (see Scatologia)
Teten, Howard, 46, 65-67, 242
Thames Centre, Ontario, 111
Thames River, 112, 124, 131, 149, 248
Thedford, Ontario, 81
Tillsonburg, Ontario, 154, 156, 257
Time Travel Murder, the, 285-286
Tissue Slayings, the, 87, 95-97, 103, 113-115, 119-120, 157, 217, 220, 256, 274, 286, 297
Toronto, Ontario, 13, 15, 54, 60, 68, 121-122, 131, 136, 169, 171, 180, 182-183, 186-188, 211, 214, 216-217, 241, 260-262, 269, 271-272, 288, 305
  Metropolitan Police, 68
Torture, 23, 31, 218, 268
Town & Country Tavern, 245-246, 252
Treasure Island Plaza, 152, 166
Trophy taking, 8, 24, 78, 81, 195
Truscott, Steven, 35, 39-46, 49-55, 59-60, 78-79, 118, 200, 203, 204, 209, 293
Tunnel vision, 42
Turkey Point, Ontario, 257, 259-261

Undoing, 95
University of Western Ontario (see Western University)
Unidentified remains, 83, 157

Unsolved crimes, 5, 12-13, 18, 26, 38-39, 45, 50, 64, 69, 83, 84, 96, 124, 128, 132, 138-139, 145, 158, 170, 181, 194, 204, 209, 214, 217, 219, 228, 255, 262, 270-271, 274, 287-288, 290, 301, 305
*Unsolved Mysteries*, 252
U.S. Department of Justice, 22, 252, 287
U.S. Interstate system, 293-296

Vancouver, British Columbia, 243
Vandalized Love Map Theory, 28-29
Veldboom, Donna, 230-233, 282
Victimology, 18, 33, 106, 140, 152, 189, 192, 257, 275
Violent Criminal Apprehension Program (ViCAP), 22, 225
Violent Crime Linkage Analysis System (ViCLAS), 22, 225-227, 274
Visionary killers, 23, 221, 282-283
Voyeurism (see Scopophilia)

Wallace, Henry Louis, 32
Warkworth Institution, 261-262
West Nissouri, Ontario, 111-112, 115
Westdale Elementary, 104, 106-107, 110
Western University, 119, 129, 131, 267-268, 289, 296
Western Fair, 139
Westminster Secondary School, 102-103
Whitechapel, 46
White, Lynda, 128-132, 154, 159, 187, 206-209, 210-212, 241, 248, 258, 261, 267, 274, 278, 305
White Oaks Mall, 166
Wilson, Simon, 122
Windsor, Ontario, 148
Winnipeg, Manitoba, 13, 71, 89
Woman in the Well, the, 83
Wooley, Jane, 136-138, 188-189, 191, 193-194, 272, 276

Yates, Bill, 148-149
Young, Detective Bob, 118, 203-204

Zodiac Killer, the, 158, 230, 255-256
Zoophilia, 26, 178[1]

In 2006, an international consortium of experts meeting in San Antonio, Texas and led by experts at the FBI revised the standing definition dating to 1983 to include <u>two</u> rather than <u>three</u> victims in separate incidents as meriting a "serial" classification. This 2006 symposium and the associated changes, as well as its ongoing implications, are relied on throughout this book.

# ABOUT THE AUTHOR

Dr. Michael Arntfield is widely regarded as the leading Canadian authority on cold case murders and serial homicide. Having served as a police officer in London, Ontario for over 15 years, he is now a criminologist and award-winning professor at Western University where he was named its 2017 Humanitarian of the Year for his work with victims of violent crime. As the 2016 visiting Fulbright Research Chair in crime and literature at Vanderbilt University, he has been an invited keynote speaker at universities and colleges across North America and Europe. He is also a member by special invitation with the Center for Homicide Research in Minneapolis, the Atypical Homicide Research Group in Boston, and a director with the Murder Accountability Project in Washington DC.

On television, he is the host and co-creator of the true crime mini-series *To Catch a Killer* on the Oprah Winfrey Network, and now syndicated internationally—a series based on his own unsolved crimes think tank, the *Western University Cold Case Society*. His other books include *Monster City, Mad City, Murder in Plain English,* and *Gothic Forensics: Criminal Investigative Procedure in Victorian Horror & Mystery*, among others.

He is also the co-author or contributing author of numerous related works, including *Homicide: A Forensic Psychology Casebook, Digital Death: Mortality & Beyond in the Online Age, Necrophilia: A Global Anthology, Criminology: A Canadian Perspective, 8th Edition,* and *A Social History of Crime & Punishment in America,* as well as over a dozen peer-reviewed journal articles and research papers. He also works as an investigative consultant and resource for various media outlets, including with the CBC's *the fifth estate,* is the co-editor of a book series on literary criminology with Peter Lang Publishing in New York and Berlin, as well as an associate editor for the journal of Homicide Studies.

He now splits his time between Canada and Arizona.
michaelarntfield.com

CPSIA information can be obtained
at www.ICGtesting.com
Printed in the USA
BVHW030813130621
609156BV00003B/224